DUNCAN HINES

Duncan Hines, standing before his huge collection of cookbooks, Bowling Green, Kentucky, Fall 1953.

Duncan Hines

The Man Behind
The Cake Mix

Louis Hatchett

Mercer
University
Press
2001

ISBN 0-86554-773-4
MUP/H584

Published by
Mercer University Press
6316 Peake Road
Macon, Georgia 31210-3960

First Edition.

05 04 03 02 01 5 4 3 2 1

∞The paper used in this publication meets the minimum
requirements of American National Standard for Information
Sciences—Permanence of Paper for Printed Library Materials, ANSI
Z39.48-1992.

Library of Congress Cataloging-in-Publication Data

Hatchett, Louis.
Duncan Hines : the man behind the cake mix / Louis Hatchett.—1st ed.
p. cm.
Includes bibliographical references and index.
ISBN 0-86554-773-4 (hardcover : alk. paper)
1. Hines, Duncan, 1880-1959. 2. Businessman—United
States—Biography. 3. Food industry and trade—United
States—Biography. 4. Hospitality industry—United States—Biography.
I. Title.
HC102.5.H56 H38 2001
338.7'664'0092—dc21
2001004756

For my Mother and Father

Contents

PREFACE

No one had ever written a biography of Duncan Hines before, so I needed a lot of help. Fortunately, a number of people rallied to my cause; I apologize to anyone whom I have omitted in the following list. The most important person to this project was Duncan Hines's great niece, Cora Jane Spiller, who not only gave me her valuable time but who enthusiastically ran down leads for me when all other avenues to my investigation were blocked. Her enthusiasm for the book was infectious and encouraging from start to finish. Every biographer should have someone like her to work with. She has been with me through thick and thin from beginning and end; without her support, I would have abandoned this biography long ago.

This book originally took shape as a thesis for a Masters degree in History at Western Kentucky University in Bowling Green, Kentucky, the birthplace and home of Duncan Hines for his first 18 and last his 20 years. I wrote the book first and then scaled it down to 120 pages for the thesis. The first draft of the book was 840 manuscript pages, which I subsequently trimmed to 740 pages.

My main thesis adviser, Dr. Carol Crowe-Carraco, was the one who provided me with the day-to-day thread that helped bring the work to completion. But perhaps my greatest contacts, particularly on arcane questions of style and format, came from Nancy Baird, Connie Mills, and Sandy Staebel, all long-time employees of the Kentucky Library and Museum, which sits on the Western Kentucky University campus. When Dr. Crowe-Carraco was not available, all three answered my innumerable questions. As I worked on this manuscript 100 miles away from their offices, I must have called them 300 times in the course of a thousand days. They always helped when I asked, and I record my deepest appreciation here.

While writing this book, perhaps the biggest treasure trove of Hinesiana came when I went to the Procter and Gamble headquarters in Cincinnati, Ohio, then the manufacturers of the Duncan Hines cake mixes, and asked to see their Duncan Hines collection. I spoke with Ed Rider, head archivist at P&G, and after a couple of minutes, his staff brought out several large files of Duncan Hines material. After going over these files for an hour, I asked the P&G staff to xerox everything and send it to me. They complied, and about ten days later I received a forty-pound box that nearly mirrored their entire Duncan Hines collection. It took almost a year to fully digest and make use of everything they sent. I offer my sincerest thanks to Ed Rider and his staff for providing me with this material. This would have been a much shorter book without their cooperation.

During my two-year effort composing this book, a number of other people also helped me along the way. I want to thank Jane Jeffries for the critique of the first 300 pages of this book. I also want to thank her for asking me to discard the first 100 pages or so, which pertained not to Duncan Hines but the history of his family. Sometimes a writer can get carried away with the research, and I was including everything I found; I finally realized that not many people would be interested in the fact that Duncan Hines's brother, Porter, put in the first sewer system in Calhoun, Kentucky in 1899.

When Jane left the project, Wendy Yates took her place in critiquing the final product. When the manuscript had been completed, she read it and thought it to be boring, and after I reread it again, I had to agree. So I took a full year to rewrite the entire thing from top to bottom—twice. To Wendy I owe profuse gratitude.

There were a number of people that I interviewed that I would like to thank. Duncan Hines's brother-in-law, Robert Wright, provided me with some valuable personal insights on Hines's character; Thomas C. Dedman, of the Beaumont Inn in Harrodsburg, Kentucky, gave me plenty of corroborative insight into Hines's influence on the lodging industry; Paul Ford Davis supplied me with a wealth of information about his former employer; Sara Jane Meeks, Mary Herndon Cohron and Wanda Richey Eaton, three of Duncan Hines's secretaries in the 1950s, furnished me with a plethora of information concerning the working conditions while employed by Hines; Elizabeth Duncan Hines, the wife of his nephew, yielded some useful information; Edward and Robert Beebe, nephews of Duncan Hines's second wife, provided me with some information about their aunt that was unknown to the Hines family; Caroline Tyson Hines, offered me additional and corroborative insights into the personality of Duncan Hines; Maj. Gen. Richard Groves, a nephew of Duncan Hines and son of General Leslie Groves ("Father of the Atomic Bomb"), gave me some critical insights into the early years of Duncan Hines's life which opened up a whole vista of understanding; much help came from Paul Moore, who prepared most of the Duncan Hines guidebooks in the late 1940s and early 1950s; Top Orendorf, who was Duncan Hines's lawyer, also had some useful insights. Duncan Welch, who was Hines's great nephew, gave me all sorts of information as well as provided me with some hilarious stories. Larry Williams, of the Williams Printing Firm was a big help in providing me the history of his business and Hines's relation to it. Finally, I want to thank William Jenkins, a former professor of Government at Western Kentucky University, for providing me with a key clue in unraveling Duncan Hines's past.

The staffs of several libraries were important to me. These people do not get enough credit. I want to thank the college library staffs of the University of Evansville in Evansville, Indiana, Western Kentucky University in Bowling Green, Kentucky, Southern Illinois University in Carbondale, Illinois for their untiring efforts in running down leads and books for me whenever possible. I also want to thank the staffs of the public libraries in Henderson, Kentucky, Bowling Green, Kentucky, and the Willard Library in Evansville, Indiana for providing me with the materials I needed to complete this project. I especially want to thank Jean Brainerd of the Wyoming Historical Society, who was of tremendous help in helping me piece together the early life of Duncan Hines.

I also want to thank the staff of *Reminisce* magazine for printing my query about Duncan Hines. From that single notice, I received a large number of responses from people who traveled across America during the 1940s and 1950s who used Hines's restaurant and lodging guides exclusively as their source for getting from one place to another in safety and comfort. Of particular usefulness were the insights of Roberta C.

Gilbert, Elinor Macgregor, Frances Wood, Shirley Wheaton, to name a few. To all of them I offer my profuse thanks.

I also want to thank Tim Hollis of the National Lum and Abner Society for providing me with tapes of the Lum and Abner story line featuring Duncan Hines (who was played by Francis X. Bushman on that particular show). Terry Tatum was of tremendous help in finding all the homes that Duncan Hines lived in during his years in Chicago. Lastly, I want to thank Dr. Virginia Grabill, a retired English professor whom I had at the University of Evansville, for deciphering several letters written by Duncan Hines's brother in the 1880s; since she is a master of this sort of thing, I knew she could do it if anyone could. She made instant sense of the scribbles I handed her. I wish I had her talent. I also want to thank Maggy Shannon, Marc Jolley, Kevin Manus, and the staff of Mercer University Press for giving me the opportunity to tell a story worth reading and remembering.

I do not think I have exhausted the subject. If I had been given a grant of several hundred thousand dollars, I could have flown all over creation to investigate every nook and cranny where Hines once trod. As it turned out, I think I did well with the slightly over $500 I spent on this project. But for the author who wants to investigate this subject further, this is a good place to start.

22 March 2001
Henderson, Kentucky

Roy Park and Duncan Hines at Sales Executive Club,
Waldorf-Astoria Hotel, New York City, September 24, 1951.

Left to right: Ruth Wakefield, Duncan Hines, Kenneth
Wakefield, Clara Hines, The Toll House Restaurant,
Whitman, Massachusetts, October 14, 1950.

Duncan Hines in Hines-Park's Test Kitchen, Ithaca, New York, October 13, 1953.

Duncan Hines at work in his office. Bowling Green, Kentucky, April 23, 1951.

Clara Hines at home, Bowling Green, Kentucky. Notice portrait of Duncan Hines above her (circa 1915), April 23, 1951.

Left to right: Willard Rutzen, Marian Odmark of *This Week in Chicago,* and Duncan Hines in front of birthday cake, 10th annual Duncan Hines Family Dinner, Morrison Hotel, Chicago, Illinois, May 8, 1951.

Duncan Hines Day, Palm Crest Hotel, Haines City, Florida,
February 12, 1953. Left to right: Edward Marotti, Walter
Jones, F. A. Randall (President Emeritus of Haines City
Citrus Growers Association), Mrs. Roy Park, Harold Schaaf,
Jim Hogge (Sales Manager), Carol Russ, R. V. Phillips, Clara
Hines, Mrs. R. V. Phillips, Roy Park, Mrs. Nichols (Manager
of the hotel), Mr. Mathias (horticulturist), Duncan Hines,
Forrest Attaway, Ruth Higdon, Tom Brogdon.

Cutting the cake for the second birthday of the Duncan
Hines Cake Mixes. Chicago, Illinois, May 11, 1953. Left to
right: Roy Park, Clara Hines, Duncan Hines, Allan Mactier
(president of Nebraska Consolidated Mills).

Clara and Duncan Hines, cutting a cake in the Duncan
Hines test kitchens, Ithaca, New York, September 17, 1957.

Roy Park addressing Duncan Hines Family Dinner members,
Chicago, Illinois, May 5, 1958. Left to right: unidentified,
Stewart Underwood, Dean Lundberg (Florida state senator),
Carlton Dinkler, Jr., Allan Mactier, Bob Shetterley (P & G),
Leonard Hicks, Senator Hruska, (Nebraska senator), Roy H.
Park, Duncan Hines, Clara Hines, Dean Meek, Bob Grison,
Matthew Bernatsky, Dean McAllister (Oklahoma University),
Wright Gibson, Ned Cummins.

Duncan Hines, with his brother, Porter Hines, at latter's home in Bowling Green, Kentucky, February 1959, just before he died.

Duncan Hines and Mr. Hackney (proprietor of Hackney's, said at the time to be the largest seafood restaurant in the world) in front of live lobster purifying pool, Atlantic City, New Jersey, May 22, 1949.

Duncan Hines and Clara at Croton Heights Inn, Croton Heights, New York, May 29, 1949.

Duncan Hines carving a turkey at home, Bowling Green, Kentucky, Fall 1953.

Duncan Hines speaking with Bill McBride, host of the Cup & Saucer Club on WOW-TV, Omaha, Nebraska, March 14, 1952.

Duncan Hines helping prepare a meal with World's Largest
Frying Pan at chicken supper given by the Poultry and Egg
Association, Schollkopf Field, Cornell, Ithaca, New York, July
5, 1955.

Bob Sebree with letters which came with the gifts from various
restaurant, hotel and motel operators around the country to
buy the Cadillac for Duncan Hines's 70th birthday, Phoenix,
Arizona, April 14, 1950.

Duncan Hines being presented the key to his new Cadillac
by Bobby Gosnell, outside of Green Gables restaurant at
70th birthday party, Phoenix, Arizona, April 14, 1950.

Duncan Hines and Roy Park, sampling Duncan Hines Ice
Cream, July 24, 1950.

Duncan Hines on the set of "Prince Valiant" at 20th Century-Fox, with Debra Paget and Janet Leigh, Los Angeles, California, August 11, 1953.

Clara and Duncan Hines at reception for Duncan Hines Day at the Town House Hotel, Los Angeles, California, August 11, 1953.

Roy Park, Duncan Hines, Merle Johnson, Jim Cathey
standing before billboard welcoming Duncan and Clara
Hines to Los Angeles, August 11, 1953.

Duncan and Clara Hines being interviewed at the World's
Largest Display of Duncan Hines Cake Mix on WBBC in
Flint, Michigan, October 1, 1953.

Mital Gaynor, Allan Mactier, presenting Duncan Hines with a
Duncan Hines cake, Blackstone Hotel, Omaha, Nebraska,
March 10, 1954.

Duncan Hines at home in the kitchen in Bowling Green,
Kentucky, 1950s.

Duncan Hines, Clara Hines and Nelle Palmer, just before
they sailed for Europe, on the deck of the S. S. Liberte, New
York, April 8, 1954. Left to right: Roy Park, Nelle Palmer
(in hat), Mrs. Roy (Dottie) Park, Clara Hines, Dr. Arthur
Hunt, Duncan Hines, Adelaide Park (the Park's daughter).

Clara and Duncan Hines in Hines's new office, Ithaca,
New York, June 28, 1954.

INTRODUCTION

Mention the name "Duncan Hines" to Americans under fifty-five today and the image their minds will undoubtedly conjure is a cake mix package. No one can blame them if they fail to recognize the significance of the man for whom the cake mix is named. Was Duncan Hines named for two men, one named Duncan and the other named Hines, who jointly created a nationally recognized brand name? Or was Duncan Hines a real person? Few know the answer.

On the other hand, mention the name "Duncan Hines" to Americans over fifty-five and a much different picture emerges. To this group the sensation upon hearing the name brings forth emotions usually reserved for one deemed reverentially special. To them Duncan Hines was a man, not associated with cake mixes, but one who recommended the best places Americans could eat and sleep when traveling along the country's early paved highways at a time when they were thirsty for such knowledge.

To the generation that followed them, the name Duncan Hines not only brings back fond memories of someone who looked after the traveling public's gustatory and nocturnal needs, it also brings to mind a name and face whose visage was affixed to over 200 grocery store products at a time when Americans were looking for something more substantial than the usual fare served in supermarket cans and packages. This generation knew that if

Duncan Hines put his name and reputation behind a particular packaged product, it was assuredly the store's best foodstuff and more than worthy of their hard-earned dollars.

Overall, though, what both groups most remember about Duncan Hines is that the name, whatever its context, meant the highest possible quality found anywhere. For example, if Duncan Hines recommended a restaurant, it was widely assumed to be one of the country's absolute best. If he recommended an inn where one could spend the night, it was instantly assumed to be one of the highest quality lodging facilities in America. If he recommended a particular recipe, few competing concoctions could surpass its taste. If he recommended an item found on grocery store shelves, it was naturally assumed to be made from the finest quality ingredients. Duncan Hines never recommended anything that was merely good or passable; his recommendation meant it was the last word in excellence.

Anyone could recommend something. And they did, long before Duncan Hines arrived on the scene. The difference, Americans soon discovered, was that when comparisons were made, the things Duncan Hines recommended truly were the best. Unlike today, his judgments of things superior did not come lightly; once mentioned, however, whatever he recommended soon became highly regarded throughout the nation. But there was another ingredient that placed him a cut above the normal dispensers of information, one instructive to all American generations: his judgments were solely his own. He let no one influence his decisions. He was fiercely independent. He could not be bought at any price—and he let everyone know it. Although restaurateurs, innkeepers and presidents of food manufacturing firms would have gladly sacrificed their fortunes for the honor of having satisfied his favor, Duncan Hines went to great lengths to isolate his emotions from any seductions they may have offered. He was determined—at all costs—to protect the integrity of his name and reputation, because he recognized their value and what it meant to the millions who placed their faith in him.

Duncan Hines rose to fame simply because he possessed human qualities many Americans wanted to see in their fellow man: character, uncompromising honesty, and integrity. For many Americans it was refreshing to find someone who had those traits. Because of the principled stance Hines took on restaurant sanitation and a whole range of other issues, Americans regarded his every word with the highest esteem; in their eyes, he was one who would never lie or deceive them. He was, they felt, one of their own and was looking after their interests. For this generation, if Duncan Hines said a particular restaurant meal made "a man wish for hollow legs," it did. And there was no argument about it.

A final factor that contributed to the American reverence for what Duncan Hines had to say was his selflessness. It was widely known among the American public that Duncan Hines turned down fortune after fortune simply because he would not sacrifice his name for financial reward. The man who said "Every man has his price" never met Duncan Hines. Nothing could sway his opinion if he thought something under consideration was even remotely questionable. For a generation of Americans, the name Duncan Hines was, as someone once put it, "the next best thing to God."

What follows is a little known chapter in the annals of America's cultural history that has never before been adequately detailed. It is the story of an average man who came to America's attention, was perceived by them as unusually trustworthy and who, because of that perception, became an American icon. Surprisingly, the public's perception and the reality were nearly identical.

1

BOWLING GREEN

There is a cartoon from the 1940s that, at one time, was every restaurant owner's nightmare. The scene is a dining room of a fancy four-star restaurant. A waiter has accidentally spilled an entire tray of food onto the head and lap of a nicely-attired customer. The customer, neatly dressed in his evening tuxedo, is trying to stifle his anger and frustration as a large lump of lasagna rolls off the side of his head. The man's indignant wife says to the waiter in a calm, controlled, yet icy voice, "Just wait 'till Duncan Hines hears about this!"[1]

This is the story of how such a potential nightmare came to be. It concerns a man with a penchant for excellence, primarily in matters of food, who raised both the standard of the nation's restaurants and their customers' eating habits by setting himself as an example of the ideal patron. In this role he exhorted his fellow Americans to demand, as he did, only the best from the nation's public kitchens.

Duncan Hines's constant search for excellent restaurants throughout America resulted in filtering out the multitude of poor and mediocre restaurants and directing attention to those truly worthy of consideration. Through his many guidebooks from 1936 to 1962 Duncan Hines favorably remarked on restaurants that were not only excellent but deserved celebration for the atmospheric and culinary enjoyment they afforded hungry and weary travelers. He made famous the restaurants that strove to put an appealing sparkle into their patron's meals. These restaurants were not only exceptionally clean, they were also noted for their high quality food. He pointed Americans toward restaurants well worth time and trouble to discover, restaurants in out-of-the-way locales too good to pass up. A Duncan Hines recommended restaurant, most Americans believed, was one where taste buds could savor extraordinary culinary delights hardly found anywhere else. For twenty-seven years millions bought his books, took his advice, and were much wiser and happier for it. The words may not mean much today, but not long ago the phrase "Recommended by Duncan Hines" really meant something.

Duncan Hines's story begins not in a restaurant but in the sleepy south-central Kentucky town of Bowling Green. Like many other families who settled in that area during the early part of the nineteenth century, Hines's forebears were originally from Scotland and England. Edward Ludlow Hines, Duncan's father, was born near Bowling Green on 5 November 1842. He was the third son of Fayette and Anne Cook Hines.[2] It was often reported that Edward Hines was a former Confederate army captain, but in fact he never rose beyond the rank of lieutenant.[3] Edward Hines enlisted in the Confederate Army at Camp Boone in Tennessee on 1 June 1861 and joined the 2nd Kentucky infantry under Col. Roger Hansen. He surrendered on 9 May 1865, as a member of Company E, the 9th Kentucky Cavalry under the command of William P. C. Breckinridge.[4] During his four years of service he was never captured by enemy Union soldiers and was proud of it. Except for a short stay in the hospital, he never left his post.[5] Edward Hines received several battle scars on his stomach as a result of his war service and this left his health in rather precarious shape. For the rest of his life, he had to take care that he did not over-exert himself and make his infirmity still more serious. As a result of this physical limitation, he never had anything resembling "nine-to-five" employment. The elder Hines's war papers reveal the confession that he joined the Confederate States of America not because he had any particular love of the South or because he had any hatred for the North but rather because, not knowing anything about the people North of the Ohio River, he naturally considered them enemies who had a tendency to look down on him and his way of life. Class envy being qualification enough to participate in the nation's most epic bloodbath, he went off to war at age twenty to battle the Yankee heathen upstarts.[6]

Hines's mother, Eliza Cornelia Duncan, was born in Warren County, Kentucky, of which Bowling Green is the county seat, on 10 August 1846. She was the daughter of Joseph Dillard Duncan and Jane Covington Duncan. Eliza, known as Cornelia, was raised near Warren County's Browning, Kentucky.[7] The story of how Cornelia met her husband is an interesting one. During the Civil War Edward Hines was riding with some troops across a field and Cornelia, running an errand for her mother, was walking to a neighbor's house. When Edward and his men came upon her and stopped her, he noticed the bottle of cordial she was holding in her hand. The bottle was destined for a neighbor's mother who was ill. Edward asked her to hand it over, Cornelia refused. When he sternly repeated his demand, she persisted in her refusal, telling him the liquid was not intended for him or his troops but for a sick neighbor. When he realized she would not hand it over; he took his horse by the reins and proceeded down the road on horseback with his fellow soldiers-in-arms. As they rode away, he confided to one soldier that he was "going to come back some day and marry that girl." And he did. After the war's conclusion, and after a romantic courtship, Edward Ludlow Hines and Eliza Cornelia Duncan married at the residence of J. D. Duncan in Bowling Green, Kentucky[8] on 11 November 1869.[9] A reception in a house on College Street followed, and an account of the wedding was published in the local newspaper the following day.[10]

Before the Civil War and after, Edward Hines sporadically attended school at various locations in Warren County and eventually graduated from Bowling Green's Warren College.[11] A career in law interested him, but since Warren College did not grant law degrees, Hines most likely read law with a local attorney and passed a bar exam to obtain his law license. To support his wife and his budding family, he was appointed to several positions, one of them being the master commissioner and clerk of the Warren County Circuit Court, a position he held for several years.[12]

With the exception of his time as commissioner and clerk of the county court, Edward Hines seems to have never been employed at any job for any considerable length. This circumstance undoubtedly was due to the stomach wounds he received during the war and which gradually worsened with each passing decade. In fact, as he grew older, the wounds eventually led to the deterioration of his health. During the time he served in his capacity as the Warren County circuit court clerk, he continued to practice law, but because of the precarious state of his health, he never handled more than one case at a time.[13]

As an extracurricular avocation, Edward Hines was active with Warren County's local Civil War Veterans group. When Jefferson Davis died in 1889, he wrote a letter to the local newspaper asserting what a fine and great man was the former President of the Confederacy.[14] Hines was "an old time Democrat,"[15] as was just about everyone from the South who fought on the Confederate side during the Civil War.[16] He was widely regarded as an educated man by the community, and everyone knew, especially his family, of the high priority he put on reading. The elder Hines even wrote a few long, interesting treatises. One of these tracts was a combination biography and war memoir; another volume by his hand explicated his personal philosophy; still another told of his world and times. He also wrote many long, philosophical letters to members of his family.[17] Edward Hines kept himself busy with one activity or another, especially when it involved Bowling Green. Regardless of his activities or whatever occupied his attention, this state of affairs remained in place until the late 1890s, when he retired to a home he had built at the mouth of the Gasper River, 10 miles northwest of Bowling Green in rural Warren County. It was in this idyllic spot that he spent his last years in comfortable contemplative isolation.[18]

The marriage of Edward and Cornelia Hines produced five sons and a daughter, plus four other siblings who died in infancy—not an uncommon occurrence in those days.[19] Duncan Hines's oldest brother, Hiram Markham Hines, was born 9 March 1871.[20] As a young man Markham worked in Bowling Green for a time before moving out west. There are two theories as to why he left Kentucky. One is that he was always in poor health, and traveling west for any disorder, then as now, was the cure prescribed. The other theory was that he was engaged to a woman in Auburn, Kentucky, who died of typhoid fever; this incident left Markham a very sad young man, and he may have left after his loved one's death. Regardless of the cause for departure, Markham's act to leave Bowling Green in the late 1880s, set an example for his younger siblings, most of whom would follow in his footsteps to seek their fortune. While Markham spent his years on the western frontier, he wrote his father and siblings frequently, often detailing for them the outlaws he had seen and the adventures he had experienced. It was a thrill for his younger brothers and sister when the postman approached the house and handed them a letter containing new stories from the land beyond the Mississippi River. When news from Markham would arrive at the Duncan household, Joseph Duncan would reply to his grandson with a letter, often allowing little Duncan to scribble notes to his older brother at the bottom of the page. One cute surviving comment from Duncan, characteristic of a boy his age, had him asking his brother to shoot a jackrabbit for him. Very little is known about Markham Hines. He moved frequently, eventually returning to Bowling Green to enter the Spanish-American War of 1898. At the war's conclusion, most of his time was spent caring for his aging and ailing father.[21] His own health was in perilous shape as well, and at age 46 on 10 October 1917, Markham Hines died in his father's home.[22]

A year after Markham's birth, a second son was born to Edward and Cornelia Hines on 8 April 1872; unfortunately, the child died on 13 May. The boy was never named.[23]

Annie Duncan Hines, Edward and Cornelia's only surviving daughter, was born on 5 April 1873. Following her mother's death, she went to Frankfort to live with her uncle and aunt, Mr. and Mrs. Henry Duncan; later she attended a finishing school for girls, the Ward Seminary in Nashville. She had many suitors but only one caught her attention, a young Bowling Green grocery merchant and distant cousin, Arthur Scott Hines. After a short courtship, they were married on 23 December 1896, in Nashville, Tennessee. Their union produced three children, two of whom bore the name Duncan. Throughout the years of their marriage, Annie and Scott Hines lived in two houses in Bowling Green, one on upper Main Street and one at 902 Elm Street; the latter residence would figure prominently in Duncan Hines's later years. Scott Hines was a popular figure in Bowling Green, and was twice elected its mayor (1925-1929, 1941-1942). He died on 19 May 1942, and Annie followed his death with her own on 4 December 1951.[24]. Annie, as a sister, was protective of her brothers, but particularly of her younger brother, Duncan, and throughout her life showed much concern for his safety and welfare.[25]

Edward and Cornelia's fourth child was named after his father. Edward Ramsey Hines was born on 14 November 1874. Like Markham, as soon as his education had been completed Ed Hines also pulled up stakes and journeyed westward. He first moved to Arizona in 1890 at the age of sixteen, but prospects for a successful life there did not materialize as he had hoped, and he later returned to Bowling Green, where he accepted a job in the Warren County Court Clerk's office under the supervision of Captain W. H. Edley. It was thought he would stay in this position, but, again like his brother, he was restless and was soon in search of another city to call home. He eventually settled in St. Louis, Missouri, where he became a legal adviser to the Railroad Terminal Association, a position he held until his death on 5 December 1935.[26] At the time of his death, Ed Hines's siblings had come to think of him as the most distinguished member of the clan. Ed had made a success of his life, and his brothers and sister were proud to claim him as one of their own.[27]

The fifth child from Edward and Cornelia's marriage, a son, William Warner Hines, was born in Bowling Green on 23

December 1875. Warner, as he came to be known, attended local public schools, St. Columba Academy, and Ogden College before serving in the Spanish-American War as a member of Company B in the Third Volunteer Infantry. Warner and his brother Markham were one of eleven sets of brothers serving in Company B.[28] After the war he married Martha Hampton Porter at her home on Upper State Street in Bowling Green on 7 October 1905.[29] Although their marriage produced no children, they adopted a son, who was already named William.[30]

Warner Hines was engaged in many forms of employment over the years, most of them related to the insurance industry. He worked for the Lamar Life Insurance Company of Jackson, Mississippi, a real estate firm in New Orleans, as an investment broker in Lexington, Kentucky, and an outfit that sold oil in Texas.[31] Later he moved to New York to work for another insurance company. In 1932, he moved from New York to Nashville where he became an executive with the Spur Oil Distributing Company, a company that owned a chain of gas stations throughout the South. Warner, a quiet, retiring Southerner, was now not far from his boyhood home, Nashville being only an hour's drive away. After his retirement from the oil giant in 1944, Warner Hines returned to Bowling Green, where he lived out his remaining years.[32] Warner had suffered from a heart ailment for years, and at 9:30 on Wednesday morning, 17 August 1948, a heart attack claimed his life. He was buried in Bowling Green alongside his brothers.[33]

The Hines's sixth child, Porter, was born in Bowling Green on 24 March 1878. Porter's birth came within the walls of the Hines home, in "a house in the 1200 block of College Street." His given full name was John Porter Hines but he was always referred to by both family and friends as "Porter".[34] Named after a Civil War friend of his father,[35] Porter went to the Bowling Green public schools and spent a year at St. Columba Academy, the local Catholic school, followed by a year at the Southern State Normal School. Porter, by his own admission, received inadequate schooling because he so frequently moved between the homes of both relatives and friends.[36]

From 1894 onward Porter Hines held a wide variety of jobs over the years, most of them involving river navigation along Kentucky's Barren, Green, and Ohio rivers. In February 1927 Porter Hines joined the staff of Bowling Green's Western Kentucky State Teachers College, a school that eventually metamorphosed into Western Kentucky University, where he became the school's chief mechanical engineer. He must have enjoyed this line of work immensely, because he remained with this job for twenty-eight years, until 1 January 1956, when he retired at age 77.[37] In 1958 Porter Hines suffered a heart attack and remained in poor health until he died at age 83 on 18 June 1961.[38]

Of all Duncan Hines's siblings, Porter Hines was the one that he was closest to, probably because of the close proximity in their ages. When they grew to be men, they were quite different in their demeanor. Porter grew to be a soft-spoken Southern gentleman while Duncan became the gregarious urbanite with scarcely a trace of Southern accent. While Porter was the picture of relaxation, Duncan was energetic, outgoing, always able to make everyone with whom he came in contact feel at ease. Like his older brothers, Porter would not use the strong language that Duncan was some-times wont to blurt out in selected moments of exasperation.[39]

The birth of Porter Hines in 1878 was followed by Cornelia giving birth a seventh time, to a daughter, on 5 May 1879. As was the case with the Hines's second child, the girl died three months later and was not named. While Duncan Hines was Edward and Cornelia's eighth child, there were two others: a ninth child, another unnamed daughter, born on 18 June 1881 who lived only three days, and a tenth child, another unnamed son who was born on 7 November 1882 in Colorado, and lived only a day.[40]

The family that Edward and Cornelia had produced was irreparably upset when at 10:30 P.M. on the Monday evening of 29 December 1884, Cornelia Hines died of pneumonia in Bowling Green at the age of 38.[41] Her death caused much unrest among the

Hines household; Edward Hines, due to his war wounds, was unable to effectively look after the brood Cornelia had left behind. Being concerned for their health and welfare, he made arrangements for his children to live elsewhere. Some went to live with members of his family; others were ensconced into the homes of friends. Indeed, the Hines household was soon scattered all across the Kentucky landscape. Duncan, then only four years old, was sent to live with his grandparents in nearby Browning, Kentucky, a village in Warren County, and it was here that his love for excellent food and his first adventure in good eating began.[42]

Born on 26 March 1880 in the 1200 block of Adams Street[43] in Bowling Green, Kentucky, Duncan Hines was the youngest of the six surviving children of Edward Ludlow Hines and Cornelia Duncan Hines.[44] Joseph Dillard Duncan (1814-1905) and Jane Covington Duncan (1817-1900) lived on a sizable farm near the Morgantown pike 15 miles from Bowling Green, then an agricultural town with light industry of about 5,000.[45] It was in this home that Duncan Hines and his brother Porter spent a large part of their childhood. The two boys usually stayed at their grandparents' house for the winter, sometimes remaining there a year before they went home for the summer to live a few weeks with their father.[46] Joseph and Jane Duncan, who raised the boys as if they were their own, owned plenty of land on which much livestock could always be found grazing. They were both well-educated, well-to-do citizens, who were active in the community's affairs.[47]

According to Hines, until he was four or five years old, he wore a dress and sported long curls, of which he was very proud. As he prepared to enter public school, his grandparents decided that he had to look like a boy. His beloved curls were cut and a little Lord Fauntleroy suit replaced his beloved dress. Seeing that he was trapped into wearing the idiotic garment, he begged them to leave him alone while he put on the raiment himself. Upon entering an adjoining room, he seized the scissors that had so disfigured his precious curls and quickly shred the offensive suit, transforming the prissy costume into a heap of ribbons.[48]

It was in his grandparents' home that Duncan Hines first learned to appreciate and covet the art of good cooking. With generations of long culinary skill behind her, Grandma Duncan, as he called her, created all sorts of wonderful things for him to eat. Unlike modern cooks, her only form of measurement was "a pinch of this and a pinch of that," and the only timer she ever owned was the one in her head. She knew intuitively when the roast or the cake in the oven was ready to pull out and serve. She used no cookbooks. Her method of acquiring recipes was by exchanging them with other ladies after church on Sunday.[49] Before this time "food," wrote Hines of his early years, "was just something to fill the hollow space under my ribs" three times a day. "Not until after I came to live with Grandma Duncan did I realize just how wonderful good cookery could be."[50] Jane Duncan rang a little bell at mealtime. Hines and his brother never let her ring it twice. They were at the table in an instant, "ready to set our teeth into the latest gastronomic delight." One of their favorites was fried bacon and creamed gravy with biscuits.[51] In the years that followed, Hines insisted one should use real eggs and real butter because they were the ingredients that made his grandmother's cooking taste so marvelous. The Duncan household consumed its share of beef and pork, as well as fresh vegetables from the garden and fish from a nearby stream. However, the good country fare that Grandmother Duncan prepared made everyone's mouths salivate. Her cooking did not consist of any special recipes. Rather, her high quality meals were the product of the long hours she put in the kitchen, supplemented with an ample portion of patience and experience that only time can mature. Nevertheless, her kitchen skills were those of such masterful artistry that it made a lasting impression on young Duncan for years to come.[52]

These were happy times for the Hines children, but particularly so for Duncan, as he indulged himself daily in what later became his great passion: eating remarkable meals. Said Hines years later,

"We ate all the time." In addition to "apple pie, pecan pie,...country ham, candied yams, turnip greens with fatback [i.e., a slab of uncut bacon], beaten biscuits and cornbread,"[53] their meals also consisted of "home-baked bread, wild turkey, venison, fried chicken, [fresh pork] sausage, and jam and molasses for biscuit topping." Duncan and Porter were also treated to meals of "marvelously prepared stuffed fowl—turkey, chicken, guinea, or geese" as well as healthy portions of hickory-smoked hams.[54] One species of Southern cooking Hines did not care for, however, was wild game other than that just mentioned. "There is a point beyond which I will not go," he admitted.

> I may be oversqueamish...but I have steadfastly declined, in spite of numerous invitations, to sample some of the 'varmints' with which our Southland abounds. I have heard of those who, with their pack of hounds, roam the fields and woods with a shotgun many a night in the hope of bringing home a 'possum or a 'coon for the table. I've seen these creatures prepared to any one of a dozen different recipes, and to me all looked equally unappetizing. This is no indictment of Southerners' tastes, nor do I mean to say that only Southerners have a tooth for such things, [but]...with all of the wonderful fluffy hot breads and pink, tender hams and Southern fried chicken at hand in my native South, [I am] perfectly willing to leave the 'possum up a gum tree.[55]

Although there was plenty to keep the boys busy on the farm, every now and then grandfather and grandsons hitched a horse to a buggy and drove into Bowling Green to get supplies, farm tools, stationery, or whatever they needed. Because Grandfather Duncan was a county magistrate, he regularly appeared in court, and on those occasions the boys visited with their father.[56] As for their education, Duncan and Porter spent their first few years attending a Bowling Green public school.[57] After a few years there, they spent a year at St. Columba, Bowling Green's Catholic school on Center Street, which was operated by the Sisters of Charity.[58] St. Columba, which welcomed children of all faiths, was an elementary and secondary co-educational institution that could accommodate slightly over 150 students. St. Columba offered students an impressive curricula, including English, foreign languages, biology and chemistry as well as needlework and guitar lessons. The $20-$30 tuition depended on what courses one took during the five-month term. At those prices, the school catered to Bowling Green's middle class, and Edward Hines made sure his two youngest boys attended. As a result of their good education, both boys could compose clear, understandable sentences, had good penmanship, and excelled at mathematics. In that less complicated day, the rudiments of a basic education were considered satisfactory. Nevertheless, the Hines boys were known for their intelligence. Duncan possessed an especially high aptitude for mathematical calculations. In later years he would always have a pen and pad handy, ready to rapidly compute any calculation that came into his head.[59]

As boys, Duncan and Porter enjoyed one adventure after another. When they were well into their seventies, they happily recalled all the "bad" things they did. During the years 1884 through around 1892 when, for one reason or another, the boys were not spending time either on their grandparents' farm or with their father in Bowling Green, they often lived for a few days with the Will Rochester family. The Rochesters and the Hines were great friends, and Duncan and Porter enthusiastically looked forward to those times when they could stay with them, especially because they had five sons to play with, two of whom were almost their age; they also had several daughters to keep their interest.[60]

This may still have been the Victorian era, but as far as Duncan and Porter were concerned, it was a joyful time to be alive and growing up in Kentucky. They loved to play pranks. When the Hines and Rochester children got together no one was safe from their mischief and merry-making. The Louisville and Nashville Railroad line ran by the Rochester' home, and the boys made much mischievous use of it. Said Porter Hines years later, "We knew the time and whistle of every train." Once, while Duncan and Porter were staying with the Rochesters, they built a snowman on the railroad track and put clothes on him. When the train came down the track, the engineer slammed on the brakes so hard to avoid hitting it that the violent action uncoupled some of the cars. "Another time there was a train of freight cars on [the side of the] track[,] just in front of the house," said Porter. "We decided to uncouple the cars so that when the engineer came to take them away he would be pulling only one. This provoked the railroad crew terribly."[61] On another occasion the boys applied a greasy substance to the railroad tracks on a steep incline, causing many a train to barely top the crest of the hill. The railroad company knew the identity of the mischief-makers and told Mr. Rochester it was imperative he control those little "eye-devils." Another time Mrs. Rochester was entertaining some children in her home, telling them a ghost story. Duncan and Porter and Mrs. Rochester's sons, overhearing the woman's dramatics in the next room, sneaked outside, climbed on the roof and dropped a dummy down the chimney and into the parlor where the story was being told. One young black boy, whose anxieties had by this time been fearfully heightened by the tale, leaped up and ran out the door, cutting his neck on a clothesline as he fled. The incident did not seriously harm the boy, but the mischief-makers received a good switching.

As he grew older, some of Duncan Hines's personal characteristics began to take shape. Duncan, in all his siblings' eyes, was the extrovert and the family's natural born entertainer. Unlike Warner or Edward or any of his other siblings, Duncan always had a good yarn to tell. As an adult, on any given summer evening, as he sipped bourbon and water, it was not unusual to find him on his porch or in his living room telling an entranced listener some fantastic tale, usually one from his adventurous childhood.[62]

When he was sixteen, Duncan Hines's primary education was completed. His father encouraged him to further his education, and so he entered Bowling Green Business College in the fall of 1896.[63] The school's curriculum by today's standards was more on the high school level than that found in a rigorous business university.[64] He spent two productive years at this institution, dutifully unearthing the mysteries of business administration. His studies, however, were suddenly and forever interrupted one day in 1898 when he went to the doctor and was given some surprising and unwelcome news.

2

OUT WEST

Late in 1898 Duncan Hines's health began to fail. He had developed "a slight wheeze" and later discovered he was suffering from asthma. "The cure for all respiratory ailments was, at that time, thought to be a move to a dry, mountainous area." After a conference with his father it was decided he should move out west immediately, lest his condition worsen.[65] Consequently, he left Bowling Green Business College without a diploma. By the standards of the day, however, two years was considered by many to be the near equivalent of a full college education. Although he had to forego the diploma for which he had worked so hard, the sacrifice seemed not to have harmed his chances for employment.[66]

Due to his mother's untimely death and his father's fragile health, maturity had been forced upon him at an early age. He therefore taught himself to be resourceful and quickly learned he was the only person who could best look after his interests. The result was a young man whose mien was much more mature and resourceful than his eighteen years belied.[67] To make his move westward he sought a job with the Wells-Fargo Express Company. Years later he told the press he took a job with the firm because John J. Valentine, then its president, came from his home town.[68] There was a little more to the story. Valentine was not only a

Bowling Green native, he was also a good friend of Hines's father who wrote Valentine and requested he find a place for Duncan within the company. Within a few weeks Edward Hines saw his son off at the Bowling Green railway station as the young man headed for a job with Wells Fargo's Albuquerque branch, located in the wilds of New Mexico territory.[69]

Following a three-day train ride, Hines arrived at his destination on the evening of 31 December 1898. He discovered streets crowded with "Indians decked out in calico and cowboys with broad-brimmed hats." All he remembered of that first night, however, was his distress. When he stepped off the train what he saw made him feel uncomfortable. "This was my first holiday away from home, my first night in a strange place. Feeling as though I had not a friend in the world, I registered at the old Sturgess-European Hotel and crept up to bed." The next day he almost decided to go home but concluded he did not have enough money for the journey. Despite his homesickness, within a day or so he began his employment with the Wells-Fargo Express firm at $40 per month.[70] Over the next few months, he quickly worked his way up the company ladder, first as a clerk, then as a railroad express messenger, then as a freight agent.[71] Eventually he was assigned to be a company relief man. In this capacity, he moved from locality to locality in the Albuquerque area when regular Wells-Fargo agents became ill or went on vacation.[72]

For recreation he soon discovered a new place in Albuquerque to spend his time and salary: a restaurant. Specifically it was one of a chain of restaurants known officially as Fred Harvey's House, but to its patrons it was simply another "Harvey House." Hines, who had never before set foot inside a restaurant—let alone eaten in one, found the experience an exhilarating one. Harvey Houses were a system of food service accommodations originally designed to cater to the public who needed transportation via the railway lines. In its own curious fashion, they helped tame the American West in outposts that heretofore were anything but civilized. Beginning in 1876 and continuing through the early 1960s, when the railroads ceased operating as a major mode of transportation, the Fred

Harvey restaurant chain offered its travel weary customers good, elegantly prepared meals in a refined atmosphere at affordable prices. Many of the chain's outlets were located along the Atchison, Topeka, and Santa Fe Railroad, the Albuquerque restaurant being one them.[73]

Unlike many restaurants of the day, it did not serve "short-order cooking"—a synonym for fried food. Instead the Harvey chain's bill of fare offered "steaks, chops, ribs, hams, and bacon...usually served with potatoes, either home-fried, hash-brown, or boiled."[74] A look at an 1888 Harvey House menu reveals what could be found in a typical dining room for a multi-course dinner costing only 75 cents. The patron could choose from "bluepoints on the half shell, filet of whitefish with Madeira sauce, young capon, roast sirloin of beef au jus, pork with applesauce, stuffed turkey, salmi of duck, English-style baked veal pie, prairie chicken with currant jelly, sugar-cured ham and pickled lamb's tongue, all accompanied by seven vegetables, four salads—including lobster salad au mayonnaise—and a wide variety of pies, cakes and custards, finished off finally with various cheeses and Fred Harvey's famous coffee." To its patrons it was a bargain, and it sure beat beef jerky.[75]

Hines usually stationed himself at the counter of Albuquerque's Harvey House, but he made an occasional foray into the dining room when he could afford it. Unlike the larger room's menu, nothing at the counter cost more than 25 cents. This happy circumstance and the large portions that the Harvey House served, combined with his $40 monthly salary afforded him the pleasure of eating "like a king." He was especially impressed with how immaculately clean the restaurant appeared; it reminded him of his grandmother's kitchen, and how she had repeatedly stressed to him the importance of "absolute cleanliness when handling food. She was almost a fanatic on the subject. She kept two buckets of water on her kitchen stove; one for cooking and one for rinsing her hands." He "never saw her pick up a pot or utensil without first dipping her hands into the rinse water." And while the Harvey Girls, the chain's waitresses, may not have had hands as clean as his grandmother's, he was highly impressed with their neat, pristine appearance, noting their uniforms were "starched and spotless," and their hair was "smoothly combed." Small, seemingly insignificant things of this nature made a large difference with him. The attention given to these matters guaranteed his continued patronage. The restaurant chain's passion for excellence was unsurpassed, and it certainly shaped the expectations he demanded of restaurants in years to come. The Albuquerque Harvey House was also a popular place to congregate with the regulars who frequented it, and he soon became one of their number; it became for him a sort of substitute home when he was not working.[76]

While Hines was working for Wells-Fargo in New Mexico, he experienced a "wild west" adventure. One day he was riding in the railroad express car with a safe full of currency to be delivered to a bank. Along a remote stretch of track, the train suddenly came to a screeching halt. Figuring something was up, Hines hurriedly opened the safe, removed the money and hid it elsewhere in the car, then filled the money bags with paper. Sure enough, it was a holdup, an incident not uncommon in those days. The bandits entered the car and demanded at gunpoint that the safe be opened. They scooped up what they thought was the money and beat a fast retreat without ever opening one of the bags to check the contents.[77] His quick action had saved the day, and to the end of his life he kept the medal he was awarded by the Wells-Fargo Company for his faithful service.

Employees who worked for Wells-Fargo knew that they would not remain stationed in one location for a protracted period, and this was certainly true in Hines's case. In early June 1899,[78] just as he was becoming settled in Albuquerque, the company promoted him and assigned him to be the relief man in the company's Cheyenne, Wyoming office. In this position, Hines soon found himself engaged primarily in deskwork.[79]

Hines had not lived in town a month when he experienced another adventure, one which he never tired of telling. "I'll never forget it," he would always begin. Hines, then nineteen, had left Denver on 1 July 1899, at about 1:30 P.M. in a new Wells-Fargo express wagon. His instructions were to deliver the horse-drawn vehicle to the company's Cheyenne office—a distance of about 90 miles.[80] It was his first run through the unfenced country. "Only a few trails wound over the sagebrush hills," he recalled.[81]

For the first few miles, Hines had no problems. He had instructions to sleep at an abandoned sheep camp, which was along the trail 14 miles from his point of origination, but he never arrived there. Hines had no idea what a deserted sheep camp looked like. He traveled all afternoon, ever hopeful that he would find what he was looking for. Eventually, as the sun began to set, he had to face the unpleasant truth: he had lost the trail. He had either passed his overnight lodging without realizing it, or he was nowhere near it. As the last glimmer of light faded over the horizon, he noticed a house not far from the trail. Confident that he would be spending the night there, he unhitched his horse and tied him behind the wagon. He walked to the house, expecting to get a bite to eat from its occupants, but he was in for a surprise. The house was deserted. He pounded on the door, but no one came. "The wind moaned around the corners of the bleak little shanty, the prairie grass rustled and whispered against the old gray boards, and suddenly the weather-beaten little cabin was the most cheerless place in Colorado," Hines recalled. The sky was now pitch black. Hines, his spirit depressed, walked back to his wagon, preparing to spend the night in it. As he walked toward it, he noticed that it had started to snow. Although summer had commenced a few days before, snow in the mountains in summer was quite common. As he tramped back down the road toward his wagon, he suddenly realized he could find neither his horse nor his wagon. They had disappeared with the daylight. He tried to listen for them, but the howl of the wind masked any movement that may have been nearby. Faced with the horror of not only losing his company's goods and horse but also of starving and freezing to death, he began to walk to keep warm. He did not know where he was going, but it beat doing nothing. He thought that perhaps he would stumble across someone or something in the dark. "I was more scared than I had ever been before" he later recalled, "I thought of a thousand reasons why I should have stayed in Kentucky." Then, as if he did not have enough to worry about, along came a new problem: coyotes had picked up his trail. "I could hear them yapping in the darkness, a few yards away." He knew they would not attack him, but he wondered if there was not always the first time for everything. Frightened, there was nothing for him to do but walk throughout the night, hoping he could survive his hunger, his ice-chapped fingers and ears, as well as his yapping companions. He walked constantly, never taking a moment to rest.

When the first outbreak of daylight made its way over the mountaintops, Hines looked behind him and squinted. There before him he could make out what looked like the silhouette of a low, rectangular house. Excited, he ran toward it, hoping to get shelter and food. But as he got closer to the structure, he noticed something about it that was strangely familiar. A realization suddenly washed over him, causing him to stop in his tracks. He had visited the same deserted house at dusk. He had walked in a big circle all night long. His horse and wagon were nearby, the animal waiting patiently for his discovery.

Thankful that he had once again regained his mode of transportation and his cargo, he remained befuddled as to where the trail to either Cheyenne or Denver lay. Besides, even if he and his horse were striding across the trail at its most visible point, there was no way to recognize it now; the snow of the previous night completely covered it. Because of the snow, he reasoned that if he tried to ride into Denver he could easily miss the city by 10 or 50 miles and never know it. Therefore, since it was closer, it only made good sense for him to attempt to find his way back to Cheyenne and deliver the wagon another day. He had one thing working in his favor: he had a general notion of which direction to travel. He knew to continue traveling uphill, because Cheyenne was situated at a higher elevation than that of Denver. Compounding his problem was his rumbling stomach, which had been without food since the previous morning.

Throughout his second day in the wilderness, he remained hopeful that he would run into some sign of life, but, alas, he did not. Therefore, he spent yet another fearful night without food, but at least he spent it in the wagon, safe from the coyotes and the icy wind.

The next morning, feeling more hungry than alive, he once again set out across the mountains. Sometime that afternoon, on 3 July he met a new obstacle to overcome. As the wagon slowly inched up a steep incline, his horse "dropped his head and stopped, spraddle-legged, in his tracks. He was played out." The animal simply could not pull the wagon another foot. Still determined to get to Cheyenne, Hines unhitched the beast, climbed on his back and poked a pin in its rear to get him to move. Despite this painful form of coaxing, the horse refused to take another step. Really desperate by this time, Hines continued his journey on foot, leading his horse behind him.

He had walked 2 miles when he came upon a house that had smoke curling from its chimney. Excited, he ran toward it. The hermit who answered the door let him in. To Hines's horror, however, his host's countenance was nothing to behold; his face displayed two large holes in both his cheeks; someone had fired a rifle at him, supposedly when he had his mouth wide open. Hines later recalled that "the thought of what must happen when he drank water aroused such interesting speculation that I almost forgot I was hungry." Before retrieving Hines's wagon as well as watering and feeding his horse, the hermit fed Hines what few sparse scraps of food he could spare. The food, however, was not nearly enough to feed a man who had been without food for nearly sixty hours. In the conversation that followed between the two over the next few hours, Hines learned that he was only 14 miles from Cheyenne. He went outside the hermit's cabin to mount his horse, intending to ride into town and devour the wares of the first restaurant he spied. Unfortunately, his horse was still too weak to carry a saddle, let alone a human being. Unwilling to let this obstacle stop him, Hines headed for town on foot, walking through 5 inches of snow.

He arrived in the frontier metropolis some time the next morning on 4 July 1899. By now he was practically starving. The walk through the snow had consumed what little energy he had acquired from the meager morsels the hermit had given him, and now he was intensely famished. Upon his arrival, he first hired a cowboy at the livery stable to retrieve his horse and wagon. With that settled, he tramped a few doors down the street to a restaurant—any restaurant. He saw a sign on one door that read: Harry Hynd's Restaurant. It was a frontier hash-house, "where the click of the roulette wheel in the back mingled with the clatter of dishes at the front counter."[82] Hines barged through the double doors.

"I want five dollars' worth of ham and eggs!" he told the counterman.

"Well, you won't get it," his host scowled back. "Nobody can eat that much ham and eggs."

Hines later conceded the counterman was right, but after four days with scarcely more than a few morsels of food, his demand seemed to him an entirely reasonable one. The ham and eggs were quickly set before him and he devoured them in no time. Many years later Hines wrote, "Nothing has since tasted as good as that platter of ham and eggs. I don't think that anything ever will."[83]

Why did he order ham and eggs? Because to the Southern palate ham and eggs was considered not only a morning meal but a standard evening meal as well. In fact, it was a meal for all occasions. Even in his later years, Duncan Hines frequently ate ham and eggs for supper.[84] Indeed, Hines always said that if a diner enters a restaurant and cannot decide what to order, the best strategy for him was to order ham and eggs, because no cook could disguise a bad egg nor spoil a slice of good ham.[85] Nevertheless, the meal he consumed that day was not, as he claimed, the best meal he ever ate; it was, more likely, that after several days without a bite to eat he was just hungry.

Afterward, Hines often dined at Harry Hynd's Restaurant. One day, while in Harry Hynd's, someone pointed out to him that the man in the corner who was eating a T-bone steak with his hands was Tom Horn, a hired gun who reputedly received $500 from local cattlemen for every sheepherder he shot. Hines was terrified. When Horn rose from his table to leave he looked slowly, casually, around the room at the other customers and, Hines said, "I tried to look as though I had never heard of a sheep."[86]

3

FLORENCE

Though only a relief man with Wells Fargo, Hines's gregarious
personality enabled him to meet the "right" people in Cheyenne
society. In 1902, Hines was invited by one of his friends, Bob Carey,
son of the former U S Senator, to spend his vacation with him on
his father's enormous cattle ranch.[87] During his short stay, Hines
and his young host got into all sorts of trouble. One day the two
young men decided to follow on horseback a Native burial party
across the Wyoming range, all the while "gathering up the
cigarettes that the Indians had put along the funeral trail to pacify
evil spirits." The victims of their prank caught them in the act and
angrily chased them all the way back to the Carey ranch. It took a
while for the elder Carey to pacify their extreme anger. A few days
later the two young men mischievously unlocked a bullpen,
enabling four-hundred of the Senator's prized bulls to happily
romp across the plains for the next several days, causing the
Senator's busy ranch hands much unnecessary vexation as they
drove them back into the gates. But it was only after the two killed
nearly all the Senator's imported Austrian quails with a shotgun
that Bob's father decided the young Kentuckian had become a bad
influence on his son. When the Senator bluntly asked Hines, "Just
when in hell are you going home?" Hines knew he had worn out

his welcome and left immediately.[88] He quickly found other things with which to occupy his vacation time. Soon after this incident, he participated in a wild boar hunt in the area between Boise and Pocatello, Idaho.[89]

One day in Cheyenne in late 1900, Hines met a woman who charmed and mesmerized him.[90] Florence Marie Chaffin was born on 10 September 1877, in the Cheyenne territory of Wyoming, thirteen years before it became a state. Her father, John Thomas Chaffin, a Virginian born in 1845, had served in the Confederate army during the Civil War. In early 1868, he married Mary Jennings Jeffres, a woman a full year older than he.[91] They had a daughter, Eva, born in Virginia in April 1868. A few months after their daughter's birth, the Chaffins, who longed for a new life in a part of America not ravaged by war, packed their belongings into a wagon and headed for St. Louis, Missouri. After an arduous overland journey to that Midwestern crossroads, the Chaffins boarded a train on the Union Pacific and rode to the point where the railway ties ceased; in 1868 this spot was Cheyenne in Wyoming Territory.[92]

The town later to become the capital of Wyoming was not quite a year old when the Chaffins arrived. In fact, there had been scarcely little civilization there only a few months earlier. Even so, by the time construction of the Union Pacific finally reached the city on November 13, 1867, approximately four thousand citizens had already established a town. Citizens might be a polite term. The town that greeted them was primarily filled with professional gunmen, soldiers, promoters, gamblers, and confidence men who enjoyed both quick money and cheap liquor, not necessarily in that order. Yet, within a short time the city matured and the rough elements went elsewhere. Within a few years, Cheyenne became the site of an expanded army post, Fort D. A. Russell. Originally built in 1867 to protect the Union Pacific workers from Indian attack, it became one of the country's largest military outposts.[93]

The Chaffin family quickly grew to become one of Cheyenne's most respected families. Upon his arrival, John Chaffin first provided for his family as the cashier at Cheyenne's Wilson bank.[94]

Later he was employed in several other positions including a stint as Wyoming's territorial assessor. This occupation kept him preoccupied for over a decade while his wife, Mary, kept house and tended to the needs of their growing family.[95] Indeed, the Chaffin family seemed to grow as fast as the town. In addition to Eva, there soon followed Fred (1870), Grace (1872), and Howard (1876). The couple's last child was Florence.[96] Sometime during the early-1880s John Chaffin left his position as the state's property assessor and became the city's major florist, an occupation he held until he died.[97]

Before Hines ever met Florence Chaffin she had previously suffered through an unhappy marriage. The marriage took place, either soon before or after 1 January 1900, to an army officer stationed at Cheyenne's Fort D. A. Russell. The marriage was mercifully brief and after their divorce, it was an unspoken rule that no member of the Chaffin family was to ever speak of the ill-fated union.

What little evidence remains of Duncan and Florence's courtship indicates that, after they met, the two began to see each other frequently. Florence, however, did not rush into his arms. Perhaps because of her previous marriage, she was a bit reticent about hurling herself into another potential disaster. But even if she had thrown herself at him, there remained one obstacle in their path to happiness: her mother. Like millions of young men before him, Duncan Hines, despite his best efforts, could not convince his potential future mother-in-law he was worthy of her daughter's hand in marriage. Mary Chaffin did not think too much of the young man from Kentucky. She liked the idea that Hines's family, like her own, had come from the South, and that his father had served with the Confederacy, but she was not convinced Duncan Hines was a good match for her youngest daughter. The two biggest strikes against him was that he was three years younger than Florence and his future looked as if it had no special prospects for a successful career—not, at any rate, as a relief man for the Wells-Fargo express office. Her parents pointed out that Florence's sister, Grace, had married Richard H. Wilson, an army officer, and Mary

Chaffin believed Florence could do just as well. It is not known if Florence temporarily acceded to her mother's wishes and tried to get Duncan to forget about her, but if she did, her efforts failed. She simply could not keep her young suitor from pestering her with his attentions. Their romance remained in an awkward, frustrated state for quite some time.[98]

Probably because of Mrs. Chaffin's refusal to let him marry her daughter, late in 1902 Duncan Hines left Cheyenne and the Wells Fargo company. He had an image problem and he was determined to rectify it. He was making a passable living, but not a great one. Therefore, he left Cheyenne not to forget Florence, but to prove to her mother he was indeed a worthwhile suitor for her daughter's hand.[99]

He did not have to travel far to find work. He moved 9 miles across the state line into Colorado where he found a job with the Coal Fuel Oil Company that mined coke, which was then shipped to Mexico.[100] Early in 1903, after a few months on the job, he was awarded a vacation and chose to go to Mexico. To get there, he boarded a trainload of coke his company was hauling across the border. The train raced through the American Southwest before coming to a stop 45 miles past Nogales, Arizona, at a "dry, dusty, hot little town" named Cananea, Mexico. After dismounting from the locomotive, Hines hailed a carriage to take him into town. He sought out the town's general store, went inside and bought some Mexican cigars. He was about to find a place to spend the night when a man approached him, asking him if he was interested in a job. He asked how much it paid. "Five hundred dollars a month—in gold." This was approximately ten times the average wage, and Hines accepted on the spot. When he asked what he would be doing to deserve such a rich bounty, Hines was told he would be a "trouble shooter in the traffic department" for the Green Copper Company, which desperately needed someone to fill the job. "The vagaries of Mexican customs and the natural slowness of transportation...often resulted in delayed shipments of mining equipment and other supplies. Delays were costly, and the company was more than willing to pay a good salary to the man who could keep the supply lines open and functioning smoothly." Within a few days he found himself a permanent resident of Cananea, working, eating and living with twenty-five other young Americans approximately his age, most of them mining engineers.[101]

While in Mexico, Hines continued to correspond with Florence. He told her of his good luck and asked her to wait for him until he became the successful man her mother wished him to be. She agreed. He spent two years in Cananea, from mid-1903 to the late summer of 1905, all the while earning a fabulous fortune and collecting for them a sizeable future nest egg. After a few months on the job, he received pieces of interesting yet disturbing news from Florence. In early spring 1903 she wrote to tell him the barriers to their potential marriage had disappeared. Her mother had died on 28 March.[102] Nevertheless, he decided to remain in Mexico. Jobs like his did not avail themselves to ambitious young men every day. He wrote Florence, asking her to continue waiting for him until he had accumulated a sizable fortune—or at least enough money that would enable him to handsomely provide for her comfort. He added it would be crazy for him to leave his job right now, certainly one paying $500 a month. Late in 1903, he received another letter from Florence that bore the news that her father had also passed away.[103] A few months later, in early 1904, she sent him another letter informing him she had taken care of her family's estate and was leaving Cheyenne. She was going to be living at Fort Slocum in New Rochelle, New York, with her sister Grace and her husband, Maj. Richard H. Wilson, who had just been transferred there from his command at Fort St. Michael in the Alaska Territory.[104] She also said her oldest sister, Eva, now an artist, would be living with them.[105]

In late summer 1905, Duncan Hines decided to quit the mining life. He had accumulated a sizable bankroll, and he was ready to get married and move on to some other line of work. He had earlier proposed to Florence via the mail and she eagerly accepted. In September 1905, after he had settled a variety of loose ends and amicably severed his ties with the Green Copper Company, he packed his bags and left Cananea by rail for New Rochelle. Never did a train ride seem so long.

4

CHICAGO

Duncan Hines and Florence Chaffin married on 27 September 1905,[106] at Fort Slocum in New Rochelle, New York, in Col. Richard H. Wilson's quarters.[107] Florence's older sister, Grace, wrote a few years after Duncan and Florence were wed: "The biggest event of our stay [in New Rochelle] was...[Florence's] marriage.... The wedding took place in our living room one afternoon. The ceremony was conducted by the post chaplain.... Then [Florence] left us to live in Chicago."[108]

Why Hines and Florence chose Chicago as their new home is unknown. Nor is it known why he chose to work in the advertising profession. He may have thought he had a talent for selling himself and sought to take full advantage of it. When the newlyweds moved to Chicago that fall,[109] Hines was quickly hired by a pioneer in direct mail advertising, the J. T. H. Mitchell company, which was a sophisticated operation for its day that had offices in Chicago's Marquette Building.[110] Before much time had passed, his gregarious personality soon made him one of the firm's best sales representatives. The Mitchell firm had a reputation for excellent service, and Hines quickly learned he had a knack for providing Mitchell's clients with what they wanted: imaginative advertising ideas that effectively sold their services and products. As a Mitchell employee, he did not call on his customers; instead when they wanted to begin an advertising campaign, they called him. He could only be reached by appointment. Although many customers were from Chicago, more than a few were from cities and towns as far away as Ohio and beyond. When he received a call from a distant client, he usually took a train.[111]

Hines liked his role as a salesman. It suited his personality, and there was prestige in what he did. His customers liked him because he was "a straight shooter" and did not try to sell them things they did not want. They found him jovially outgoing in his demeanor and not irritatingly aggressive—unlike some salesmen they had encountered. He made his customers feel comfortable and relaxed when he was around. In fact, he was almost courtly toward them. Hines was gentle but firm, and his customers always wanted to buy something from him. This was the secret to his success.[112]

Although Hines was now living closer to his Kentucky home, his family did not see much of him. He visited them once a year, but that was all he could manage to arrange.[113] After five moves in seven years, in 1912 he and Florence found a permanent residence in an apartment house at 5494 Cornell Avenue;[114] it remained their home for their marriage's duration.[115]

Hines and his boss, John T. H. Mitchell, got along fabulously; quite often they called on distant corporate clients together. So highly did Mitchell regard his employee's ability as a salesman that it was not an uncommon sight to see them together, bustling down the Midwestern breadbasket's highways in Mitchell's car, with the boss at the wheel and Hines in the passenger seat. Although Hines could not drive, this lack of knowledge did not seem to bother Mitchell, who enjoyed his company.[116]

Sometime between 1910 and 1914 the Mitchell company chose to discontinue its involvement with direct mail and plunged itself into the printing business. Within several months the company became a major Midwestern printer. Hines's role within the reorganized company was unaffected by the changeover, because Mitchell could always use his valuable selling talents. The printing industry, however, intrigued him, and Hines sought to extend his knowledge of it. He learned as many facets of the trade as he could, and within time the industry regarded him as one of its more knowledgeable experts. Before long Mitchell gave him new duties. Although officially still a salesman, Hines soon found himself designing, writing, and producing corporate brochures as well as books and catalogues for the industrial firms he called on, which increasingly were outside the Chicago area. As he came to realize, the time he took to learn the many aspects of this new trade proved a valuable asset.[117]

It was while traveling for the Mitchell firm that Hines first began jotting down in a memorandum book the names of good places to eat. He traveled through so many cities and towns over the years that writing them down and noting what they served seemed to him a sensible practice; he could revisit them when he was next in town. He even extended the practice when he went on vacation. One of the places he investigated on a 1915 vacation via train through the Midwest with Florence was the Golden Lamb restaurant in Lebanon, Ohio, just north of Cincinnati.[118] He stepped through its doors because friends had told him it was the oldest hotel in the state and had "a great deal of historical romance connected with it." However, he also went inside because he "was curious to know what kind of food they served."[119]

Over the years, the entries in Hines's restaurant memorandum book grew as he found more good restaurants in which to dine. When on a sales appointment in a town he had not visited for a year or two, a quick look at his notebook told him where to go to devour a delicious meal. By the late 1910s fellow salesmen who knew of his notebook gave him their lists of favorite eating places in exchange for his. They, too, were interested in such restaurants; few places serving good food existed, especially beyond large cities. When he investigated a particular place and found it of high quality, the restaurant's name and address and what it served were recorded in his memorandum book for future reference. His colleagues in sales had good reason to ask for and keep such lists. They did not want to die of restaurant food poisoning, as many did. Any seasoned man in sales then knew that knowledge of a good, clean restaurant was treasured information. "More people will die this year from hit-or-miss eating than from hit-and-run driving," Hines stated repeatedly over the years, and everyone in the business knew it.[120]

Sometime in late 1914 Hines left the J. T. H. Mitchell Company.[121] He was a resourceful young man, however, and by early 1916 he was once again working for another employer. His well-known skills as a salesman in the printing field were quickly appropriated by Mitchell's rival, Rogers and Company, another Chicago printing firm.[122] They employed him until late in 1927 when Rogers and Company was purchased by the Mead-Grede Printing Company.[123] At the new company's request, he remained for a few months as a Mead-Grede employee. As he had with the Mitchell company, his duties with both the Rogers and Mead-Grede operations involved selling. In addition to the usual printing wares, he also sold creative "advertising specialties," items such as key chains, erasers, calendars, fans, pens and pencils that featured a company's logo.[124]

One day in the summer of 1918, while discussing food with some acquaintances, the subject turned to lobsters and the best way to prepare them. Hines's friends kept telling him of the wonderful flavor New England lobsters possessed, that it was simply heavenly, that there was no finer in the world, and that he ought to come to New England with them to discover this truism for himself. He became intrigued with the idea and his friends agreed to take him and Florence on a gastronomic tour of New England—from Provincetown, Rhode Island, to Portland, Maine. An eating tour seemed to him an enjoyable way as any to spend a summer vacation. Therefore, a few weeks later, Hines and Florence climbed into the back seat of their friends' roadster and headed for New England. Within a few days they were well into their quest, visiting "every notable seafood restaurant" along the New England coastline, with an emphasis on exploring the many varieties of lobster. Hines remembered it well: "For days I devoured lobster in every shape, manner, and form of preparation,...but we never did decide which was the best way to prepare" lobster.[125] As a result of the trip, however, Hines could see the advantages of owning a car—something he had been putting off for years. Until he left the Mitchell Company, his primary means of transportation in Chicago was either by foot or train. Before 1915, all of his long distance excursions by automobile had been while sitting in the passenger seat; now he was without a boss to chauffeur him around. Once he joined Rogers and Company in 1916, he discovered he could not call on some clients because they were in small towns without rail service. He spent several frustrating years working around this problem, but after much hesitation, he finally decided to purchase an automobile. Although he considered learning how to drive a car a formidable challenge, he also believed he needed one if he was to remain a successful salesman. It was becoming evident in his eyes that, except for very distant sales calls, non-ownership of an automobile was becoming a handicap he could ill-afford to suffer. Therefore, in late 1919, he bought his first roadster and, at age 39, began mastering its use. Over the years his taste in cars would change a bit. He traded in his old car for a new model every year. His "first car was a big, expensive, hearse-like contrivance," but by 1938 he favored automobiles that were light and fast.[126] By the 1950s his taste in cars returned to larger models, especially Cadillacs.[127] Nevertheless, once he had mastered driving his vehicle, he made the most of it. When he met a client in a distant city, he no longer took the train; instead he drove to the client's factory. The more he drove it, the better he liked it. Soon, for him, driving his car was a way of life.[128]

Hines kept busy during the 1920s. He was in his car or on a train nearly every weekday. As the 1920s unfolded and as more roads were paved, he increasingly forsook train travel for the pleasure driving his car afforded him. It was not unusual in those days to see him steering his car down the road to his next appointment, the vehicle stuffed full of "advertising specialties" and printing catalogs. He traveled to "manufacturing plants in the Middle West." On a typical train trip he might go from Chicago to Buffalo, New York, on Monday; from Buffalo to Bradford, Pennsylvania, on Tuesday; from Bradford to Wheeling, West

Virginia, on Wednesday; and from Wheeling to Huntington, West
Virginia, on Thursday, before heading back to Chicago on
Friday.[129] After 1925 he began to travel well beyond the
geographical confines of the Midwest, often traveling into the Deep
South or the far Western states. Regardless of where he was, after
keeping his daily appointments, he busily familiarized himself with
the town's restaurants by asking its residents about the best places
to eat and recording their comments.[130]

The Hines's Chicago apartment was home not only to them but,
from time to time, to Florence's sisters. The 1920 census shows that
Eva, Florence's oldest sister, was living with them.[131] Florence's
other sister, Grace Chaffin Wilson, had a daughter, whose name
was also Grace, a fact that no doubt created much confusion. In
February 1921,[132] Grace's daughter married Leslie R. "Dick"
Groves, an ambitious West Point graduate and engineer. When
Leslie and Grace Groves were living on the grounds of Chicago's
Fort Sheridan, where he was stationed, they frequently enjoyed the
company of Duncan and Florence Hines. In fact, Leslie Groves and
Duncan Hines became not only compatible in-laws but great
friends; the two men had a lot in common in their outlook on
life.[133]

In 1916, during the first World War, while Col. Richard H.
Wilson, was in Mexico chasing Pancho Villa across the Mexican
landscape to no avail, Florence's sister, Grace Wilson, lived with the
Hines for more than a year. After the war, Florence Hines and her
niece, Grace, spent much time in each other's company, usually
shopping in Chicago's many stores.[134]

Ten years later, during the last weekend of November 1926,[135]
Leslie and Grace Groves came to Chicago to attend the Army-Navy
football game held at Soldier Field. During their stay, Leslie Groves
had business elsewhere that day, so Grace Groves visited the Hines
in their Cornell Avenue apartment. At one point Grace and her
aunt Florence decided to leave the apartment to see a movie, and
Hines was asked to baby-sit for the Groves' son, Richard, whom
they called "Little Dick." Before he could change his mind, they
were gone, leaving him alone with the child. Hines only had one

problem with this situation: he had no idea what to do with the boy. What followed was a scene reminiscent of an Edgar Kennedy movie short, as Hines tried to cope with the mischievous child. Not long after Florence and Grace had left, Little Dick, who was about five years old, snuck up behind Hines while he was reading the newspaper and hit him square in the chest. The boy "bust the dickens out of me," Hines said later, and even broke his glasses. This was probably not the best way to win Hines's favor. At one point Hines told the boy to go to bed. The child dutifully went to his bedroom but stayed there for only about five minutes before becoming restless. Little Dick was lugging around, in Hines words, "this dog-goned monkey," and the child began using the stuffed creature as a stratagem to resist going to sleep. Little Dick told Hines that his monkey, Snooky, wanted a drink of water. So Hines got up from his chair, went into the kitchen, and brought the child the requested glass of water. But neither little Dick nor Snooky would touch it. "Then about five minutes later," the child would squawk, "Snooky wants a drink." Hines, once again, complied with the child's request, getting the boy another glass of water. This was only the beginning. The boy asked twice more for a glass of water for his thirsty pet monkey and twice more Hines acquiesced in the boy's request. But after several more requests for water and several more trips to the sink, Hines became exasperated. So he went to the sink, filled up a scrub bucket of water, and said "All right, Little Dick, are you sure Snooky wants a drink?" And with that he took the monkey "by the legs" and "shoved him...in the bucket of water," letting him have all the refreshment he wanted. The situation then became very unpleasant. The boy began to bawl and "he finally wore himself out and went to sleep." When his mother returned home with Florence and heard his explanation of what he had done, she was not amused. Hines later rationalized away his behavior, saying, "Not having any kids of my own, I didn't know what to do with them except give them candy or something like that."[136]

After being separated from his wife all week, Duncan Hines did something many traveling salesmen still do not do. Instead of flopping down on the sofa and refusing to travel another mile, he and Florence spent their weekends together in their car, traveling the highways of America. In the introduction to an early edition of his book *Adventures in Good Eating,* Hines related how he and Florence first became interested in traveling on weekends:

> My interest in wayside inns is not the expression of a gourmand's greedy appetite for fine foods but the result of a recreational impulse to do something 'different,' to play a new game that would intrigue my wife and give me her companionship in my hours of relaxation from a strenuous and exacting business. She [did] not play golf, [was] not addicted to bridge or to society functions and apparently like[d] to 'go places' with her husband better than she like[d] any other kind of relaxation…. The nature of my business oblige[d] us to live in Chicago, although we would [have] like[d] a house in the country. One day on the golf links I suddenly realized the fact that it was unfair of me to find my relaxation in something which my wife could not share. I decided to reform. We had both been accustomed to refinements in good living and on occasional automobile trips together I had noticed that she was especially interested in these provisions for the comfort and pleasure of tourists. This gave me the idea of giving our recreational motoring trips the spice of definitive objective. Why not make a game of its resources in inns and tourist accommodations?

Therefore, when he returned from business on Friday evening, they "hit the tourist trail, sometimes driving all night to enjoy the scenery by a bright full moon."[137]

When Florence Hines was not keeping herself busy with housekeeping, she was either having her many friends over for coffee and tea, or she was shopping with them. Hers was an enjoyable, uneventful life. But as soon as her husband came through the front door, she spent all her time with him. Each was the other's best friend and trusted confidant. When Hines found his business was increasingly keeping him on the road, she did not demand that she travel with him to keep an eye on him. Duncan Hines was not that manner of man and she knew it. Besides, he was not always gone every week, all week long. Nor was he always in some distant city. Sometimes he spent the whole day meeting clients in Chicago. Every week was different. But when the weekend came, they were inseparable.[138]

During the 1920s, the two made it their habit to spend their weekends together "motoring." Within a few weeks, they had "tasted the narcotic of touring" the country.[139] Their weekend sojourns were spent burning gallon after gallon of gasoline as they drove across the country in a vehicle that freed them from all thought of geographical confinement. Every weekend brought them the pleasure of being able to zip down rural roadsides at high rates of speed, all the while gaping in wonderment at America's rural and urban beauty. Every weekend they stopped at a multitude of roadside restaurants to eat something before finding a tourist camp or hotel by nightfall. This was their hobby, and because they had no children, their expenses were few.[140] From the early 1920s through the late 1930s, their travels together averaged between 40,000 and 60,000 miles annually, this in addition to approximately the same number of miles he traveled during the week. Despite the mileage he accumulated over the years, he never had a traffic accident. Year after year he would preen himself as a model driver. Explaining his secret in 1938, he said he rarely drove at night and "I obey the signs." He also never tried to drive either at dusk or early dawn, the time when most traffic fatalities occur.[141]

Over the years, as Hines criss-crossed the continent while working for his various employers, his search for good restaurants was a matter of trial and error. Although he always had his restaurant memorandum book with him when he traveled, quite often the places listed in it were nowhere nearby. On these occasions, he was at the mercy of chance and luck. He knew there were many restaurants around, but he had no way of knowing which were the sanitary ones with good food. Since he had to eat somewhere, the only course of action left to him in the early years was to walk into a restaurant that looked half-way clean, order something, and hope the kitchen's chef did not poison him. He experimented at least once a day in this way, relying on serendipity in his quest for a good solid meal that would satisfy his taste buds. Sometimes his meals were good, sometimes they were not. Sometimes the reputation of an establishment lived up to its good name, but just as frequently it turned into a disappointment. When the meal was not worthy of his fastidious standards, however, he groused and remembered never to enter the restaurant again. When he began to explore America's restaurants, he noted there was usually "good food in the cities, but in small towns and along the highways the average restaurant was a place of dirty tablecloths, crankcase coffee and pork chops cooked to a cinder."[142] Once while dining in a roadside inn, he was served "soggy French fries and battleship-gray beef"; his response was to immediately stand up, pay the bill, and walk out without tasting it. If the food did not look good, it probably tasted worse.[143]

When Hines and Florence spent their weekends traveling, his restaurant memorandum book always accompanied them. With this in hand, he and Florence kept "check lists" whereby they "judiciously balanced the succotash of one inn against the smothered cabbage of another."[144] They were "determined not to wander too far from good provisions." After all, they did not care where they went—or how far, but they knew the joy they received from traveling would be robbed if the food they ate was inedible.[145]

As they explored the continent, they made a game of their restaurant hunt. First Florence suggested a place to stop and eat, then later Hines suggested another. In this way, meal by meal, they slowly made additions (and subtractions) to his already sizable notebook. Sometimes their weekend food "safaris" took them to eating spots as far as 250 miles from home, "stopping two or three times a day for waffles, sausage and eggs, and at least as often for fried chicken, baked clams or black-bottom pie."[146] Sometimes, however, the food they were served was simply dreadful. Hines later remembered "the library paste served as gravy in some 'short order' places was a personal insult."[147] One trend they noticed in their travels was that, more often than not, much of the unpleasant roadside fare they were served was fried. Once, while passing through a little town in Mississippi, they discovered a restaurant that even fried custard.[148]

The roadside restaurants they frequented contained many perils and surprises, and Hines and Florence endured their share. Sometimes the meat they consumed was adequately refrigerated, but sometimes it had lain out too long in the warm air and had spoiled—but was served nonetheless because many restaurant owners believed there was no sense in letting meat, even if it was spoiled, go to waste. Food poisoning in restaurants was quite common. The reason so many people went to their graves after eating in restaurants was because local health inspectors rarely visited them—especially those outside metropolitan areas. Therefore, when someone visited a dining establishment, he could expect the possibility of "undercooked pork chops and decaying salad amidst a decor of greasy walls and flypaper." A visit to a restaurant was not always a delightful experience. In fact, save a sanitary oasis here and there, the filthy condition of most restaurant kitchens were often sickening when not simply appalling. It was quite common to walk into a restaurant or a railroad depot lunch counter in the early 1920s and—just as had been the case seventy years earlier—be served the usual mealtime fare: "rancid bacon, eggs preserved in lime, bitter coffee made with the local strongly alkaline water, ancient beans, leaden biscuits accurately called 'sinkers', and 'antelope steak', so tough you couldn't get your fork in the gravy"—in short, meals often prepared by chefs who had no idea what they were doing but needed a job.[149] Restaurants—especially those in rural areas—were usually nothing more than dirty roadhouses with a kitchen tacked on as an afterthought. They were unkempt, unclean, and unsanitary; quite often they served their guests dirty utensils.

Restaurant sanitation meant a great deal to Hines, and his concern increased with every passing year.[150]

As Hines and Florence traveled more extensively, they discovered others shared their thoughts. Wherever they stopped to eat or rest, they found themselves exchanging comments with many motorists. "Where's the best place to eat?" was almost always Hines's opening comment upon meeting them. This question was usually followed with a lengthy discussion of the subject followed by his dutifully jotting down their suggestions in his notebook. In this way, Hines gained a wealth of knowledge.[151] By 1930, many years after he had first begun compiling his first restaurant lists, his memorandum book had swelled to approximately two-hundred listings.[152]

This keen interest in fine dining establishments soon marked Hines as an expert on the subject. Eventually his interest in good restaurants became well-known. Chicago businessmen asked him for recommendations—and what to eat there. Over the years, in a slow but ever growing procession, hundreds whom he had met in his travels (and sometimes perfect strangers whom he had never met in his life) came to him before heading off on a long journey, asking advice on not only the best places to dine but the best places to sleep as well. On any given day, Hines might receive a call which would start, "I'm off to Nashville—where should I eat?" or "I'm going to Boston—where is the best place in town I can get a steak?" And he supplied his questioner with an answer. He told those who asked his advice of countless superb restaurants of which he was acquainted, such as the "elderly woman of reduced circumstances [who] ran a superb tea room on the road south of Louisville...or a couple who grew all their own vegetables [who] did wonderful things with sauces at an unassuming inn near Syracuse," New York. Whether it was Fort Worth, Boston, or Indianapolis, he knew where all the good restaurants were, and with every passing year more people came to agree.[153]

Though he was now firmly ensconced in Chicago, Hines's siblings in Bowling Green never forgot him, nor did he forget them. Hines and Florence tried to visit Bowling Green once or twice a year—usually for a week in summer and again at Thanksgiving or Christmas. Family members always gave the Chicago couple a warm Southern welcome when they arrived in town. Once they had unpacked their bags, the Hines sometimes spent their whole day at Annie's home. But usually Hines and Florence went their separate ways. Hines spent most of his time with his sister and her family at her Elm Street home, but sometimes he would walk a few blocks downtown to loaf around the courthouse square. Meanwhile the ladies of Bowling Green usually treated Florence to such Southern social customs as noontime luncheons, bridge parties, and teas which were pleasant, serene, social events that usually extended well into the afternoon. Toward evening, Hines and Florence dressed for dinner, which was usually held at Annie's home or one of their many friends. After they had eaten, they gathered in the living room for a long chat, punctuated by a variety of humorous stories, which lasted well into the evening. When Duncan and Florence were not calling on others during their Bowling Green visits, they were being called on by old friends who had heard they were in town. Many evenings were spent entertaining many of Hines's contemporaries in Annie's parlor.[154]

By late 1928 Hines became dissatisfied with his new employers at the Mead-Grede Company, so he took a similar job as a salesman with the Columbian Colortype Company, another printing firm just a block away.[155] He hit the road again, traveling extensively, making calls on industrial and commercial clients who requested to see him. He stayed with this firm for two years. In 1930 he left Columbian Colortype for a similar position with the Gentry Printing Company;[156] he stayed with them for four years.[157] In 1934 he left Gentry to work as a salesman for another printing concern, E. Raymond Wright, Inc.[158] Regardless of which firm he worked for, he continued to sell his printing wares primarily in the American Midwest. His non-train travels outside the Midwestern states usually took him no farther south than the Ohio River, no farther west than the Rocky Mountains and no farther east than Buffalo, New York.[159] More often than not, he traveled a thousand miles a week. Although he had no fixed hours with any firm he worked for, by his own admission he worked quickly and efficiently and was often through with a day's work "before any one else" in his profession. He was a "salesman's salesman," and would have remained one for the rest of his life had it not been for fate.[160]

After many years of watching him play supper sleuth, people began to take Hines seriously. Someone with his precision for accuracy in restaurant recommendations could not be kept a secret forever. And, as usually happens when one has specific knowledge about a particular subject, he becomes an expert the newspapers want to write about. In 1934 a Chicago newspaper reporter learned of his repute and asked him for permission to write an article about his unusual hobby. Hines saw no harm in the request and granted an interview.[161] After the article appeared, however, his life was never again the same. Soon his apartment phone was ringing all day long, and this time the calls were not just from businessmen. They were also coming from hundreds of seasoned travelers who had found their trips completely ruined or made wholly unenjoyable because they had dined in a badly managed, unsanitary restaurant. He later claimed that "executives bound for conferences, musicians going on the road, honeymooners choosing their destination—perfect strangers all—called for advice."[162]

Toward the end of 1935, thanks to the newspaper article, his reputation as the man who knew the best places to eat and sleep throughout the country had grown to such an extent that one day Hines realized he was spending all his time answering telephone queries. While he was dispensing advice one morning, the thought occurred to him to design some literature that would cut down the time he spent answering his mail and talking on the phone. After all, time was money. No one was paying him to answer questions. Therefore, in November 1935 he and Florence compiled a list of the 167 best restaurants they had dined in over the years, covering an area of 30 states. They included only the ones that never failed to leave a highly favorable impression. Hines then ordered 1000 copies printed on a heavy stock of blue paper. The couple included these lists inside their Christmas cards and mailed them to everyone they could think of, including all his friends, business associates, and just about "anyone who had pestered him for a restaurant recommendation." He entitled his restaurant list "Adventures in Good Eating."[163]

The list was condensed from his original notebook of "superior eating places," which by this time had grown from between 700 to over 1,000.[164] He had hoped widespread use of this list would give him some time to return to making a living. He was not prepared, however, for what happened next. Before too many weeks had transpired, friends began deluging him with requests for still more copies of his restaurant list. And so did their friends—in one wave of requests after another. Hines had created a monster. Everyone, it seemed, wanted his restaurant list. To keep from going broke in printing costs, he began charging a dollar for it. No one seemed to mind. As far as they were concerned, it was a price well worth paying.[165]

5

LEAVE ME ALONE
OR I'LL PUBLISH A BOOK!

As people across America were tacking up their January 1936 calendars, Hines kept receiving more letters from people who wanted a copy of his restaurant list. "We got hundreds of requests for cards from people we had never heard of," he later recalled. "It made me realize that we had done something that had never before been tried in this country— because there were no authoritative and unbiased guides to good eating. I felt that I could perform a real service to the public by giving them an appreciation of fine food and telling them where they could get a decent meal."[166]

After witnessing favorable public reaction to his Christmas card, Hines resolved to put his restaurant knowledge in a book. He may have toyed with the idea earlier, but now he had seen enough evidence to conclude a sizable number might be willing to pay for his knowledge. He had to do something. By mid-January his hobby had transformed itself into a nightmarish phenomenon he could not control. He could have thrown all the letters and telegrams he received about restaurants in the garbage. Likewise, he could have slammed down the phone every time someone asked him about a restaurant. But he did not. Despite their increasing number and that it handicapped his ability to make a living, he felt duty-bound to answer every communication. Still, he no longer seemed to have any time of his own. His knowledge of American restaurants had become an albatross that somehow had to be governed. It was under these circumstances that his book, *Adventures in Good Eating*, was born.

Hines rationalized his decision to publish a restaurant guide by later recalling there "were book reviewers to tell us what we should read, art and drama critics to advise us on what to see—but there were no authoritative and unbiased guides to good eating.... And the reaction to my 'card' indicated that people were eager to have someone perform the service of telling them where to find good food when they were away from home. Why not myself?"[167] He therefore resolved to take matters into his own hands. He hand-addressed and sent out multigraphed copies of simple questionnaires to all the notable restaurants that had accumulated in his memorandum book.[168]

In his questionnaires, he asked restaurant owners the usual questions, such as their address, times and days open, average price for breakfast, lunch and dinner, if they were air-conditioned, and the house specialty. Ninety-percent were answered; half made it into the book's first edition. The responses were sent either to his Cornell Avenue home or to the Wright Printing Company.

After Hines sifted through his 900-plus replies, he realized he had far too much material to produce an inexpensive book. He therefore decided to cut his material down to size. To determine which restaurants to include in his book, he compared the replies he received with his comments in his notebook. When he was unsure of the validity of the information he possessed on a certain restaurant, he relied on newspapers and other literature as well as menus sent to him by friends.[169]

Even while compiling his book, he was already planning ahead. If response to this volume did well, he wanted to produce an updated edition annually. As many restaurants across the country appeared and disappeared each year, he believed an annual publication of his restaurant guide would prove useful; it would enable its users to keep up with the latest changes. With this in mind, Hines began to assemble a plan that would ease him out of the printing business and into the publishing world.[170]

Hines never worked on his book during business hours; it was all done on his own time. He was fortunate, however, in having a very generous employer, E. Raymond Wright, the owner of the Wright Printing Company. Wright was more than willing to let him pursue his publishing objectives so long as he brought in revenue for his firm. In fact, Wright helped him with his experimental venture by letting him use his company's address as the incorporation site for Adventures in Good Eating, Inc. and even became his business partner. In addition to Wright, who served as the corporation's vice-president, another Chicago native, known only as Mr. Hueser, served as the corporation's secretary.[171] Both men owned shares in Adventures in Good Eating, Inc. Hines was listed as the company's president and treasurer. The company issued ten shares of stock with each share being worth $100. Hines held six shares while Wright and Hueser each owned two. In 1937 Hines bought out his partners, making him sole owner of the company.[172]

After several weeks of typing, cutting, and pasting the manuscript in his Cornell Avenue apartment, his compilation of his expanded Christmas card soon emerged into the first edition of *Adventures in Good Eating*. Aside from Florence, his friends, Harold and Eleanor Beebe, also gave Hines much help with his project; Eleanor was one of Wright's secretaries. Also helping in the endeavor was another secretary employed by Wright, Eleanor's sister, Emelie Tolman.[173] Hines placed his printing order with the Wright Company on 9 June 1936, and soon 5,000 copies of his 96-page book rolled off the presses. Wright charged him $1,131.07 for the job.[174] He wanted his book to have the look of quality, yet he could not afford to produce one with a hardback cover. Therefore, the format he finally chose was neither hardback nor paperback. Instead, large, perforated holes ran down the publication's left side; enmeshed through them clung a cylindrical, bright-red plastic binder. The first title of this thin, pocket-sized edition was *Adventures in Good Eating for the Discriminating Motorist.*

In addition to writing and editing his book, Hines now had other duties. He effectively became his own publisher and distributor. "He had no regular channels of distribution, but he did permit restaurants which he had recommended to sell his book." The Chicago bookstores also put it on their shelves. If one could not purchase the book through these avenues, Hines sold him a copy by mail. To defray printing costs, he sold it for $1.00. But it was not an overnight success. Despite the fact he sold all copies by year's end, he lost $1,539.[175] But its publication did serve one useful purpose; the constant stream of daily phone calls from restaurant hunters ceased; there was no excuse to call him now. Within a few weeks appreciative letters commending him for his effort replaced the daily phone queries. Little did he know what he had set in motion.

In his short introduction to *Adventures in Good Eating*, Hines conveyed his mission when he wrote that when he first took to the road:

> The highways were crowded with gasoline pilgrims whose main interest seemed to be the relative merits of inns. They fairly oozed information about the places we ought not to miss.... Most of these tourists produced private lists of 'best places' and nearly all of them remarked that there ought to be a reliable directory of the most desirable inns available to motorists. Being a printer, this idea intrigued me. After years of travel over the highways I found I had the names of several hundred inns, scattered over the country, the desirability of which was enthusiastically vouched for by those who had patronized them.... This recreational quest has revealed the fact that...there are thousands of these gasoline pilgrims to whom the price of a meal is a minor consideration.... Tourists are free spenders and 'eating out' amid country surroundings is the...prevailing recreational fashion. Millions upon millions of dollars are spent throughout the motoring season in these

roadside inns. To make this expenditure more satisfactory is the purpose of this directory.

He followed his introduction with a cautionary note on the book's accuracy. He wrote that although he made a valiant effort to create a book free from errors and as current as possible, he could not control restaurants' destinies. Some changed management. Others went out of business without warning. Some lost their cooks—and thus their reputation for fine food; this was especially true if their chefs ran off with the restaurant's recipes. One reason he lost money on the first book was because he spent a considerable sum making sure his book was error-proof. Despite his best efforts, Hines reasoned the average diner would not expect perfection. If the cook dropped dead or was discharged or whatever, and a restaurant patron subsequently had an unpleasant meal, he was confident his readers would not blame him for these misfortunes. "No doubt they will be generously overlooked; any other reaction would be unreasonable." He cautioned his readers that any restaurant, even a good one "...may seem to have the automatic perfection of a machine. But it isn't a machine; it is a coordination of the efforts of a group of human beings—and occasionally this fact will demonstrate itself in imperfections."

Hines closed his introduction with a short litany that soon characterized and defined his persona in the minds of the American public. In time, these words would forever earn him the public's trust, and they contributed to his emerging fame: "I have never accepted a free meal or any other consideration from any inn. Those mentioned are included because, in my judgment, they are entitled to be listed on the merits of their food and their service. Until a meal has been eaten and paid for, no mention of the directory is made—and then only if the inn meets its standards."[176]

Duncan Hines's ability as a writer also contributed to his book's success. Few could so succinctly inspire daydreams of dining on wondrous meals in distant locales as he. Those who read his book found charming wordage that tempted them to hop in their car and investigate the culinary delights told thereof. Of Stute's Chick-

Inn, a restaurant in Hot Springs, Arkansas, he wrote, "Imported Italian foods the specialty here. But it is their good, old, American menu of thick porterhouse or broiled milk-fed chickens that has made Stute's famous. And their beaten cream biscuits, the like of which you have seldom tasted."[177] Of his favorite Kentucky restaurant, the Beaumont Inn in Harrodsburg, Hines described it as a "white-pillared mansion built in 1847" that for 20 years had served..."Southern hospitality at its best. Their food specialties are fried yellow-legged chicken, two-year old, genuine country-cured, hickory-smoked ham...delicious beaten biscuits, [and] an ample variety of fresh vegetables."[178] Designed for specific information as well as simple browsing, one could spend an afternoon with his guidebook, reading his concise, enjoyable descriptions of restaurants and leave the experience feeling as if he had taken a culinary tour.

There were restaurant guides available, even in Duncan Hines's day. No doubt he and Florence tried to use these a time or two, but to no avail. They were useless because they were unreliable. David Schwartz writes,

Adventures in Good Eating was not the first restaurant guide intended for defenseless wayfarers. The *Guide Michelin* had already come to the rescue of discriminating French travelers...but the American guides were mostly a sham, financed by the very establishments they purported to review. Hines, on the other hand, snubbed all offers of advertising. He fiercely guarded not only his independence but also his anonymity, making reservations under an assumed name and, in the early days, frontispiecing his books with a 20-year old photograph of himself as a natty young blade. But most important, *Adventures in Good Eating* oriented itself to the automobile at a time when owning one was coming to be regarded as an American birthright. Although Hines included big-city restaurants in the book, his was a trailblazer in featuring the small-town places, the uncelebrated inns and tea-rooms and taverns that his urban audience *needed* to know about in order to eat well between one city and another. And he told them about these places without the slightest trace of snobbery or literary affectation in a style that exuded humor and humility.[179]

Not long after the book was released, a Chicago newspaper printed a profile of Duncan Hines. Chicagoans learned he was probably that city's only resident who thought nothing of making a round-trip to Detroit by car in a single day just to eat lunch. He also revealed he frequently drove over 400 miles to Nashville, Tennessee, to dine in a restaurant that served America's best apple pie, the crust of which Mary Gotscholl prepared by mixing chicken fat with the shortening.[180] At the article's conclusion, Hines let loose with a volley of opinions, exclaiming that, overall, food was "cheaper in Chicago than in New England, and cheaper on the Pacific coast than in Chicago." He said San Francisco had more restaurants than any other city, New England had the highest concentration of them in America, Southern food was "too greasy," and any restaurant sign bearing the words, "Home Cooking" was "a delusion."[181] Quotable statements as these, in city after city, soon made him a favorite with newspaper editors. His newspaper interviews were calculated to make the public wonder about him, to ask, "Who is this man, anyway?" Surely, they reasoned, a man who drives 400 miles to eat in a restaurant must know something others did not. The curiosity he created about himself was transformed into book purchases. His method of attracting attention surpassed anything an advertising agency could devise.[182]

To discover new restaurants he may have missed, Hines devised a way to learn of them. Between the last page and the back cover of his book appeared three perforated postcards pre-addressed to Wright's Chicago printing firm. For the price of a one-cent stamp a reader could send him the names of other restaurants he believed merited investigation. Across the top of the post cards read the words: "Editors: I found dining at the following places an unusually pleasant and satisfactory experience. I believe that their standards of food and service entitle them to honorable mention in the next edition of *Adventures in Good Eating.* They are recommended for your consideration." This was followed by space enough for three recommendations which asked for the name of the establishment, its exact location, and its distance from the nearest city. The endorser could check a box if he wanted his name acknowledged in the next edition.[183] Although he had earlier accumulated a number of contacts for new restaurant recommendations, it was from this postcard that he found a new generation of individuals whose passion for fine roadside dining surpassed even his own. His interaction with them soon gave birth to an informal society, a group later dubbed as his "dinner detectives."[184]

6

THE DINNER DETECTIVES

With each passing week the postcards Hines had provided for his readers poured into his office in growing numbers, each giving him new restaurant leads to investigate. The task of trying to organize this mass of information eventually became overwhelming. By early 1937 Hines realized he had to rely on others of like taste and temperament if he were to investigate all leads that came across his desk; the job of inspecting every potential restaurant that met his criterion had become too large an endeavor for one man. To tackle this problem, he recruited friends who shared his opinions on matters of good food.[185] Many were more passionate about quality dining than even he, and they made his job of compiling information much easier. Several approached Hines soon after buying the first edition of *Adventures in Good Eating*. After they tested Hines's veracity for detecting wonderful dining experiences, they began to correspond with him regularly, recommending other places for him to include. They formed with him a common bond of friendship. If he tested several restaurants a culinary compatriot had recommended and found the correspondent's standards in dining to be equal or superior to his own, he relied on his judgment thereafter. He encouraged the correspondent to keep him informed of other delectable restaurant "finds" that would intrigue him and the discriminating public. Afterward, he usually heard from the correspondent two or three times a year. One by one, this is how Hines's informal network of "dinner detectives" evolved.

One aspect to recognize is that his dinner detectives were usually successful people. In Hines's day, people from this social strata tended to travel frequently enough to experience "adventures in good eating"; hoi polloi did not. People who had succeeded in life, Hines felt, could be trusted; they had competently managed their careers and finances to the point where they were considered honorable members of society. By extension, when these people traveled, they did not just eat or sleep anywhere. They were discriminating; they were picky; they were much like himself. Thus, in his eyes, successful individuals had superior tastes when it came to the finer things in life—such as good restaurants.[186]

There was another reason why the "dinner detectives" were valuable to Hines. His guidebook was published annually and he was keenly aware that no matter how good a restaurant's reputation, its maintenance was nothing less than a daily gamble. Anything could put a restaurant out of business quickly—even a good restaurant—such as a fire, a flood, a rerouted road, the death of the owner or, perhaps, the death of the chef whose knowledge of the restaurant's recipes died with him. Anything could happen. Therefore, he tried to keep abreast of any restaurant changes he listed so as to assure his readers they still measured up to his exacting standards. For this reason alone he needed his "dinner detectives" to keep tabs on them. Thanks to his correspondents, each new edition of *Adventures in Good Eating* was kept current. By early 1937, "many purchasers [had] a standing order with Hines for all new editions." Hines decided to print a second volume due to the enthusiastic support his book received from those who found it a godsend when traveling.[187]

During 1937, Hines tried to juggle both his printing duties with the Wright company and his guidebook business. It was an exhausting experience. While his book's second edition was being prepared, he was also on the road all the time, albeit working for

Wright less and himself more. Even if Wright had paid him to spend his entire time investigating restaurants, there were simply too many leads coming in to follow up; he could not begin to answer the enormous volume of mail that daily flooded his office. Something had to be done. During the latter half of 1936, Hines had used a secretary on a part-time basis, but now he needed one full-time. Therefore, in the spring of 1937, he hired an unidentified secretary to come to his Cornell Avenue home to handle his voluminous correspondence and answer his phone while he was out of town. When he was home, though, he rolled up his sleeves and helped her. He wrote out in longhand or dictated for his secretary as she typed all the descriptive matter found inside the book. He also laid out its design.[188] Despite his help, Hines's secretary was overwhelmed. There was too much mail coming in each day to adequately answer it with care. Therefore, within a few weeks, he hired several more women to answer his correspondence. They worked out of his home after business hours. Two of them were Wright's employees, Emelie Tolman and Olga Lindquist. Later they left the Wright company to work for Hines full-time.[189] There were days when his secretaries wished they had never taken the job. By the middle of 1938, they were answering as many as a thousand letters a week.[190] As to what Hines looked for when hiring, a former employee said, "I think he was rather impulsive." He would hire someone "if he decided he liked somebody's looks. There wasn't any rigorous testing." But if he discovered they could not do precisely what he wanted and in the way he wanted it done, he quickly replaced them with someone who could.[191]

The second edition to *Adventures in Good Eating* was published early in 1937, and for the second year in a row, Hines lost money on it, but by a much smaller margin. The second edition, which now listed almost 500 new restaurants, sold 16,000 copies. "Aside from [his] traveling expenses and the cost of a tremendous personal correspondence, [Hines] managed to lose only $584." The biggest factor for the much narrower loss on the second edition was his decision to raise the price to $1.50. In addition, as month followed month, word-of-mouth slowly closed the gap between deficit and profit. He published a third edition of *Adventures in Good Eating* in the early summer of 1937, and from this point forward, his profit and loss ledger remained comfortably in the black, much to his relief.[192]

A look at some surviving invoices for which the E. Raymond Wright Company billed Hines for its printing services between August and December 1937 gives a glimpse into the nature of what it cost Duncan Hines to produce his guidebook. In mid-August, Hines ordered 1,000 copies of a booklet that he wrote entitled "A Frank Statement," a publication that advertised his unimpeachable character. Hines gave these booklets away at appropriate opportunities in his travels to interested individuals and institutions. This was part of his continuing campaign to introduce and sell himself to the public. Wright charged him $34.52 for these booklets.[193] Another order in late September for 5,009 additional units of the third edition of *Adventures in Good Eating* cost Hines $799.07.[194] Hines had other printing expenses besides the book. A mid-November invoice for 1,000 questionnaires cost Hines $52.87. The purpose of these questionnaires was to obtain new restaurant information and to receive updated facts and figures on those establishments previously listed.[195] Wright charged Hines similar or higher amounts for stationery and envelopes. In addition to what Wright charged him, his business expenses included, stamps, secretarial salaries, meals, and gasoline, as well as a host of other incidental expenses. Hines may have made some money on each book, but when his profit and loss statements are examined, it is easy to see that his income was not a stupendous figure. The money he earned from his venture was just enough to provide his wife and himself with a comfortable middle-class existence.

Although Hines increasingly found it harder to devote less time to the printing firm, Wright let his enterprising employee use his business address through at least December 1937. Although Wright was a stockholder, his meager $200 investment cannot fully justify his favorable treatment of his employee. Only a deep friendship can explain a business relationship like this one. On the penultimate page in the second edition of *Adventures in Good Eating*, Hines wrote that "the publication of this book would have been a far less delightful enterprise without the enthusiastic cooperation of my business colleague, Mr. E. Raymond Wright.... Instead of regarding it as an intrusion, Mr. Wright could not have been more interested in it had it been his own project."[196] Hines did not officially leave the Wright firm until sometime after March 1938, when he could safely predict the continual success of his venture.[197]

The second edition of Adventures in Good Eating contained a few improvements over the first. Whereas the first edition listed 475 restaurants, the second edition listed 1,250. The interior pages were marked by a heavier, more serious-looking typeface. The new edition even listed Hines's home phone number on the first page: (MONroe 0006).[198] A slightly altered introduction to the book written by Hines was included, which concluded with these words: "PLEASE NOTE. If you find any place listed in this book that should definitely be eliminated from future editions I shall appreciate your advice in detail."[199]

Another new feature in the second addition was the listing of twenty-six of his "dinner detectives." Those listed included Cameron Beck, the director of the New York Stock Exchange Institute; Gordon McCormick, a life-long friend; Gluyas Williams, the cartoonist; Forrest A. MacGibbon of Marshall Field & Co.; C.A. Patterson of Hotel Monthly and Restaurant Management magazine; and Frank J. Wiffle, secretary of the National Restaurant Association.[200] This select group eventually grew to 300-400 volunteers who constantly monitored the restaurants Hines listed. Not only did they keep him apprised of the places he recommended, they were constantly searching for new discoveries. One of Hines's most enthusiastic dinner detectives was a young millionaire who, in the late 1930s, had the pleasure of traversing the ends of the earth for him, tirelessly searching for the best in mashed potatoes. The young man, a native of the western United States, frequently telephoned Hines at his home, always beginning the conversation by asking how the reprint of "our book" was progressing.[201]

The dinner detectives came from all walks of life. Corporation executives, bankers, and university professors were just a few occupations that comprised their ranks. One notable detective was Metropolitan opera singer Lawrence Tibbett, a figure popular with the public from the 1920s through the 1950s. Tibbett frequently traveled about America giving concerts. While he and Hines did not see each other socially, there was much correspondence between the two. Hines was always very grateful when Tibbett recommended a restaurant because he knew the opera star's refined tastes mirrored his own. Another famous dinner detective was radio commentator Mary Margaret McBride.[202] With a daily audience of six-million listeners by 1948, McBride was network radio's most-listened-to host of women's programs.[203] An attractive heavy-set woman who somewhat resembled Kate Smith, McBride began as a dinner detective in the late 1930s after she interviewed Hines on her CBS radio program. He always tried to appear on her broadcast when he visited New York. Hines had an entertaining persona and McBride was glad to have him as a guest. His genial, almost folksy, manner won him a larger following with every appearance. When he appeared on her program, his many years as a salesperson came in handy. Through the medium of radio, his well-modulated, gentle voice proved a useful instrument when he sold himself and his message to millions of listeners.[204]

Not long after the first edition of *Adventures in Good Eating* was published, it was prominently featured in a display window in Chicago's Marshall Field department store. Early in the summer of 1936 Warren Gibbs stopped through Chicago while making his seventeenth transcontinental automobile trip across America. While walking by the display window, he discovered Hines's book and immediately bought a copy. He wanted to test it as he made his way to New York. As a result, Gibbs undoubtedly became the most committed of all the dinner detectives. In the introduction to the second volume, Hines recalled Gibbs' enthusiasm for it: "When he read the descriptions I had written about places where he had been, he felt that here was something very much worthwhile for the tourist, for he had never found a travel guide recommending good eating places upon which he could always depend." Gibbs was so overjoyed at possessing the book, he took it to heart and made a point to visit as many places in it as he possibly could. After a few weeks, so impressed was he with Hines's uncanny ability to recommend nothing but superior restaurants, he visited him in Chicago on his return trip home.[205] Gibbs told him, "You've got something worthwhile here. I've been to many of the places you recommend, and I quarrel with your judgment in only one instance. I had planned to do a book like this, but you've beaten me to it. The book fills a real want, and I'm willing to turn over to you all data I've collected." He then offered to become a dinner detective. Hines warmly accepted and, as their discussion progressed, he appointed Gibbs his Western Representative for *Adventures in Good Eating,* Inc. and made him his West Coast book distributor. The only thing Gibbs accepted from Hines in the way of payment for his services came in the form of barter: "a bottle or two of rare liquor and a Kentucky country-cured ham." Therefore, beginning in August 1936, Warren Gibbs drove at least 11,000 miles a year for Hines, and all for the love of letting others know where good meals were to be found.[206]

There were other restaurant sleuths, all of whom were ardent Duncan Hines supporters. One was Carveth Wells, the well-known explorer and lecturer affiliated with the Conoco Travel Bureau.[207] Still another nationally-known figure was Julian Street, a gentleman who specialized in wines. Hines made good use of Street's knowledge of the vineyard. In each edition of the restaurant guide through 1946, Hines included a short, annually updated essay by Street on wines designed to help the prospective diner choose the best recent vintages.[208]

Although many of the era's celebrities were great resources, his best source for new outstanding restaurants came from the tens of thousands who annually bought his books. They recommended scores of new places for him to investigate, and they warned him when one of his listed establishments was about to change hands or was negligent its responsibilities.[209]

While the dinner detectives also discovered many comfortable lodgings for travelers to sleep, their primary interest was in locating excellent restaurants. Although hotels and motels had problems, those could be overcome; but an unsuspecting traveler could not overcome a fatal restaurant meal. Therefore, it did not matter that the dinner detectives emanated from all walks of life and practiced thousands of disparate professions. The social glue uniting their gleeful participation in assembling the contents of *Adventures in Good Eating* was their fear of the unsanitary kitchen practices found in restaurants across America. Why should anyone, they reasoned, have to eat from an unwashed plate or drink from a dirty glass or be served unfinished portions from another customer's plate? Why indeed?

7

FLORENCE HINES'S LAST YEAR

Sometime in 1937 Florence Hines went to the doctor and was diagnosed with inoperable cancer. A Christian Scientist,[210] she sought no surgery for her troubles and accepted her coming demise as part of the natural order of God's world. Evidence shows, however, that the last year of her life was not spent in agony on a couch or in a bed. Surviving hotel receipts indicate that she accompanied her husband wherever he went, and their travels were frequent and extensive. The final months of Florence's life was one in which no expense was spared. The moments Hines shared with his wife were no doubt ones that were forever cherished by him long after she departed.[211]

Hines's travel log shows that on 10-11 April 1937, he and Florence were in Milwaukee, Wisconsin, visiting several restaurants, most notably Mader's German Restaurant, of which Hines had high praise. He wrote in his guidebook that Mader's was:

> unique, not because it is a German restaurant, but because it serves the unusual traditional German dishes you never find in so-called German-American restaurants, [e.g.,] Deutscher Apfel Pfannkuchen, and many others. One of the most popular,

Munchner Kalbshaxen, Deutscher Speckbraten with dumplings, which even the most fastidious enjoy, is fried pork shanks (weighing at least two pounds) with sauerkraut. The shanks are parboiled first and then fried to a beautiful golden brown. Wonderful! And, too, each glass, dish and silver sparkles with cleanliness; they are thoroughly washed and sterilized after each serving.[212]

Hines so greatly enjoyed Mader's pig shanks, branding them "the best I've ever found," that he frequently arranged to have a dozen sent to his home.[213]

One week later (17 April), Hines and Florence drove 40 miles west of Chicago to Geneva, Illinois, to dine at the Mill Race Inn, a pleasant restaurant surrounded by a peaceful setting. The following day (18 April) they drove to Aurora, Illinois for an elaborate feast. They followed this trip three days later with one to nearby Winnetka, Illinois, where they enjoyed the gastronomic amenities of The Hearthstone House near Green Bay Road. This air-conditioned restaurant was, in Hines's words, "one of the outstanding eating places in the Chicago area, managed by Mr. and Mrs. Donald Robertson. Their staff of women cooks is famous.... Evenings you will enjoy a delicious chicken or steak dinner—a man's size meal—with a variety of hot breads and jam.... An unusual treat at luncheon is the Hearthstone fruit salad with their famous French dressing.[214] Hines raved about that fruit salad for years, declaring it to be the best he had ever devoured. The following day (22 April) he and Florence took another day trip, this time for a hearty feast in St. Charles, Illinois. On 28 April they were back in Geneva, Illinois, to dine once again, this time at the Little Traveler at 404 Third Street.

Beginning April 30 and continuing through 2 May the Hines took an extended culinary tour, one that led first to Detroit and Cleveland and then back to Chicago, a journey that covered 740 miles and one which left them sated for a fortnight. Not until 15 May did they venture out again, this time to pay another visit to the Hearthstone House. Two days later (17 May) they visited

Bensenville, Illinois, then located 20 miles west of Chicago but which has now been swallowed by urban sprawl. That evening, at the corner of Church and Green Streets, they dined at Plentywood Farm, a rustic restaurant which was "a low log house at the end of the lane with a porch facing a garden."[215] The next day (18 May) they took another short trip, this time to enjoy the culinary joys to be found in suburban Lake Forest, Illinois.

Wanting to visit some of their old haunts that were strung across middle America, the couple packed their bags two days later and drove 120 miles to LaGrange, Indiana, where they dined and spent the night before moving on the next morning. They spent the following day (21 May) in transit, driving 230 miles to Toledo, Ohio, where they had dinner that evening at one of Hines's most coveted restaurants, Grace E. Smith's Restaurant Service and Cafeteria, located at the intersection of Madison and Erie Streets. Hines said of this wonderful establishment, "This is the place that changed my attitude toward cafeteria food. It is owned and operated by Grace Smith, an outstanding person among America's most successful restaurant operators. It is located in a new air-conditioned building—has five attractive dining rooms on the ground floor, in which you can get table, counter, cafeteria and fountain service. The striking feature is the superior type of food—cream soups, juicy and tender meats, wide variety of salads, fresh vegetables, delicious home baked rolls, breads and top desserts. Their lemon pie alone will make you want to return again and again. All cooking done by women, supervised by Home Economics graduates. I never go through Toledo without stopping here for at least one meal."[216]

A lengthy journey of 1,200 miles consumed the Hines' days on 22-23 May 1937. On the first day, they drove to Columbus, Ohio, to examine some potential restaurants for his guidebook as well as a recommendation for an inn. When Hines had completed his examination, the couple drove southward, through Cincinnati, Ohio, and Lexington, Kentucky, before finally spending the night in Harrodsburg, Kentucky, at that city's famous Beaumont Inn. That evening, in the Beaumont's spacious dining room, they consumed heaping plates of fried chicken and hickory-smoked country ham, as well as several delicious beaten biscuits, before washing down their meal with generous portions of sweetened iced tea and pushing themselves away from the table. They spent their second day driving back to Chicago digesting the previous evening's sumptuous repast.

The couple did not venture onto America's highways again until 11 June when they drove 664 miles, first to one town and then another, before arriving in Gallatin, Missouri. Once there, they consumed a superb meal at another of their favorite haunts, Virginia McDonald's Tea Room. This restaurant, officially known as the McDonald Tea Room, located halfway between St. Joseph and Kansas City, Missouri, was an establishment the couple often pined for in their idle moments at home. Said Hines in his guidebook, "It would require more than one full page of this book to tell you of the many good things to eat prepared by Virginia Rowell McDonald."[217] 12 June was spent driving 305 leisurely miles back home, long enough to gab the day away while savoring the after-effects of Mrs. McDonald's culinary skills. Hines and Florence did not take any long distance trips together again until 26 June, when they took a day trip to Chalet, Wisconsin, but the trip did not forfeit a memorable meal.

The Hines spent 1937's Independence Day in Milwaukee, Wisconsin, probably dining that evening once again at Mader's German Restaurant. The following day (5 July) they drove to the north side of Rockford, Illinois, and stayed overnight but not before sampling the cuisine at the Sausage Shop and Rathskeller; Hines apparently believed the drive worth the effort because he was extremely impressed with the establishment's variety, writing that for "years they have been specializing in 70 kinds of Milwaukee sausages and luncheon meats, and 70 kinds of imported and domestic cheeses, as well as serving them in at least 70 kinds of ways...in sandwiches."[218] Less than two weeks later (18 July) the Hines found themselves 70 miles away from home in Union Grove, Wisconsin, enjoying the surrounding scenery and food offered there. The next week (24 July) they dined once again in Winnetka, Illinois at the Hearthstone House.

Seven days later (1 August) the Hines dined in splendor near their apartment at Chicago's Pa Petit Gourmet restaurant[219] where they feasted on spaghetti, salad, and French onion soup. One week later (8 August) they had lunch in Barrington, Illinois, in an atmosphere that evinced anything but splendor. It was an outdoor restaurant and gift shop, located five miles west of town on Sutton Road; patrons who dined here were served on the lawn as they sat in folding chairs. Its owner called the establishment My Country Cousin.

Six days later (14 August) the couple found themselves in Crown Point, Indiana, in the dining room of Lamson's Tea Room, a restaurant opposite the court house; here they ate steak and fried chicken. The next day (15 August) they feasted at another of Hines's all-time favorite spots, the White Fence Farm in Lemont, Illinois. Hines spoke of this restaurant in his guidebooks in copious terms and drew an almost pastoral portrait of the function that country restaurants once served. Not only were restaurants as these once major destinations for travelers, but they also served a communal function as well, one that—in the sense described below—has evaporated with the passage of time. As Hines relates in his description of the White Fence Farm, "dining out" in the country was a singular, memorable experience for city dwellers.

One of Chicago's foremost citizens, Mr. Stuyvesant Peabody, had a theory that many people would enjoy a simple menu of superior food when served in an attractive atmosphere on a good-looking farm. It is evident that his theory [was correct], for more than forty-thousand came the first four months it was open, and now the place has been enlarged considerably. If you like good food, tasty sandwiches, rich Guernsey milk, homemade ice cream pies and about the best chopped steak sandwich you'll find anywhere, I am sure you will like this place to eat. One of the pleasant features is that while awaiting a table or after eating you can play shuffleboard, croquet, ping-pong, pitch quoits, or simply sit on the terrace and enjoy the music of an exceptionally finetoned Capehart installation.[220]

One week later (21 August) the Hines journeyed to nearby Hinsdale, Illinois, about three miles west of LaGrange. There they enjoyed the cuisine of another of their favorite haunts, the Old Spinning Wheel Tea Room. Like the White Fence Farm, this, too, had a rustic, open-air, attraction about it. Wrote Hines, "No sophisticated city dweller can resist the urge of a low log cabin set far back of an old rail fence among the trees and flowers, a spacious lawn and comfortable rustic chairs where one, after a bountiful dinner, may sit and enjoy the twilight.... It is very inviting, and the steak or chicken dinner with hot corn sticks is served just as attractively as one would serve his guests in his own home."[221]

The following day (22 August) the Hines dined once again at the Hearthstone House in Winnetka, Illinois. They refrained from old haunts on their next culinary tour. On 28-29 August they ate only in new restaurants. On their first day out they frequented the doors of the Pink Poodle, a restaurant 40 miles from Chicago; the following day they drove all day until they arrived in Goshen, Indiana to investigate another new dining facility called the Pine Tree Inn. No reports exist of what they found there, but it must not have passed muster because, like the Pink Poodle, Hines never mentioned it again.

The couple had primarily visited restaurants near their home since mid-July, but now that it was Labor Day weekend, it was time to take a long trip to a restaurant and lodge which, they were soon to learn, few could compare. On 4 September they packed their bags and headed for the Lowell Inn in Stillwater, Minnesota.[222] Billed as "The Mount Vernon of the West," the Lowell Inn was located in a little town of scarcely 8,000 people, 19 miles from Minneapolis, Minnesota. "I'd heard much that was good about the Lowell Inn long before I published my first book," wrote Hines years later. "Because I was always on the lookout for good food and fine eating places, I wired Arthur Palmer, the proprietor, for a reservation. He wrote back immediately, saying that the bridal suite was all ready for us." When Hines and Florence arrived, they were staggered by the building's beauty. "Not only [was] the bridal suite" beautiful, Hines wrote, "but every room in the place had been redecorated and through it all could be seen the fine hand of a woman—a woman of extremely good taste." Hines was always attracted to people who took care in looking after the smallest details and he soon met that "woman of extremely good taste," Nelle Palmer. From her they learned the history of their hotel and their "fierce devotion to quality."[223] As they related their story, Arthur and Nelle Palmer made a great impression on Duncan Hines, one that blossomed into a friendship that lasted for many years.

Duncan Hines's mention of the Lowell Inn in the 1938 edition of *Adventures in Good Eating* really put it on the map as a coveted destination for travelers. In his guidebook, Hines praised the institution the Palmers had created, noting, "their Colonial Dining Room is furnished in authentic Southern Colonial reproductions and antiques. In the Garden Room [the dining room], there is a hewn stone fountain which pours forth sparkling spring water into an illuminated pool where guests may catch brook trout, which are then fried for them."[224] Hines jovially stated that catching the fish was great fun, and that the best part of fishing for them was that guests did not have to worry about the game warden.[225] Hines was also impressed with the Lowell Inn's main dining room and its "lovely arched ceiling" but he was especially drawn to the food served there. It was not just the hotel's salad that mesmerized him; it was also their recipes for chicken, steak, and lamb chop dinners. The menu item that impressed him the most was the plate of hot rolls the inn served, the virtues of which he extolled in his book for decades to come. While the rolls were, in his opinion, the best to be found in America, his favorite dessert entree at the Lowell Inn was its pecan pie, which was, Hines stated with an air of finality, "the best I have ever encountered."[226] Another after-dinner entree of which he was most fond was the Lowell Inn's blueberry pie, which he said was excellent "because the berries are shipped specially from South Carolina."[227] The Lowell Inn remained a restaurant Hines swooned over until the day he died.

On 5 September Hines and Florence spent their day driving through the Minnesota countryside before stopping for the night in Ft. Atkinson, Wisconsin. On 6 September they drove through Milwaukee and on to Chicago, arriving home that afternoon. The last leg of their trip reminded them of another journey they had taken from Milwaukee to Chicago a few years before. Hines had promised a friend in Chicago[228] that he would bring him several pounds of Limburger cheese. Before he left for Chicago, Hines carefully wrapped the foul-smelling edible so it would remain cool in his car. "It was a warm day, and that Limburger ripened in a hurry," said Hines recalling the story a quarter century later. "The aroma lingered on long after I'd delivered the cheese, and finally I had to sell the car in self-defense." He always wondered if the next owner ever got rid of the smell.[229]

Five days later (11 September) Hines and Florence dined again at the White Fence Farm. On 12 September they headed north and drove approximately 40 miles until they stopped in Walworth, Wisconsin, 2 miles southwest of Geneva Lake, to dine at Buckley's Tea Rooms, where the chicken, in Hines's estimation, was far above the average for what was usually served in tea rooms.

The couple waited until 19 September before visiting another Chicago-area favorite, one they had not recently patronized. On this day, they took a leisurely drive in the country, first to Lake Forest, Illinois, before heading to nearby Northbrook, where they sat down in Phil Johnson's, a large restaurant 21 miles north of Chicago on Waukegan Road. As usual, there was a crowd. In his guidebook Hines told readers about it, remarking that "from a modest beginning this place has grown until it now frequently serves 2,000 or more people a day. Their specialties are barbecued chicken and unusually good broiled steaks, served with a generous portion of excellent fresh French fried potatoes, bread and butter, and a slaw salad.... Their kitchen is immaculate.... A favorite place to take the entire family."[230] One week later (25-26 September) Hines and Florence traveled to both Monroe and Madison,

Wisconsin, to investigate more new restaurants; they spent the
night there before returning to Chicago the following morning.

   Hines and Florence remained dormant in their travels for a
while, but after fourteen days they were ready to once again satisfy
their wanderlust. On 9 October the Hines left for an extended four-
day trip to Tennessee. It was on this occasion that their photograph
was taken. The picture was of Hines standing by his car with
Florence seated in the passenger seat, and it was one that he put in
later editions of his guidebook. The couple drove to Nashville and
stopped at Kleeman's, one of the few Southern restaurants that
Hines really enjoyed, where one ate a "Supreme Toast Sandwich,"
i.e., country ham and chicken on toast, while the other ate a "Sliced
Chicken Egg Bread Sandwich," another hearty concoction, over
which was poured a delicious sauce. After consuming their mini-
feast, they continued their journey through the Volunteer State
until they arrived at their destination of McMinnville, Tennessee;
no record exists of why they went there, but they were probably
visiting friends. The next day, 10 October, they made a quick day-
trip to Bowling Green, Kentucky, to visit Hines's family, before
heading off for nearby Glasgow, Kentucky, to investigate a
potentially good eating facility there. They finally stopped for the
day in Lexington, Kentucky, where they consumed supper at the
best dining facility in town, the Canary Cottage.[231] There they ate
country ham and fried chicken served with homemade rolls and
corn sticks.

   On the morning of 11 October they drove through Cincinnati to
Columbus, Ohio, to eat lunch in what he and all his "dinner
detectives" believed was one of the finest restaurants in America,
the Maramor[232]. Hines told his readers, "Don't feel that you have
to have on your best bib and tucker. The weary motorist is equally
welcome as the formal party guest." It was here, Hines wrote, that
the nation's best fried chicken was served. He was also impressed
with the Maramor's adjacent gift shop, where "you can get some of
the best candy and cookies I have ever tasted."[233] He had nothing
but the highest praise for the Maramor's owners, Mary and
Malcolm McGuckin, and he entreated his readers to pay the

restaurant a visit, even if it was out of their way; many Americans did, to the McGuckins' delight. From Columbus, Ohio, the Hines drove across the Ohio state line into Indiana that afternoon and headed north to Fort Wayne, where they spent the night. The next morning (12 October), they left Fort Wayne and arrived in Chicago early that afternoon.

The Hines did not take any more lengthy trips together for the rest of the year, but they took a few day-trips. On 23 October they dined one last time that year at My Country Cousin, taking advantage of the location's rustic atmosphere before cold weather made the outing too uncomfortable to enjoy. The next day (24 October) the couple traveled to Heaven City School, Wisconsin, located about 60 miles north of the Chicago city limits. Six days later (30 October) they visited the White Fence Farm in Lemont, Illinois, one last time before it closed for the year.

The last two dates from Hines's travel log for this year show that he and Florence went to Burlington, Wisconsin, on 6 November and to LaGrange, Illinois, the next day. The purpose of the latter trip was to eat at the Green Shutters restaurant on LaGrange Road, a well-known tea room that featured a wide, screened-in porch for those days when dining outdoors was preferable. When they arrived there, however, they had to eat inside; the cool, brusque nature of Chicago's early November winds precluded their dining on the restaurant porch.

At first glance, the Hines' traveling might seem inordinately expensive, but even by 1937 standards, their expenditures for both food and lodging were relatively modest, most likely because that year they did not often venture too far from home. Their lodging expenses for the year came to $23.90; their most expensive room, the one in Gallatin, Missouri, cost them $2.75. Their meals for the year cost $102.50, each of them averaging between $2.00 and $2.50. Their recreational travel totaled 8,808 miles that year, considerably less mileage than their usual quota of 40,000 to 50,000 per year. Hines wanted to spend as much time with Florence as possible before she was nothing more than a memory and he did not travel much during 1937.

Richard Groves, son of Leslie Groves, remembered Florence Hines as a very charming person, outgoing, exuberant, and the world's greatest cook. Groves, attending secondary school away from home, frequently spent the day with Duncan and Florence when he was traveling through Chicago between semesters. He spent a week with them in the summer of 1935, and saw them again in the spring of 1936. Later that summer he and his mother came to Chicago where they were the Hines' guests, but when he returned to their doorstep in December of that year for a pre-Christmas visit, Hines spent time with Groves but Florence did not. Florence, Hines told the young man, was too ill to see him.[234]

Despite Florence's illness, the frequency of Hines' travels in early January 1938 began to increase. On 8 January, the couple traveled to Evanston and Winnetka, Illinois, to eat lunch. They did not dine out for the rest of the month. Hines traveled to Winnetka, Illinois, on 15 January to visit the Hearthstone House for business reasons, but he did not eat there. The only time Hines and Florence dined out in February came on 6 February, when they ate at the Normandy restaurant in Oak Park, Illinois. Most of Hines's time during the second month of the year was spent in preparation for the 1938 edition of *Adventures in Good Eating*.

By January 1938 Hines's book orders finally exceeded the production abilities of Wright's firm. Shortly after, Hines soon amicably parted company with Wright, both as client and employee. For a new printing facility Hines chose one of the biggest in the business, R. R. Donnelley & Sons Company.[235] A measure of how well Hines's publishing venture had blossomed in a little less than two years is revealed in a contract with the Donnelley company. Hines told them to print 11,500 copies of *Adventures in Good Eating*. The expense left him with $3,068.10 less than he had the day before, but after Hines sold the entire print run, his gross sales came to $17,250.[236] From this it is easy to see he was earning a comfortable, if not an extravagant, living. By the time this edition of *Adventures in Good Eating* was published in mid-1938, word-of-mouth advertising had increased the book's sales to such an extent that his enterprise was making money on its own—and he had scarcely advertised it. *Adventures in Good Eating* was a self-contained engine of self-promotion. From this point forward Hines never again worried about losing money as a publisher.

As winter gave way to spring and the weather began to clear, Florence indicated that she felt strong enough for yet another long trip. Therefore, on 15 March 1938, the couple left their Chicago apartment and headed down the road in search of new restaurant adventures as well as old haunts. On 16 March, the Hines arrived in Lebanon, Missouri for a meal. On 17 March, they drove to Little Rock, Arkansas, and to the corner of Capitol Avenue and Fifth Street, where they dined on spoon bread and escalloped chicken at the Freiderica Hotel with its owners, the Pecks. On 18 March, they set out for New Orleans to dine together one last time at Antoine's Restaurant where they consumed perhaps that restaurant's most famous dish, Oysters Rockefeller. From there, they called on as many culinary haunts as their schedule allowed. They stayed at New Orleans' St. Charles Hotel through 19 March [237] and left town on March 20 for Memphis. Crossing the Tennessee border late that afternoon, they dined that evening on English muttonchops in that city's Little Tea Shop on Monroe Street. On 21 March they left town for St. Louis, Missouri, dining early that evening at the Oltz House, 8 miles past the city limits, where they were feted with "roast duck with wine and orange sauce and guinea under glass with a slice of Virginia ham."[238] They returned to Chicago the next day on 22 March, satiated with good cuisine and many memories. For the first three months of 1938, their traveling expenses totaled $28.60 for lodging and $44.69 for meals.

April of that year left Hines consumed with business, as he arranged to get new editions of his book into as many outlets as possible. The official release date for the latest edition of *Adventures in Good Eating* was 1 April, but because of last minute pre-publication problems, distribution did not begin until 10 April. The Donnelley Company agreed to handle all the shipping for him, and this aspect of the business underscored why he felt it necessary to leave Wright. The smaller company was simply unable to handle the enormous distribution effort Hines's book required.

Of the books printed for the next edition, Hines kept 766 copies for himself. On 10 April he received them in several boxes, via Chicago's Picket Truck Line, which he kept scattered in secluded corners of his Cornell Avenue home over the next several months until he eventually sold them to his many correspondents across the nation. Hines sent these books to interested individuals who had heard about his efforts as well as those listed establishments that desired to sell the book on their premises. At Hines's instruction the Donnelley company sent Warren Gibbs 700 copies. Whenever a new printing came off the press, Donnelley also sent several hundred copies to the Marshall Field department store in Chicago and to the Dearborn Inn in Dearborn, Michigan. Aside from these two high volume locations, most distributors received the usual number of copies, which ranged from 5 to 100.[239]

The books having been disbursed and their distribution now comfortably in Donnelley's hands, Hines and Florence decided in late May to take another trip across the country; this time they pointed their automobile toward the Northeast. On 21 May 1938, they stayed at Philadelphia's Walnut Park Plaza;[240] that evening they supped on red snapper chowder at Bookbinder's Restaurant, while they watched their steaks being broiled over the restaurant's open fireplace. From there they traveled to New York, a city that Hines, during his lifetime, was to visit in excess of 150 times for culinary adventures; Hines liked New York because it offered over 30,000 restaurants to choose from.

Hines and Florence stayed at the Hotel St. Regis for three days.[241] Although the Waldorf-Astoria was Hines' favorite hotel in the 1940s, in the 1930s he favored the Hotel St. Regis. In his guidebook Hines wrote of the St. Regis that "for fine living in New York this hotel ranks high among the very best. It is beautifully equipped and beautifully run (not overcrowded with large conventions)." There were several restaurants within the interior of the St. Regis, and Hines was most impressed with all of them, particularly their special policy regarding wines, one guaranteed to leave few empty hotel beds. He wrote that "their wine list is undoubtedly outstanding in America. Far too many places charge too much for wines. The St. Regis makes a sincere effort to popularize wine drinking by pricing really fine wines at extraordinarily low prices." Of the hotel's restaurants, Hines was quite charitable toward them all, writing that "The Iridium Room…is fashionable, has a fine orchestra. The Oak Room…is a charming, quiet dining room….The Maisonette Russe provides… Russian atmosphere, [along with] excellent Russian and French cooking. On the roof, for summer, is one of the most charming eating places in New York, with a lovely show."[242]

Hines said of New York restaurants that there were so many good ones that he could write a book devoted to them alone. One of these haunts was Keen's English Chop House on West 36th Street. Walking into it was like walking into a British ale house of a century earlier. The establishment was "paneled in dark wood. In winter, stout logs blaze[d] merrily in a cheery open fireplace. The chairs and tables [were] made of oak." But the restaurant did not live in the past. On one visit, Hines discovered it was offering its patrons something quite novel: 3-D viewers by which diners could view and then select a variety of mouth-watering entrees.[243] After three days of gorging themselves with the best food they could find, Hines and Florence returned to Chicago, stuffed and happy.

Upon their return home, Hines's mail revealed some good news. The Donnelley company reported that the print run of the latest edition of *Adventures in Good Eating* was nearly exhausted and public demand for the books was still running high. They were filling orders for them every day. Sales were so brisk that Hines, frightful of being caught short, ordered Donnelley to print another edition. On 1 July Donnelley presented Hines with the bill for his request: $2,107.18 for 11,595 copies.[244] Considering what his expenses were and what he was making from each book, Hines considered himself extremely lucky to have a printer who could operate this quickly.

While Hines's book was a profitable venture, he saw he could increase his income by printing another annual volume on his other area of expertise: good places to sleep. In the summer of 1938, just as Florence's health began to worsen, he published the first edition of *Lodging for a Night*, which was a guide to 3,000 superior hotels and motels found in the continental United States. It was Hines's intention for both books to complement the other.[245]

In the 6 August 1938, issue of *Publisher's Weekly*, the book publishing industry's trade magazine, there appeared a two-page story about Hines's success in self-publishing. The story noted that since the April publication of the latest edition of *Adventures in Good Eating*, 11,500 copies "literally sold itself…with only word-of-mouth recommendations to push it along." The article also said Hines had recently been granting a considerable number of newspaper interviews and had appeared on both Ruth Wakefield's and Mary Margaret McBride's radio shows to tell the public about the book and why they should buy it.

The article also reported that earlier in the year, when Hines had visited Philadelphia in May, a reporter for the Philadelphia Evening Ledger interviewed him and the resulting piece was printed shortly thereafter. The public response to the article was so popular that the newspaper published 20,000 enlarged copies of it and mailed it to interested individuals. But the one fact about Duncan Hines that caught everyone's attention and impressed them was his refusal to accept advertising. One restaurant offered Hines $10,000 for an advertisement; Hines refused, "preferring to keep his book uninfluenced by any commercial considerations." This principled statement came while the country was still mired in the Depression and impressed the public even more. The *Publisher's Weekly* article concluded by informing readers of Hines's new book, *Lodging for a Night*.[246]

In the latter part of the summer of 1938 Florence Hines ceased traveling with her husband. Surviving hotel receipts list Hines as a hotel guest but without his wife to accompany him. Apparently, she was in severe discomfort with cancer spreading throughout her body. There is no doubt Hines would have preferred to stay by her bedside, but, Christian Scientist to the end, Florence likely asked him not to worry about her and told him to continue working on his guidebooks. So he did. But, with a couple of exceptions, his travel records show he did not stray too far from home, and he did not leave the house regularly.

On 11 August, Hines spent the night at the Deshler-Wallick Hotel in Columbus, Ohio,[247] and that evening he once again dined at the Maramor restaurant, consuming—but perhaps not completely enjoying—a dish of broiled calf liver with bacon, celery, and almonds supreme.[248] Eleven days later (22-23 August) Hines lodged at the Commodore Perry Hotel in Toledo, Ohio,[249] and dined on chopped livers in Zimmerman's Restaurant.[250] He also stopped in Grace E. Smith's Restaurant and Cafeteria to eat the special of the day.[251]

Shortly after noon[252] on 6 September 1938, Florence Hines died of cancer in their Cornell Avenue apartment, her husband at her side. Funeral services were held on 8 September, and she was buried in Chicago.[253] Two days later Hines returned to Bowling Green and spent two weeks with his brother and sister.[254]

While Hines was mourning the loss of Florence, events were taking shape elsewhere that shortly defined the rest of his future. A few weeks before Florence's death, Hines made a quick trip to the Northeast to check on some dining recommendations. While in Madison, Connecticut, a little town on the Connecticut shore, he dropped in on a "dinner detective" friend of his who just happened to be entertaining another friend, Ernie Pyle, the noted correspondent for the Scripps-Howard newspapers. They took Hines to one of their favorite restaurants and suggested he order a lobster dish, one that came to the table bathed in butter. When his meal was brought to him, the two held their breath and waited for the verdict as he put a sizable portion of the shellfish into his mouth. Hines looked off into space for a long, pensive moment. Finally, he turned to them and nodded, murmuring softly, "Very good, very good." Soon afterward, Pyle wrote a column on him. Pyle's syndicated column was widely read during the late 1930s, and Hines's exposure in the journalist's newspaper column was the first time a large segment of the public had been introduced to him and his interesting line of work. According to Pyle's article, printed 10 September, Hines's home-office during the past year had been humming with activity. Pyle reported he now employed three to five women in his Chicago apartment, all of them answering his ocean of mail as well as the telephone calls. Pyle also observed he had become something of a "messiah" to travelers across the country, and his "little red book" was their road map and protector from harm. Some of these travelers wrote him every day about new restaurants to include in his next edition. Hines told Pyle that one man once wrote him six letters in one day. When Pyle asked Hines how many meals he sat down to daily, Hines said as many as six, although he added that he did not consume every last morsel on his plate. Rather, Hines said, he just picked at the meal, testing its worthiness or non-worthiness before paying his bill and departing for the next restaurant on his list. He told Pyle he ate only one real "whopper" of a meal each day. This led Pyle to ask him if making a profession out of his hobby did not spoil the personal pleasure of eating. Hines said it did not, because he did not overeat.[255] Pyle's column stirred great interest among the public. Soon Hines's secretaries were inundated with requests for their employer's book and information about Hines himself.

After Florence's death, Hines returned to Chicago and threw himself into his work in an effort to forget his misfortune.[256] He spent most of his time investigating potential recommendations for his two guidebooks. In late November, on the day before Thanksgiving, Hines drove for six hours through a blizzard from Chicago to Bowling Green to join his family for the holidays. That weekend he and his brother, Porter, went quail hunting in the Warren County woods. The following Monday, however, he resumed his life on the road. He drove to the Ranch Hotel in Stratford, Missouri, to see if it was worthy of inclusion in *Lodging for a Night*. On Tuesday, Hines was off to Tulsa, Oklahoma to see the owner of Dolores' Sandwich Shop, a tea room one of his correspondents had recommended. On Wednesday he traveled to the Dallas-Fort Worth, Texas, area to check on a number of recommendations. Such was the life of Duncan Hines. He got up in the morning and put his pants on like everyone else. He had nearly forgotten an interview he had sat for in May and had no notion it would ultimately change his life. In fact, he had no inkling of the good fortune he was about to reap.

When Hines had been in Philadelphia in May, he stopped by the offices of the *Saturday Evening Post* to visit his friend Wesley Stout, the magazine's editor. Stout thought his magazine's readers would be greatly interested in reading about Hines and his unusual but worthwhile business. So he commissioned a journalist, Milton MacKaye, who often wrote articles for the *Post*, to write a feature piece on Hines.[257] Before the month was over, MacKaye sat down with Hines in his Chicago apartment for an extensive interview, one which lasted for several days. As is the nature of magazine articles, there was a long delay between interview and publication, and MacKaye's article had by this time practically vanished from Hines's memory.

During the last week of November Hines received word the *Saturday Evening Post* issue which featured the article on him was about to be published. He complained to his secretary, Ms. I. A. Bench, "I do not know why the *SE Post* did not let me see [a] proof of [the] article. I gave MacKaye enough material for half dozen stories. So I do not know what they are printing."[258] Three days later he found out. On 30 November, the 3 December 1938 edition of the *Saturday Evening Post* article hit America's newsstands. Inside its pages appeared a lengthy article of how Duncan Hines's little hobby of visiting good restaurants had mushroomed into an annual guidebook now very much in demand by the reading and traveling public. As soon as the magazine appeared on newsstands, Hines bought several copies so his friends and family could read the article.[259] On the same day the article was being devoured by the *Post's* readers, Hines received a telegram from M. Lincoln Schuster of Simon and Schuster, which read:

New York City Nov. 30, 1938 Duncan Hines 5494 Cornell Ave. Chicago Congratulations on Saturday Evening Post article. All of us here doubly interested because we have been making

independent researches for years toward an american eating
guide book. If you are interested in making a deal with an
established publishing house like ours for distribution and
promotion would like to explore possibilities with you. We
have done a number of books in this field including complete
wine book by Bates and Schoonmaker and Ida Bailey Allen's
Cooking with Wines and Spirits. When will you be in New
York or could you see Mr. Simon in Chicago later in December
otherwise suggest we discuss this further by mail. M. Lincoln
Schuster Simon and Schuster[260]

Hines scribbled on the telegram a note to his secretary, "Have
written him. D. H." A meeting between the two men was arranged
for January 1939, but for one reason or another, they never met.
Schuster's partner, Richard Simon, also tried to acquire Hines as a
client. But to no avail. Hines had good reasons to shy away from
large publishers, despite the advantages they possessed in
advertising and distribution. In a letter to his New York agent for
national book distribution, Frank M. Watts, an employee of the
New York book-publishing firm, W. W. Norton & Co., Hines
explained why he was reluctant to have publishers take over his
business. "I receive letters from publishers from time to time,"
Hines confided to Watts, "all offering to take over the publishing of
my books, but the one thing that they do not understand is that the
book has to be revised all the time and [do not realize] the
enormous cost [it entails].... [I]f I turn[ed] the book over to
someone on a royalty basis I would go broke in a hurry.... If I
could turn the books over to someone under some arrangements
whereby the cost of all this detail work would be paid, and then net
me a sufficient royalty, I might consider it."[261] For the present, he
believed his best interest was to leave things as they were. More
than a decade passed before he would find a suitable business
arrangement.

8

THOSE WHO MAKE US
WISH FOR HOLLOW LEGS

Book publishers knocking on Hines's door was only the beginning. For Duncan Hines the *Saturday Evening Post* article was his life's seminal event. Overnight he was transformed from a small-time book-publisher into America's most authoritative voice on the best places to eat. In a very short time he was an American celebrity. He was in demand to give talks and make appearances before audiences of all kinds. The public's regard for him and what he had to say was so high that his sphere of influence eventually extended well beyond recommending restaurants. The only explanation that can account for the phenomenon of his sudden popularity and his instant—almost eager—acceptance by the public is that he was the right man in the right place at the right time. Americans were ready for a Duncan Hines, and he was ready for them.

Hines seized the sudden respect the public bequeathed to him and quickly turned it to his advantage. In an era of social reforms, he would also become a social reformer, one who acted on behalf of the dining public. At age fifty-eight he had a great career ahead of him, and his only regret was that Florence was not there to share it with him. Nevertheless, this was his moment, and he made the most of it.

Despite the attention he suddenly received, his personal life changed little. Success did not go to his head. Hines remained level-headed about his transformation from common to famous citizen. For the next few months he continued working out of his Chicago apartment-office. The cult of celebrity, however, did affect his book publishing business—for the better. Even before the *Post* article hit the newsstands, he had been forced to hire three and sometimes five secretaries to help him with the avalanche of mail that daily greeted his mailbox.[262] When Milton MacKaye interviewed him, he described his Cornell Avenue apartment as "a houseful of antique furniture." Florence had been the household's collector, but circumstances had forced him to displace some of her antiques to make way for desks, typewriters, filing cabinets, and other needed office furniture. By late 1938 his incoming correspondence averaged more than "400 letters and cards a week," and he made sure his employees answered every piece. When not on the road inspecting new restaurants, Hines routinely spent his time answering his mail, preparing new editions of his two guidebooks, as well as working on a new publication, a cookbook.

Even before the appearance of the *Saturday Evening Post* article, Hines was not always able to travel about the country with complete anonymity. After the publication of *Adventures in Good Eating*'s second edition, some restaurants he had previously listed anticipated another visit. "Now that he has a national reputation among food people," MacKaye wrote in his *Post* article, Hines's practice of dropping in on kitchens "takes some strength of character, for if it were known that he was dining at any given place, you may be sure that his service and food would be attended to personally."[263] Despite this handicap, Hines regularly investigated potential new guidebook entries. When not engaged in his search, Hines re-inspected previous entries. If he noticed in his mail a pattern of complaints, he subsequently investigated; if he found his worst suspicions confirmed, he deleted the entry from the guidebook's next edition— usually forever, unless he received information to warrant it another chance, (e.g., new owners).

One of the myths Duncan Hines deliberately perpetuated about himself over the years was that he might at any moment enter a restaurant's kitchen through the back door and inspect it before he dined. According to Hines, he had a technique he claimed could ferret out any ill-omened restaurant, particularly if it was imaginatively unclean. This method of separating good restaurants from bad, if practiced at all, was probably honed during the 1920s, when he and Florence first traversed across America's few paved roads. As previously stated, roadside restaurants of that era were usually unsanitary affairs, so they had to watch where—and what—they ate. Nevertheless, well into the mid-1950s, Hines had Americans believing it was his regular practice to park his automobile outside a potential restaurant and head for the back door. "First I sneak around to the back to see what the garbage situation looks like," said Hines in a typical interview. "If that's bad, I stick my nose in the kitchen," perhaps detecting unpleasant odors of food served two days earlier. "If I smell rancid grease, then I back out. I know it must be one of those" restaurants "where if you get anything to eat after the cockroaches are finished, you're lucky."[264] Of these back door excursions, Hines said he often encountered some really revolting sights, such as the time he slipped through the rear entrance of one restaurant and discovered "the family cat sleeping on the bread dough."[265] This story was one Hines told repeatedly over the years. The image of him lurking around the back doors of restaurants, discovering public hellholes serving unsanitary food too dreadful to contemplate, created an image of Hines that remained embedded in the American consciousness for more than two decades.

Although it will never be determined if Duncan Hines visited many restaurants via the back door, it really did not matter. He frequently wrote of doing it, he always said he did it, and he made enough personal restaurant inspections to make the public and restaurant owners think he did it. In addition, he periodically had himself photographed inspecting restaurant kitchens, and these pictures invariably were printed in scores of magazines and Sunday newspaper supplements to further the image he intended to create. Everyone believed he did it, and that was enough for Hines. Perception was reality. Every restaurant was on notice. Duncan Hines, they feared, might step through the back door at any moment. He might catch them with a dirty kitchen and spoil their potential chance to have an endless stream of customers via his guidebook. It was a great system for cleaning up restaurant kitchens throughout America, and it no doubt afforded Hines many private cackles.

When he was pressed by reporters, however, Hines made no secret of his method of investigation. He told them that when he went into a restaurant he never advertised his entry. He just came in and sat down like anyone else. This was easy enough to do. Hines looked like an unremarkable, conservatively-dressed businessman with short, silvery hair sporting wire-rim glasses. He was a solidly-built individual of fifty-eight, with a ruddy complexion, weighing 178 pounds. Some Americans, who knew him only by his photograph, wondered if he were over six feet tall, but in fact he was surprisingly short; Hines stood five feet, eight and a half inches.[266] One of his secretaries described him as "a short, squat man," a physical characteristic also found in most members of his family.[267] If his figure displayed any paunch, this was seen only in his later years. Although he was photographed regularly, many restaurateurs did not recognize him because Hines always took off his glasses when the flashbulbs began to pop.

When Hines made a reservation, he always used an assumed name. When he sat down and ordered a meal, he usually chose "two soups, four entrees and at least three desserts." This alone should have been a tip-off that an unusual patron had entered the premises, but apparently few ever caught on. To the waitresses or the management he was just an unusual guest who could not make up his mind what he wanted to eat. When his meal was served, he sampled a little bit of everything, "usually eating only one dish of each course." After he paid for his meal, he usually asked to inspect the kitchen. If the restaurant management complied with his request, Hines was given a personal tour, the manager at his side. If after his careful examination the restaurant was found to have comported itself with his strict standards of both culinary and sanitary excellence, Hines left the premises, never bothering to reveal his real name. If the restaurant passed his inspection, its management was informed a few weeks later by his office that it had become the latest addition of the "Duncan Hines Family" of quality restaurants.[268]

Some restaurants were not so lucky. If the restaurant refused to comply with Hines's request for a kitchen tour, he paid his bill and left the premises immediately, knowing full well they were hiding something. Hines suspected that if a restaurateur refused to show his customers the kitchen, he was probably shielding some dark horror. If the restaurant possessed some unsavory, unsanitary secret, Hines never discovered it; but, consequently, he never let the public discover the restaurant, either. Sometimes, though, Hines never inspected the restaurants he visited. This honor, of course, was relegated to a small number he had previously listed which had not received a series of customer complaints. When dining in one of these, if he asked to see the kitchen at the conclusion of his meal and was instantly granted access to it, it was all he needed to know, reasoning their open invitation was "evidence [enough] that there was nothing to hide."[269]

To understand why the American public developed an almost instant affinity for Duncan Hines, it is necessary to understand the public persona they encountered via newspapers, magazines, and radio. They discovered a man who was, in many ways, quite appealing to the popular imagination: colorful, sometimes eccentric, never dull. He reminded many of them of an uncle they had somewhere in the family tree.

Like many uncles, Duncan Hines was full of opinions, and he espoused them at every opportunity, using the various media outlets of the day as his pulpit. A transcript of his conversation reveals that it was his tendency to flit from one subject to another. An example of this can be found in a 1954 interview with Hines during the preparation of his autobiography. As Milton MacKaye discovered sixteen years earlier, the subject of Hines's conversation could easily bounce around from one topic to the next. In five minutes or less Hines would cover restaurant sanitation, the proper method for preparing fried chicken, fine wines, and the best way to carve a turkey. There was no apparent explanation for the character of his thought patterns; he was just an impulsive individual with an overactive mind. It is possible that he acquired this speaking trait early in his career as a salesman and had refined it over the years. To a degree, he was almost impossible to interview.

An example of his thought patterns can be found in his interview with MacKaye. At one point in their conversation, Hines remarked that restaurants in America—and the preparation of food and cooking in general—had improved over the past twenty years. He recounted how it was impossible, by the end of World War I in 1918, to find a good cup of coffee anywhere. One of the reasons for this, he declared, was that most people had never tasted good coffee and therefore had no criterion by which to make an evaluation. Hines said that "there can be only two reasons for a poor cup" of coffee—not enough coffee in the pot or brewing it too long. This remark led his mind to wander into a new topic for discussion—a relatively new trend in restaurant food: salads. Hines observed that, over the years, there had grown among the public the general acceptance of salads and "the increasing use and wider choice of fresh vegetables." Salads somehow led him to think of wild game and steak. Hines noted how the public's penchant for wild game had "retrogressed," that the supply was very limited, and only a few chefs in America knew how to prepare it with any skill.[270] This train of thought led to another nearly unrelated subject; in his estimation, he stated flatly, "the states between the Mississippi River and the Pacific Coast are pretty much the Gobi Desert so far as good cooking in the small towns goes. The worst steaks," he pointed out, "are always to be found in the cow country, where they butcher grass-fed cattle and have never heard of aging meat."[271] Hines's sometimes contradictory nature surfaced in the next moment. He complained about being unable to find a high quality steak and then turned the conversation toward a subject that, he said, completely befuddled him: Americans' love affair with meat—particularly steak. "Why should I eat steak in Butler, Pennsylvania, when I can go to the Nixon Hotel and have pure pork sausages, buckwheat cakes and piping coffee served on distinctive china with charming hospitality?"[272] It could be that Hines just wanted a good steak *when* he wanted a good steak, regardless of where he happened to be. Nevertheless, this was what it was like to have a conversation with Duncan Hines.

The 1938 edition of *Adventures in Good Eating* listed about 1,800 restaurants that conformed with Hines's exacting standards of cleanliness and excellence. By his estimation he had visited 70% of them, with the remaining 30% being comprised of recommendations that had withstood the critical examination of his dinner detectives.[273] *Adventures in Good Eating* may have been a guide to the nation's best restaurants, but a few critics charged it was not necessarily a guide to eating cheaply. Although the audience Hines had in mind when he conceived the book was a clientele who could afford to travel and eat well, one criticism it received was that it was of little use to travelers with limited food budgets. While the book had a scale of menu prices with each entry, some critics were not mollified. One claimed that in 1938 that Hines listed only those restaurants that charged more than seventy-five cents per meal. Anyone who opened a copy of *Adventures in Good Eating* knew this was untrue. While his guidebook listed many restaurants with prices above seventy-five cents, it also listed a great number which offered meals under that figure. Overall, the average price for a recommended meal in the 1938 guidebook was $1.25.[274]

Critics apparently overlooked the case of a restaurant run by Mary Rowton. In the 1936 edition of *Adventures in Good Eating*, Hines wrote: "Once in a while I encounter a sixty-cent meal for two dollars. But I have never had a two-dollar meal for sixty cents." Not long after its publication, Hines received three letters, "one from San Francisco, one from New York and one from Memphis." Each said Hines was wrong, "that at Paris, Arkansas, in the Ouachitas, a two-dollar meal could be had for not sixty but fifty cents."[275] To see if this was true, Hines drove there to investigate. When he arrived, he "met Mary Rowton, a seventy-year-old Irishwoman, who" served "meals in her home. Hines had a noon dinner. The price was fifty cents. The food was plain, but good." At this sitting Hines sampled "radishes, onions, chicken, country ham, whipped potatoes, candied sweets, macaroni, baked beans, spinach, rice, Southern cabbage, stuffed eggs, cottage cheese, three kinds of pickles, homemade relish, coleslaw, two kinds of cake, mince pie, grape pie, custard pie, [and] ice cream."

After pushing himself away from the table, Hines turned to the proprietor and exclaimed, "My dear Miss Rowton, you can't make money selling such a meal for only half a dollar." She nodded in agreement. "No," she said. "As a matter of fact, I owe about twenty-seven dollars in back taxes now." He observed the diners who filled the dining room, then remembered the many out-of-state license plates he had seen in the parking lot. He observed that more than a few had come many miles to enjoy her cooking. "They were well-dressed travelers, drawn there by the food and not by the price." He tried to reason with her, all the while trying to understand the reason for her stubbornness. All she had to do, he said, was raise her prices to $1.50. "It's worth it," he said. "You won't lose a single customer." She still declined. She explained "three local men had been her boarders since she started business." She charged "them thirty-five cents a meal" and "if she raised her price, she would lose them." This seemed nonsensical to Hines who reasoned she would make up the lost revenue with the payment from a single customer. Then came Miss Rowton's admission. "The truth is that I don't care whether I make money or not. I've been in business forty years and I am too old to change. The only things I care about in the world are cooking and going to church." There were more than a few restaurant proprietors in his little red book who shared similar sentiments. They cooked for the love of it.[276]

In Hines's day, as now, the cuisine of New England was noted for its clams, lobster and chowder. One delectable place he never tired of visiting, after he discovered it in 1937, was a restaurant near Boston in Whitman, Massachusetts that was owned by Ruth and Kenneth Wakefield. They called it the Toll House.

Ruth Graves Wakefield was a high school cooking teacher and dietician and her husband, Kenneth, worked in a meat packing house when they decided to open a restaurant dedicated to serving plain, hearty food superbly cooked. In August 1930 the Wakefields bought an old 1709 Cape Cod house, which was first a stagecoach way station, then a home to a succession of families and then, finally, was an unsuccessful tea room. After purchasing it, they immediately went to work fixing it up. Within a few weeks they opened their doors to the public, crossed their fingers, and prayed they would not quickly deplete their bank account's accumulated savings of fifty dollars. The couple almost lost everything on the first day. "On opening day a woman ordered luncheon for a number of guests; the Wakefields spent thirty dollars on supplies. The lunch was served and the hostess walked out without paying," which left them with twenty dollars in the cash register.[277] The following day "the Toll House opened for business with eleven dollars in the till." They had spent nine dollars earlier that morning for the procurement of more food. As the noon-day meal approached, they became anxious. Finally "two elderly people from Pennsylvania" became their first "tourist guests." They had driven to Whitman to see the house in which they had grown up in as children and remained for lunch when they discovered it had become a restaurant. After their guests departed, the Wakefields became depressed over the fact that no one else had visited them for lunch. The rest of the day proved fretful. The Wakefields, "the lone waitress, and Jack, the young chef, sat around and worried all afternoon. Every time a car slowed, they would all run to the window to see if it was going to stop." They wondered if their efforts were nothing more than a fool's errand. But their luck changed within a few hours. "That evening eleven more people came to dinner." By evening's end, after they had shut their doors, they breathed a sigh of relief as they counted their small but tidy profit. There was money enough to pay their help and buy food for the next day. Egged on by hope, they prayed they would be in business for many years to come.[278]

Their hope crystallized into a bright reality. By 1938, the Wakefields had ninety employees serving guests at sixty-four tables. The place became so popular that reservations for a Thanksgiving Day dinner there had to be made by 15 May. These Thanksgiving Day meals were not ordinary affairs by any stretch of the imagination. When a turkey was served, the bird weighed no less than twelve pounds. As an extra courtesy, when guests left the restaurant they were "handed a basketful of cold remnants of turkey" to nibble on after they arrived home.[279] By 1955 the restaurant's original building had been transformed into a lounge, and on weekends it was not unusual for the Wakefields to feed a hungry crowd of between 1500 to 2500 guests.[280]

It was the Toll House that gave rise to Hines's oft-quoted remark, the full text of which is "It makes my mouth water to think of the baked Injun Porridge as it is prepared at Toll House, in Whitman, Massachusetts. That's the kind of dessert that makes a fellow wish for hollow legs."[281] Baked Injun Porridge was not the only dish Hines devoured when he ate at the Toll House. He liked everything they served. He wrote, "Every year I go to this charming place, which becomes more attractive each time. They have added several dining rooms, and in the summer you may also dine outside amid flower gardens, shrubs and trees. The real emphasis here is on their noted food; such good things as Ruth Wakefield's famous onion soup and chicken soup, broiled live lobster, boneless fried chicken, charcoal broiled steaks and salads that taste as good as they look, lemon meringue pie and many other tempting desserts. This is indeed one of my particular favorites."[282] Ruth Wakefield may not be widely known today, but one of her recipes is still an American favorite. Indeed, her restaurant's name is embedded in it. Nearly everyone has tasted a Toll House cookie.[283]

One question that Hines consistently found himself answering concerned the location of America's best restaurant. He responded that there was no such place. It all depended on what one wanted to sink his teeth into. The Middle West was the best place to find a pie. "The best dog-gone lemon pie in the world," Hines declared, was made at Stone's Restaurant in Marshalltown, Iowa, a dining facility that had been in operation since around 1905.[284] Hines wrote of this "quaint little dining room," which made its first appearance in his guidebook's 1937 edition. "Don't be dismayed by the obscure location—almost under a viaduct 'down by the winegar woiks.' One bite of Queenie's angel food pie—and you won't care where you're eating. The restaurant is unpretentious but for fifty years Stone's has been searched out by transients."[285]

Mrs. Anna Stone, the proprietor and widow of the founder's son, made valiant efforts to keep the restaurant as clean as her own kitchen. A few years later, when America's entry into the Second World War commenced and wartime rationing, food shortages, and the lack of manpower ensued, Mrs. Stone, like all Americans, tried to cope as best as she could. But in early 1945 she temporarily closed her doors rather than compromise her ideals and the restaurant's integrity. When most of the wartime domestic problems created by the war subsided, she reopened in April 1946, much to Duncan Hines's delight. Stone and Hines remained close friends for many years, and Hines did all he could to let others know about her operation. Stone's Restaurant was just one of many roadside dining facilities Hines could recommend to his critics; travelers could purchase a meal there for under seventy-five cents. But that is not why he dined there. For him the attraction was still that mile high lemon pie in the middle of Iowa, and it brought him back to the Midwest repeatedly.[286]

The slow disappearance of the tea room in the 1930s saddened Hines. Milton MacKaye, in his *Post* article, described his own irrational knee-jerk tendency when he saw one: "Many men—and I number myself among them—have what may be described as spinning-wheel trouble—that is, when they approach an inn with a spinning wheel or a couple of green glass bottles in the front yard, they step on the throttle. Hines says that this phobia against tea rooms, as such, makes many men miss a lot of good eating. Some of the best inns are cluttered up with antiques and collections of Aunt Sarah's quilt designs, and if one will brave the whimsy, he may find the finest type of home cooking." One of the most famous tea rooms of this character, still in existence, was the McDonald

Tea Room in Gallatin, Missouri, a town about 60 miles from St. Joseph, Missouri, and about 80 from Kansas City.

Its proprietor was a woman Hines admired greatly. In about 1920, Virginia Rowell McDonald became very ill and stayed in bed for nearly eight years. In 1928 she became well enough to lift herself from her sickbed, and from that moment forward she made the most of the remainder of her life. In the years that encompassed her illness, she had consumed her husband's collected savings. She felt obliged to somehow repay him for his sacrifice, but she was stuck for an idea as to how to do it. She recalled that her mother was deemed by many as a great cook; Virginia, however, believed her own cooking skills surpassed that of her mother. One day in the summer of 1928, Virginia announced she was going to open her own restaurant. Her husband, a realist, pointed out that no one in Gallatin patronized restaurants, that they were several miles off a main highway, that they had no place for a restaurant, and that they had no silver or dishes. But Mrs. McDonald had answers. Tourists would drive off the highway for good food, she could borrow dishes from friends, and there was an old blacksmith shop that would serve nicely, if he would put a floor in it and build the tables and chairs. On a Monday they were ready to open. Mrs. McDonald suggested that her husband shave and put on a clean pair of overalls and go downtown and ask every traveling salesperson he saw to come to the tea room and eat free. It was a shrewd move. Dyspeptic salesmen [were] always hunting for a good place to eat, and they spread the good news among their fraternity.

After a few weeks "a sizable number were finding their way to Gallatin and to" Virginia McDonald's Tea Room. By 1938, her tea room was a tremendous success, serving more than 250 customers at a time. Particularly famous were her relishes and corn muffins. It was through his friends in Chicago that Hines first learned of her legendary kitchen skills. Always ready to check out a good tip, Hines "drove four hundred miles over to Gallatin one day just to see if the food was really as good as everyone said it was."[287] Many years later, Hines said he never regretted the trip. In time, her tea room expanded into "a fine, modern restaurant." Hines liked her corn muffins so much he printed the recipe for them in his autobiography.[288]

Another of Duncan Hines's favorite restaurants was "in the hill country of central Florida," four miles north of Lake Wales off U. S. 27 in a beautiful triple-leveled hotel and restaurant "ten minutes away from the famous Bok Singing Tower."[289] This was the Chalet Suzanne, "a rambling structure set in the midst of 230 rolling acres of orange trees and lily pools near the shore of little Lake Suzanne."[290] Its architecture was not Swiss but, rather, featured "a potpourri of architecture and decorations from all over the world. The tables in the dining room [were] of tile from Mexico, Spain, Egypt [and] Italy. The patios, hung with Spanish moss and bright with bougainvillaea," suggested "Spain or the tropic isles of the Caribbean. The furniture [was] English, the crystal Egyptian."[291]

Hines marveled at the human spirit behind this unusual place and championed it as frequently as possible. The Chalet Suzanne was a one-woman enterprise run by Mrs. Bertha Hinshaw. She began her business from the rubble of a series of personal misfortunes. She and her husband "lost almost everything they had in the market crash of 1929 and spent their few remaining dollars trying vainly to raise rabbits for a living. Then Mr. Hinshaw died suddenly of pneumonia, and [Bertha] was left to face the depression and the raising of two children with no assets but her resourcefulness and a background of gracious living. She thought she might put the latter to work for her, since in her travels with her husband she had collected a number of unusual and outstanding recipes and some lovely furnishings. She thought she might combine these in an unusual guest house and restaurant." Since there was no money for an architect, she became her own.[292]

On the day she was ready for business in 1931, "she trudged" four-hundred yards "from her home to the main road and posted a small, hand-painted sign that read: MEALS SERVED. The cars, however, whizzed on by. Then one day a man and his wife ventured up the driveway. Mrs. Hinshaw served them. A week later the wife returned with four companions. At the same time two of

Mrs. Hinshaw's friends telephoned and asked for dinner. "But I can't cook properly for more than five people," she said, "agonizing over this sudden rush of business."[293] Through sheer determination, however, she survived the next few months. As word of her marvelous cooking skills spread among the transient public, her qualms about feeding large numbers of peoples dissolved. When she realized the public would gladly travel long distances just to eat her meals and sometimes sleep in her guest house, Bertha Hinshaw hauled her two children into her car "and headed north on the existing roads, tacking up Chalet Suzanne signs along the main highways."[294] Before long those who had tasted her cooking told others of her culinary abilities, and word of this remarkable woman spread rapidly, first throughout the state, then beyond its borders. Afterward, her home grew into the Chalet Suzanne which—even today—is by far Florida's most eclectic and enchanting restaurant-inn. Bertha Hinshaw literally built it herself, adding "room after room" in her spare time. She personally laid the tiles which paved her restaurant's lovely patio. By 1938 her guest house had blossomed into a 25-room affair which featured boating and bathing for patrons who took advantage of the nearby white sandy beach.[295]

It was the food, though, that made Bertha Hinshaw's restaurant famous, and its popularity eventually brought Duncan Hines to her doorstep. So charmed was he by the fairy-tale exteriors which surrounded him as he enjoyed his wonderful meal he kept returning over the next two decades to relish the experience. His favorite dishes included baked grapefruit and steaks with mint ice; and he always swooned when he devoured their orange souffle.[296] Guests seldom saw Mrs. Hinshaw because, despite her enormous success, she insisted—even decades later—on personally preparing the meals.[297]

Hines had many other favorite restaurants, ones which he treasured for good eating experiences above the rest. One of these was Crane's Canary Cottage at Chagrin Falls, Ohio, which was located in a residential home twenty miles south of Cleveland. "I doubt you will find more delicious food in the country," he wrote.[298] Expounding on this culinary find nearly ten years after its discovery, Hines told Phyllis Larsh of *Life* magazine why he was so enthusiastic about it: "First," he said:

> they bring in these crisp, hot little finger rolls and you think you are just going to eat a dozen of them, they're so good. But before you get started, they've brought in the watermelon pickle—the best in America—and three kinds of soup. You have to keep moving back from the table to disguise the loosening of your belt. They serve a salad—it's so doggone beautiful you hate to destroy it. The dressing has lumps of Roquefort cheese the size of the end of your little finger. Oh, honey, that's the one place where you absolutely bust.[299]

Another of his enthusiasms, one that remained dear to his heart was Mrs. K.'s Toll House Tavern at Silver Spring, Maryland, just north of Washington, D. C. He wrote:

> Here's an outstanding place in a two-acre garden that possesses unusual charm. You dine in the past here—so far as surroundings are concerned. Nothing is changed apparently from the Revolutionary days when it was built. Even the pretty girls who wait on you in Colonial dress seem to have been miraculously preserved from a more leisurely age when dining was a rite not to be passed over casually. It may be crass to speak of food in this genteel atmosphere but their Virginia ham and fried chicken are the best there are. Mrs. K. superintends the cooking herself, particularly the hot breads and the pies and cakes that have made the place famous. The kitchen is one of the most immaculate I ever inspected. Try a Planked Steak dinner.[300]

Finally, although New York City boasted many fine restaurants, few could compare, in Hines's estimation, with the Krebs at Skaneateles, New York. The Krebs was operated by Fred Krebs until his death in the late 1930s. Its ownership was taken over by

Frederick W. Perkins, a twenty-four-year Krebs employee and his wife, who for many years afterward gave hungry travelers some of the best food in New York State. Located in a town of less than 2000 population in the region's Finger Lakes section, in its day the restaurant often served more than 1000 people daily. People would "drive up from New York for one meal"; reservations had to be made months in advance. Milton MacKaye, describing its riches, wrote: "Here, from April to December, food is presented in prodigious quantities; coffee in half-gallon pots. The lobster Newburg is famous, and may be served along with a choice of soups and desserts, a half chicken, a slice of roast beef three eighths of an inch thick, five vegetables, and a sherbet. It's marvelous, but it's brutal."[301] Hines swooned over this culinary institution, never making up his mind which of their many dishes he liked best. "Perhaps it is the lobster, perfectly marvelous," he opined, which was served "along with a superlative cut of roast beef and fried chicken, or perhaps it is the amazing popovers that greet you for breakfast."[302] Whichever it was, he always tried to show up when he was in the neighborhood.

However, as Christmas 1938 rolled around, not quite a whole month after the publication of the *Post* article, Hines was not necessarily thinking about his next roadside meal. Now that he was alone with no one to care for him, he was increasingly thinking about returning to his boyhood home. But it was not an easy decision. He had been away for forty years.

9

BACK HOME AGAIN
IN BOWLING GREEN

In early December 1938, Duncan Hines sent a note to his secretary, counseling her not to become too depressed over the tremendous amount of work she was suddenly facing. He wrote:

> It is possible that we may have the new *Lodging* [guidebooks] ready by February 15, but I am not yet certain about doing it so quickly. I like the way you have handled things during my absence. I never worry about business. All any of us can do is to be loyal & do the best we can. Then if things do not turn out right, worry won't help a bit. You go ahead & have the girl assist you whenever she is needed. Perhaps one of the most important things to remember about the conduct of any small business [is that] to make a profit you must keep expenses down. That is why this business has been conducted from my home. By May 1st we will move out of the apt. & have an office somewhere.... You should handle [office business] any way you desire so long as you have a record of invoices & labels to send to Donnelley for shipment from their plant in Crawfordsville. All the accumulated orders should be shipped by Donnelley &

perhaps books can reach customers by Xmas.... I leave here tomorrow night 12/12—8 P.M. Arrive in El Paso 12/14—10 A.M. will go to Hilton Hotel for laundry & mail. Then start for gulf coast.[303]

On 20 December 1938, after traveling most of the month through the Southwest, Hines's car pulled in front of his sister Annie's Bowling Green home. He spent Christmas there, trying to relax as he decided how to manage his time and newfound fame.

Hines may have had thoughts of opening an office in Chicago, but his sister had other ideas. During his Christmas visit, Annie, ever-protective of him, insisted he leave Chicago and return to Bowling Green. She told him that, since Florence was no longer around to look after him, she wanted to take her place. "What if something happened to him?", she asked. "To whom would he turn?" Hines hesitated making a commitment, but Annie insisted he seriously consider her suggestion. He therefore gave it some prolonged thought, turning over in his mind the myriad problems and organizational turmoil such a move would entail. Returning there did have some merits. He was almost 59 years old and not getting any younger, and since he and Florence were childless, there were no close relations in Chicago he could turn to in case of emergencies. In this light, Bowling Green offered some security. Then another factor entered his mind's calculus. Now that he was financially secure, he no longer needed Chicago and its myriad printing firms to secure lucrative sales jobs. But perhaps the most important argument that clinched his decision, made by both Annie and his brother, Porter, was that he had been away from home too long. It was time to come home. After several days, Hines agreed to return to the city of his birth in the spring.[304]

Before he could move, though, there was much work to do. Hines spent the winter of 1938-1939 preparing his new guidebook editions. The days passed quickly. On 1 February 1939, Hines gave the Donnelley company the proof-sheets for the new 1939 editions of *Adventures in Good Eating* and *Lodging For a Night*. He ordered Donnelley to print 10,000 copies of the lodging book and 25,000 copies of the restaurant guide.[305] Both editions had become considerably fatter in appearance since their last printings. So much new information had passed across Hines's desk during the preceding year that both guidebooks had to undergo many changes, additions and subtractions. It was hard work but worth the trouble. The new edition of *Adventures in Good Eating* now had over 2,000 listings, and it had expanded, as had the lodging book, to 288 pages. In all subsequent printings, Hines tried to hold his publications' page length to that number.[306]

His printing bill for the restaurant guide cost him $4,936, while the bill for the lodging guide cost him $1,789. Depending on the size of the order, additional printings of 5,000 or 10,000 units cost him between $1,100 and $1,800.[307] Fortunately, Hines could now afford such expenses. By his own estimate, within forty months after the appearance of his first book in 1936, the cumulative number of units published under his name came to a figure that well exceeded the 100,000 mark.[308] Of *Adventures in Good Eating* alone, Hines estimated that by the end of April 1939 it had sold 75,000 copies.[309] Upon completion of releasing his latest guidebooks to the public, Hines turned his attention to moving to Kentucky.

The decision to move back to Bowling Green was not an easy one. Despite the desire to return to his boyhood residence, Chicago had been his home for the past thirty-four years; leaving it meant leaving his friends behind. One of the move's drawbacks was that few of his boyhood friends still lived in Bowling Green; most had either departed for other cities or had died. Still, the choice of returning there was his, and Annie and Porter Hines made sure he never regretted it.[310]

On 31 March 1939, Duncan Hines's nephew (Annie's son who was also named Duncan Hines) and his young wife, Elizabeth, journeyed from Bowling Green to Chicago to help their famous relative move his belongings to Kentucky. In Elizabeth Hines's view, helping her husband move his uncle back to Bowling Green was an odd experience. Hines was a stranger to her. She had only met him once a few years earlier, when he and Florence had stopped through Bowling Green for a quick, one-hour visit. She felt a little uneasy about helping a man she barely knew move into her already crowded home. Elizabeth lived with her husband's parents, Annie and Scott Hines, and though their house was a sizable one, it was not large enough to easily accommodate five people. She feared the addition of a distant relative from Chicago would create tension within the household. Still, the Hines family was a very close-knit one, and loyalty to family came first, and for that reason she agreed to accompany her husband to Chicago. Annie could not make the trip because her husband had a delicate heart condition and could not exert himself enough to travel that far without serious repercussions. Due to this circumstance Annie insisted her son and daughter-in-law go in her place. The young couple's trip took all day. When they arrived at his Chicago apartment that evening, Hines was waiting for them, ready to go.

Before they headed south for Kentucky, however, Hines took the young couple out for a night on the town. He "thought...that the Morrison Hotel was the best place to eat in the whole world," said Elizabeth, recalling the night they departed. "I remember going to the Morrison Hotel for dinner."[311] Afterward, the three returned to their uncle's apartment and picked out items to be sent by freight to Kentucky, then waited until Hines made arrangements by phone to have the articles collected and shipped. With that completed, they packed his remaining belongings into both Hines' automobile and their own, and as the moon shone high above them, headed southward through Indiana down U. S. 41 for Kentucky. Said Elizabeth Hines, fifty-four years after the event, "I can't believe that we left at night." Her husband drove the lead car, while, at his insistence, Hines drove the second vehicle, with Elizabeth at his side. It snowed on the way down, and throughout the trip Elizabeth believed Hines to be "the worst driver in the world that night.... It was a snowy, blustery night—terrible."[312] Despite her opinion of Hines's driving skills, on the following morning, 1 April 1939, both cars arrived "safely home" in Bowling Green without incident.[313]

With the exception of the downtown area, Bowling Green in 1939 was markedly different from what is there today. There was no by-pass encircling the compact town, nor was there an interstate highway and a toll-road intersecting near the city. The town square, known as Fountain Square, served as the metropolis's focal point. Surrounding it were the bank, the post office, the courthouse, and a variety of offices and stores, which were surrounded by the city's residential area.[314] For a few months after his arrival, Hines lived with his sister Annie at 902 Elm Street, just a few short blocks from Fountain Square. He temporarily used her home as his business location until he could find an office. Once Hines settled in, though, he returned to his natural state: perpetual restlessness. He missed the daily hustle of city life. To counter the tranquility he found in Bowling Green, he began to pursue various hobbies when he was not working. Weeks after his arrival, Hines and his namesake nephew, Duncan, tried curing country hams in barrels of brine. For some reason the venture was not terribly successful. Nevertheless, Hines was not idle. "I don't think there was ever a time when his mind wasn't clicking," said Elizabeth Hines.[315] When he was in town for a week or two, Hines and his brother, Porter, who lived a few blocks away on Park Street, spent much time together. They were wonderful companions, sometimes spending two or three evenings a week in Annie's living room or on the front porch, swapping riotous stories of their boyhood days. Like most close-knit Southern families, the Hines clan gathered for formal dinners on Easter, Thanksgiving, and Christmas. On these occasions, Porter Hines carved the ham while Duncan simultaneously carved the turkey.[316]

To make Hines feel more at home when he was with them, family members kidded him about being "the head rooster." This nickname, which Hines proudly wore, eventually led family members to giving him toy roosters as gag gifts. The inside joke with roosters even extended to Hines's employees. One of his secretaries once asked him to autograph a cookbook; Hines complied with her request, scribbling his signature along with the initials, "H. R." When Hines was away on long trips many years later, it was this same secretary's responsibility to watch the office all day alone. To show her his genuine appreciation for her loyalty, Hines frequently brought her little gifts from his travels. After returning from one trip, Hines, with a twinkle in his eye, presented her with two ceramic roosters.[317]

His relatives did what they could to make him feel welcome; they cordially invited him to their annual outdoor activities and were delighted when he came. The Duncan family always had a July picnic in Browning, Kentucky, at the home of Dillard Duncan, the grandson of Joseph Dillard Duncan. It was Dillard Duncan's tradition on these occasions to prepare a wonderful noon-time barbecue; other family members supplemented the feast with their own home-made dishes. Little get-togethers such as these went a long way to prevent Hines from missing Chicago. He may have had some initial qualms about returning home, but after his first summer there he never regretted it.

Regardless of how warmly he was received upon his return, Hines still had plenty of work to do. He had to find an office and quickly reorganize it if his guidebook business was to operate smoothly. Some of his business problems were handled by others. Before he moved to Bowling Green, he hired a Cincinnati advertising agency to handle general public relations for Adventures in Good Eating, Inc. Then he hired a Chicago firm to handle his books' publicity upon their publication. He also retained his regular attorney in Chicago, James Black, should he need legal advice.[318] All during April he searched for permanent headquarters. Within a few days he found an office in a single room on the second floor of the American National Bank.[319] Once Hines set up shop, any visitor could reach his office via the stairway from the banks back entrance. The visitor who entered his office could always find a secretary seated at the front desk, answering his voluminous pile of mail, while another secretary was filling innumerable book orders for his thousands of customers. The bank building was a much better location for an office than his apartment in Chicago had been, but before many weeks had passed, business volume forced him to expand into the adjacent room.

Still, even with this improvement, so heavy was the volume of mail, it soon became apparent that a larger office was needed. In fact, so much space was taken up by filing cabinets that there was scarcely any room for Hines and his two secretaries. Some cabinets contained files on each recommended restaurant, hotel, and motel, while others held the scores of letters that daily cascaded into his office. When Hines answered a letter, a carbon copy of his reply was always made and filed in the appropriate folder, and this took up still more file space. For these reasons, coupled with his desire to increase the number of institutions covered in his guidebooks, the need for a larger office became acute. Due to the spatial limitations, Hines began to consider building a combination of house and office.[320]

Because his business was inundated with mail each day, Hines could ill afford to start from scratch and train a completely new staff. Most of his time was spent on the road investigating new leads and he did not have time to remain in the office and explain how he wanted it to function. Therefore, before he moved to Bowling Green, he persuaded two of his Chicago secretaries, Olga Lindquist and Emelie Tolman, to also move there. Shortly after the newcomers had ensconced themselves in their new environment, Ms. Lindquist and Mrs. Tolman became the talk of the town; the newcomers impressed the Bowling Green natives with their business-like efficiency. In a geographical area of the country where all matters were approached in a sometimes overly relaxed fashion, the two secretaries' matter-of-fact demeanor commanded attention, if not always outright respect. When at the office, neither engaged in much conversation during business hours. This was somewhat jarring for Bowling Green's citizens, because it was the habit of the average female employee there to tell all within earshot fifty things about her family before she ever waited on a customer. What the locals did not realize was that Olga and Emelie did not have time to talk; there was too much work to do. The mail just kept pouring in from all parts of the country, and they had to answer it. So much of it came in into the office that, quite often, Hines took it on the road with him, where he answered it from the desk of the hotel or motel room of wherever he happened to be. When he answered his mail, he sprinkled his replies with excuses like "I've been away" or "My desk is piled high." Recipients of his correspondence could usually pinpoint his location by the letter's postmark.[321]

No doubt all this work and the frenzied coordination it involved sometimes drove Olga and Emelie nearly crazy. If one wonders what it was like working for Duncan Hines, very few secretaries are still alive to impart that information, but those who survive sum up their experience in one word: Busy. A typical day for one of them might begin by examining the various notes that Hines had left on her desk; these were usually responses to letters he had read the night before. After typing these for the outgoing mail, her day's activities could involve numerous chores. Every day was a little different. Whatever she faced that day, her hectic pace did not stop until the office closed that evening. When she went home, her day may have been over, but it was not for Duncan Hines; there was simply too much work to do. Sometimes he worked well into the night, answering as much mail as he could before placing his replies on his secretaries' desks and going home to bed. When he arose early the next morning, he quickly went to the office to answer the remaining mail before going to the post office to fetch another sack load.

While Hines dictated some of his letters, Olga and Emelie answered those not requiring his personal attention. Despite the volume of mail, though, Hines carefully considered any document that bore his name. He adamantly refused to sign any letter without knowing its full content and significance. No secretary in his pay ever gave him a stack of letters to sign quickly. Hines insisted on reading each letter carefully before it was dropped in the mailbox.[322]

Although there was only one telephone in his office, Hines rarely used it. When he was away from the office, he almost never bothered to call in. Said one secretary, "We didn't hear from him from the time he left until the time he got back."[323] Quite often he could be away for two or three weeks. One reason for his reluctance of using the telephone was that there were few people he knew well enough that warranted a phone call. "Why call someone on the phone, when a letter would serve the same purpose?" he reasoned. Calling someone long distance on the telephone, in Hines's eyes, was an unneeded expense, an extravagance, and one he could do without. Besides, he wanted to keep a record of what he had said to whom, something he could not do if he used the telephone.[324]

Sara Meeks, one of his secretaries in the 1950s, explained what it was like working for Hines. "We never sat around," she said. "We always worked. We took an hour off for lunch...Sometimes we would bring our lunch, but usually we wanted a break. We wanted to get out....We never ate or had coffee or anything while on the job."[325]

Hines put both Olga and Emelie in charge of keeping his files in meticulous order. And they did, because Hines was very serious on this point. Sloppy paperwork could sabotage all his efforts. His business was not, he stressed, a flippant one. There were people out there who depended on him. "Caution," therefore, was the office watchword. Hines stressed to them that if they were indifferent to what his books meant to so many—and if their attitude was reflected in their paperwork—he could lose the public's trust and thus his business. This, however, was the least of his concerns. He could always return to the printing business. He could not, however, win back his name once it was tarnished by lackadaisical office practices. Every time he published a recommendation, his integrity was on the line—and to him losing it was a worse fate than losing his business.[326]

Adventures
— IN —
Good Eating

Perhaps as an antiquarian, you have known the thrill of uncovering some long forgotten treasure of New England master craftsmanship. Or maybe it was the lure of "first editions" that sent you rummaging through second hand bookstores. No less does the hope of turning up some rare "pre-cancelled" items cause others to fumble through musty stamp collections.

So it is with joy akin to that of the collector that I have pursued the quest of unusual places to eat, where food of outstanding quality is served. It is with a feeling of mingled temerity and pleasure that I reveal the following list to my friends—a list compiled from memoranda accumulated in various travels and journeyings oft. Those places which have not been personally tested and tried, have been vouched for by discriminating friends.

I am passing this information on to you, hoping that it may yield enjoyment and delectation, should you find yourself in the vicinity of one of these "harbors of refreshment" as you travel hither and yon. Should you suffer disappointment, as one traveler to another, be good enough to tell me in order that I may be less enthusiastic in my endorsement in the future. Again, should you have nominations of your own, I invite you to submit them, that other weary wayfarers may share the unusual food and hospitality. (A detachable page is added for your convenience.)

I realize that this list is neither comprehensive nor complete—it is just the sketchy jottings of my occasional rambling through the country side. Whether it ever reaches a second edition depends on you. As in other realms of endeavor, fine food and true hospitality are just as often found in the wayside tavern and roadside home receiving guests as in the more ostentatious and formal hotel in town. If you care to join me in compiling this very intimate American register of "Le Cordon Bleu," I welcome you.

DUNCAN HINES
5494 Cornell Ave., Chicago, Ill.

10

LIFE CHANGES

Lodging for a Night, first released in 1938, was an outgrowth of *Adventures in Good Eating.* This guidebook, while not as popular as its predecessor, was just as vital. It was prepared in response to his readers' many requests that there be a companion volume to *Adventures in Good Eating.* T. C. Dedman, owner of the Beaumont Inn in Harrodsburg, Kentucky, knew Hines well. His inn was always listed in both of Hines's guidebooks as an excellent place to eat and sleep. "He was very important to us," said Dedman, speaking of Hines's influence on his industry.

> Of course, you could not pay Mr. Hines. There was no membership charge. You were in [his book] or you were out, and there was nothing you could do about it except improve your situation to please him....You could not entertain him. Many times he [stopped to eat at] our place, and we'd say "Mr. Hines, we'd like to pick up your lunch" to which he would reply, 'absolutely not.' You could not. He just wouldn't have that at all....He came fairly often. Even when he was in Chicago, he used to come by the inn once or twice a year. And, of course, when he moved to Bowling Green, why several times a year we would always see him. But his books, *Adventures in*

Good Eating and *Lodging for a Night* were certainly most influential so far as all inns or eating places all around were concerned. In other words, we felt that he definitely help put us on the map.

Though little has been written as to how the lodging industry viewed Hines, his opinions and suggestions, according to Dedman, were taken very seriously by innkeepers. "Those who were not in [his guidebook] pooh-poohed it a little bit, saying it wasn't important. But it *was* important! It was *very* important." The reason it was important could be revealed by those who strolled in as guests. Said Dedman, "People would come by and say, 'We're traveling by Duncan Hines' books." A plethora of such customers was motivation enough to keep most innkeepers on their toes because such travelers annually put an extra $25,000 to $50,000 in an inn's bank account.

Dedman witnessed Hines's lodging inspections. "He stayed overnight a few times at our place—in fact a number of times," he said. "But when he didn't, he would ask to see" two rooms "and sometimes three or four." Hines "would ask to see one on the second floor and one on the third floor. Or a couple on each floor. And he would go up and say, 'Oh, could I see in this room?' He would pick the room. He wouldn't just take our key." Hines "would look in the bathrooms. He would look around [the room for] cleanliness, feel the beds, and that sort of thing." Though Hines was a frequent guest, Dedman and his family were never sure what the verdict on their inn would be until the next edition of *Lodging for a Night* was published. Their experience was duplicated a thousand-fold by other innkeepers every year.[327]

Within the pages of his dark-blue lodging guide, Hines developed a criteria that shaped his lodging recommendations, which he asked his readers to adopt while traveling. When the time came to choose a place to spend the night, these "required" qualities, said Hines, made it possible for any traveler to determine an accommodation's worthiness. As Hines's reputation as a trustworthy authority grew, hotels and motels were foolish to ignore his words, because his readers were soon demanding innkeepers adapt his criteria, which consisted of: cleanliness throughout—not only clean linen but clean bedding; quietness, such as freedom from traffic and other noises, as well as disturbing movements or conversations of other guests; comfortable beds; courteous, adequate and unobtrusive service, and hospitality, which Hines said was the defining ingredient that made "a traveler's sojourn pleasant" and created within him "the desire to return again."[328]

In the first edition of *Lodging for a Night* Hines acknowledged it was weighted with a preference for hotels. He attributed this prejudice to "habit" because "a first-class hotel carries an establish-ed reputation and offers certain recognized conveniences." But just because he tended to favor hotels as a place to sleep did not mean he was unwilling to let them off the hook. If he saw things he did not like, they did not get listed. Most hotels, he said, had innumerable deficiencies, and every seasoned traveler would agree with him. The fact that Hines went to the trouble to lay out a reform agenda for hotels is a telling comment on the state of the hotel industry in the late 1930s. In many instances, Hines said, hotels might as well have had a motto that proudly boasted: "The public be damned. They've got to sleep somewhere." Hines instructed the public, should they find any such institutions, to let him know. If a pattern emerged, they would not be listed. Those who were excluded soon started paying closer attention to what he said.

There were places to spend the night along the road other than hotels. One new development in the late 1930s was the infant motel industry. When *Lodging for a Night* was first published, this primitive form of public accommodation was struggling to emerge from its initial disreputable incarnation, i.e., horrible little places on the side of the road which, more often than not, were makeshift houses of prostitution that operated within the limits of the law. By the time the lodging guide garnered the public's attention, motels were slowly becoming respectable places. Even so, travelers still needed to discriminate; sometimes lovely exteriors could mask an ugly interior—or something worse. In this respect, *Lodging for a Night* proved for many to be an invaluable traveling tool.

For a motel to be included in *Lodging for a Night,* Hines developed a criteria. Not surprisingly, some of his guidelines duplicated his expectations for well-run hotels. But there were a few differences. Travelers who wished to stay in a motel, he said, should expect and demand: a clean, inviting atmosphere; restful beds; clean bedding; clean linen; full lavatory and bathroom facilities, including plenty of hot water; convenient parking to unload personal belongings; a quiet location away from traffic and city noises; and a room that is "comfortable by reason of cross ventilation—a real advantage in sultry weather." A couple of aspects that quickly gained his approval concerning motels was that there was "no occasion for tipping—and more often than not the prices [were] more reasonable than the hotel rates."

Although many motels eventually established a code of ethics, Hines wrote his own code for them. It was, he insisted, one motel operators should follow to the letter—that is, if they wanted any business from him or his readers. Many motel operators appreciated his efforts, even if it required increased expense on their part. Hines said while his code was short, it was identical with those prevailing in first class hotels. Once put into practice, he said, travelers would quickly find motels and motor courts an attractive option. His code insisted that: only guests with baggage should be accepted; guests should register in the regular way and remain all night; drinking on the premises should not be permitted; and all questionable trade refused.[329]

Hines repeatedly stated that his book of lodging facilities, like his restaurant guide, was not complete. His contribution to guidebook literature consisted of those inns which had been brought to his attention and inspected. However, because they were found to be void of defects, he listed them until a pattern of complaints made it necessary to dispense with their inclusion. He advised his readers to always tell the innkeeper that *Lodging For a Night* led them to his door. He also suggested that, whether or not they enjoyed their stay, the innkeeper should know their opinion of his establishment. That someone took the time to say anything at all, Hines believed, would make a difference in the long run. Their comments also gave the innkeeper some indication of what customers wanted in their accommodations. There is no doubt many readers complied with his request.

The last page of the 1939 edition of *Lodging for a Night* printed two pictures. One was of Hines standing next to his automobile. In the passenger seat was Florence with their Boston terrier, Peggy, in her lap. It was taken just as they were about to start off for their last trip to Tennessee. For Hines, the photograph had a sentimental quality. Accompanying the photo was the caption, "I deeply regret to say this is the last picture taken of Mrs. Hines." In the ensuing years Hines frequently traveled to Chicago, where on many occasions he visited Florence's grave. Below this sad reminder was another photograph of his current home.[330] In that house another annual Duncan Hines publication was about to be born. Its birth was only months away. But there was something different about this one. It was not a guidebook.

On 25 April 1939, Jack Bruce, the man in charge of book production for R. R. Donnelley, wrote Hines and commented that "the sale of your books must be 'red hot.' I presume that you are progressing very nicely on the new cooking book."[331] Indeed he was. Almost a year earlier, Hines had decided to supplement the income from his two regular guidebooks with a third publication—a cookbook. Its origin grew out of repeated requests for one from those using his restaurant guide who wanted to duplicate the same dishes in their kitchens that they were consuming in public—and believed Hines could persuade the originators of these wonderful concoctions to give them away. This was a most unlikely prospect, and Hines knew it. Most restaurants were afraid to publicize their prized secret recipes for fear that, once the public knew how to create them, they would no longer patronize their businesses, preferring instead to eat them at home. Hines, however, was never one to miss an opportunity, so he began visiting restaurants, asking for recipes. He had no idea whether or not he would be successful in collecting enough material.

To his delight, he had no trouble at all. He should not have been surprised. What restaurant owner or chef would dare refuse a request from Duncan Hines? He calmed all fears by announcing he had no intention of publicizing prized recipes; he merely wanted a tasty dish or two that would satisfy the public's demand for something unusual, something not always found in the home. A single recipe, he said, could do no harm, and it might do plenty of good; when it appeared in his cookbook, both restaurant and chef would be given credit for its creation. Many restaurants were delighted to give him a couple of their cherished culinary secrets. It was the least they could do for a man who had done much for them and was working hard to elevate their industry to new heights of respectability.[332]

Hines also prevailed upon his relatives and co-workers for recipes. The book even included some culinary treasures his grandmother Duncan had made for him as a boy.[333] Many of the book's 460 recipes were first tested in his sister's kitchen. After each dish had been approved, Hines's secretary, Emelie Tolman, typed it up on a slip of paper, all of which were assembled into a manuscript. Hines read through the final draft, made suggestions for amending the text, and soon sent it to the printers. The result of this effort came to fruition on 1 October 1939 with the publication of *Adventures in Good Cooking and The Art of Carving In The Home.* Shortly after the cookbook was published, the public bought 15,000 copies.[334]

He knew covers with primary colors increased a book's sales so Hines selected bright yellow for his newest publication. It must have helped because, for a while, the cookbook outsold his guidebooks. Its recipes did not consist of the American home-style variety, i.e., the often tasteless and vapid culinary hodgepodge found at church socials. Instead, they were easily some of the richest foods many Americans had ever encountered. A few of the recipes were a bit sophisticated for the average homemaker, and sometimes their unusual ingredients were not always readily available at the corner grocery store. But there was no doubt that, when prepared exactly as directed, they produced delightful results.[335]

The 256-page book broadened Hines's name recognition beyond his usual customers. It also associated his name with good food as never before. There were not too many cookbooks on bookstore shelves in the late 1930s, and that fortunate circumstance enabled Hines's effort to stand out among its competitors. The book stirred interest. The concept of a book collection of recipes from famous restaurants was, at the time, unique.

Although Hines's secretary, Olga Lindquist, was not unattractive, it was his other secretary, Emelie Tolman, a blonde, Northern-speaking, slightly portly woman of Scandinavian descent in her mid-40s, who was more frequently found in his company. There was such a backlog of mail piling up on his desk and so little time to answer it that Hines began taking Emelie on the road with him. Emelie spent so much time with him that, after a few months, they decided to get married.[336] Although Hines's family had their reservations about his intentions to marry again, they did not reveal their thoughts. They were perhaps concerned about the differences in their ages, but that was the extent of it.[337]

Emelie E. Tolman was born in Chicago, Illinois, on 18 October 1896. Her father's name was Peter Daniels; her mother's maiden name was Catherine Oberhofer.[338] In 1920 Emelie Daniels married Lee Tolman; the marriage was an unhappy affair and ended in divorce about a decade later. Emelie no doubt hoped that her second trip down the aisle would be more successful when, at age forty-three on 9 December 1939 in Rockport, Texas, she became Mrs. Duncan Hines.[339]

As Emelie adjusted to Bowling Green's customs and conventions, she made several friends, although none were close. The Hines were on the road so much that intimate friendships with the citizens of Bowling Green were hard to form. When the two did meet, though, they noted that she talked a little differently than they did. Overall, in their estimation, Emelie was a well-organized, neat, efficient career woman, but they didn't get to know her very well. Emelie, almost from the first, hoped they wouldn't live in Bowling Green forever. Used to Chicago's fast tempo, she found Kentucky's slow pace of living tiresome. It was so different from the speedy environment to which she was accustomed. She also did not like the clannish tendencies she detected in Hines's family.

As to why Hines married Emelie in the first place, his reasons are not difficult to understand. He was lonely. He had not adjusted well to life without Florence. He needed a traveling companion, someone who could fill his emotional void—and someone who could handle the sackfuls of correspondence he carried around the country in his car. He needed a wife, and in Emelie he found what he was looking for. She understood the peculiar sort of work in which he was engaged and could accommodate its occupational vagaries. It is not for certain they deeply loved each other, but each provided the other with the lure of security. She needed a husband to provide her with a measure of protection; he, on the other hand, was sort of helpless without a woman about the house. In short, it was a marriage of convenience.

There was another aspect that determined his decision to marry Emelie. Despite Annie's help, without a wife it was he who had to do those myriad things about the house for which he had no talent or, more likely, no patience. These were things Florence had handled over the years with aplomb and efficiency. Emelie filled a void here, too. Even before their marriage, she was sending out his laundry and taking care of the whole panoply of his other daily needs. So it should not have been a shock to anyone when, after a few months, their decision to marry was, more or less, a natural progression toward an obvious conclusion for two people who did not have anyone but themselves. Though their marriage was not built on a solid emotional foundation, Hines, for a time at least, was happy. Thanks to her, his life slowly stabilized, and that, at least, was enough to soothe the past year's pain and anxieties.[340]

Although life had not been uncomfortable for Hines while living with his sister, he hated imposing on her. Just before he married

Emelie, he moved a few blocks away into a recently constructed, late Tudor architecturally-styled, efficiency-apartment complex known as the Arms Apartments.[341] It was a convenient location, as it was two blocks away from Hines's office and three blocks from Annie's home.[342] Even before Hines moved into it, he knew it was only a temporary home. He had no intention of remaining there long. He wanted an abode of his own, one where he could sit on the front porch in the evening and chain-smoke cigarettes while watching the cars go by. For these reasons and others, he decided to build a house in the country. Since summer he had spent his spare time exploring the Warren County countryside in search of a tract of land to build not only a home but a structure which would serve as the location for his ever expanding business.[343] In September he finally found a piece of property that suited him. On 11 October 1939, he bought a parcel of land located 2 miles north of Bowling Green on the southeast side of highway 31-W, known locally as the Old Louisville Road. E. F. Wilkinson and Edgar and Irene Walker sold it to him for one dollar; construction commenced immediately.[344] For a month or so after he and Emelie were married, the couple made his apartment their home.

While waiting for construction of his new home to be completed, Hines and Emelie continued to ply the roads of America in search of new guidebook additions. No matter where they went, Hines almost never failed to drop by the local newspaper office to spread the gospel. For example, in early December, when he visited Oklahoma City, in addition to revealing some of his personal habits, such as writing his books at 3:00 A.M. because it was the only time that "people don't drop in, the telephone doesn't ring and ring and ring, and one can concentrate" and letting it be known that more than 300 "dinner detectives" were currently checking places for him, he mostly discussed restaurants. He began by pointing out that when one chooses to dine in a restaurant, its atmosphere was not the only factor to consider. There were three others. First, was cleanliness: "If a place is not clean," said Hines, "it can't be good." The public, he said, should also consider *who* cooks the meals; he shuddered when he thought of how much good food untalented cooks ruined. The third thing to look for was food quality; many kitchens routinely produced over-or undercooked food made from poor quality ingredients. "If people knew the poor quality of [the] food so often proffered them," Hines lamented, they would not "touch it with a ten-foot pole." He also stated that so long as the customer paid his bill, most restaurant personnel didn't care. He concluded the interview with a dig at male cooks, the thought of which made Hines laugh. "Men can't cook, they don't know how and never will learn.... They have the notion that cooking is women's work and that the men's distinction comes in squeezing icing in curlicues on top of cakes. That's not cooking. It's a mess."[345]

By year's end Duncan Hines had become one of the nation's best selling authors with a distinction: he was also his own publisher. As the nation began lifting itself out of the decade-long Depression, his books were fast becoming a fixture in the glove compartments of hundreds of thousands of American cars. Thanks to the war in Europe and other social, political and economic factors, Americans began to regularly put money in their pockets. After a decade of economic drought, many Americans now pursued a little leisure—and for many that meant an occasional meal in a nearby good restaurant. Also, by year's end, Hines books had collectively sold almost 100,000 copies that year, "a figure that could then be claimed by only thirteen other best-selling authors."[346] Eighty percent of Hines's books were sold from his Bowling Green office; the rest were sold by vendors who supplied bookstores and newsstands. At the end of the year Hines gave his publishing representative in New York, Frank M. Watts, the number of books sold through those vendors: *Adventures in Good Eating* 12,430 copies; *Adventures in Good Cooking* 2,017 copies; *Lodging for a Night* 5,949 copies, bringing total sales to 20,396 copies.[347]

The R. R. Donnelley Company produced excellent work for Duncan Hines through early 1940, but the long distance between Chicago and Bowling Green made continued involvement with the company difficult. If a problem with the books developed during

production, Hines could not give it immediate attention. What he
needed was a highly competent book publishing firm near Bowling
Green. The problem was where to find one. Which company could
he turn to? He had seen many incompetent publishers over the
years and was unwilling to hire just any firm.

For the past several years his brother, Warner, had lived in
Nashville, Tennessee. Now that he and Duncan lived only an hour's
drive from each other, the two visited more often. One evening late
in 1939, while Hines was visiting him, he complained of his
publishing problems. Hines said he wanted to switch to another
firm, but he had to be cautious for fear of being saddled with an
incompetent publisher. If he hired a firm that proved to be inept at
book production, the good will the public placed in him might
suffer. After all, they expected quality from everything associated
with his name, including the sturdy quality of his books.
Fortunately for Hines, Warner had just the printer for him. He told
Hines of a printing firm that handled his oil company's business,
and assured him that they were both fair and competent. Warner
gave him the printing firm's business card and told him to call
them. Duncan said he would. When he left for his hotel that
evening, he had already predetermined they would publish his
books. As far as he was concerned, if it was good enough for
Warner, it was good enough for him.[348]

Warner Hines was a vice-president of Nashville's Spur Oil
Distributing Company. The firm he had recommended his brother
to investigate was that city's Williams Printing Company, which
handled Spur's print advertising, particularly its ubiquitous
billboards.[349] Larry Williams, who later became the owner of the
Williams firm, explained how the marriage between Duncan Hines
and his company came about. "It was a Saturday afternoon," he
recalled, "when Duncan Hines called the Williams Printing
Company from [Nashville's] Hermitage Hotel." James R. Overall
answered the call. Hines told him, "Come up here. I've got a box
full of copy for a book I want you to print." Overall said, "Thank
you very much," and hung up the phone. Tom Williams, one of the
company's vice-presidents, who was sitting across from Overall's

desk, asked, "Who was that, Jim." Overall replied, "Aw, some nut. He called from the Hermitage Hotel. He told me to come up there and pick up some copy. I ain't gonna do it. I'm goin' home." Williams, thinking he might not be a nut, decided to go to the hotel to check out the potential client. Williams' hunch proved fortuitous, because the meeting between the two men began a long, fruitful relationship. After a quick handshake, Hines thrust into Williams' hands two large envelope boxes which contained his manuscript. Williams asked him if he wanted a price on it. Hines said he did not. Williams asked him if he wanted to know something about his company. Hines said, "I know all I need to know." Williams said, "Mr. Hines, what do you want me to do?" Hines replied, "I want you to print this book. Go back and go to work." Williams brought the two boxes back to his office and set them on his desk. After examining its contents, a collective agreement was made among the executives that the project was too large for their small company to handle. So they arranged to have the Methodist Publishing House[350] print the book for them. A few days later, after Larry Williams and Paul Moore, another Williams employee, proofread and prepared the book for printing, they sent it to the larger printer, which quickly produced it to Hines's specifications. The books were shipped across town to the Williams firm, then put on a truck, which delivered them to Hines's Bowling Green office. Through an arrangement made with Hines, the Williams firm sent the other volumes via the postal system to book distributors across the country. The quality of the work so impressed Hines that he transferred his entire printing business from the Donnelley company to the Williams firm.[351]

Although in the beginning Tom Williams was responsible for Hines's books, by the mid-1940s most of the work fell to Paul W. Moore, a young man in his early twenties. Moore, a business-oriented individual who possessed a light sense of humor, began working for Williams in 1939 at age 21 by cutting linoleum plates. Tom Williams grew to like the young man and eventually he made him his personal assistant. Drafted in 1944, Moore served two years in the U. S. Army. Upon his discharge in 1946, Moore, now 28, returned to Williams to resume his regular duties. It was at this time that his involvement with the Duncan Hines books became more pronounced.

Tom Williams gave Duncan Hines the special attention his famous client demanded. But after the war, increasing bouts of illness kept Williams from his duties. As a result, Moore was put in charge of handling his employer's correspondence and proofreading duties. If Williams could not tend to Hines's needs, then he sent Moore in his place. Hines accepted the situation and was altogether comfortable with the arrangement. When Williams died in 1949, Moore took over as Hines's account representative. From that point forward, Moore not only handled the production of Hines's books, he even handled printing his business cards. Hines insisted that Moore personally travel to Bowling Green to pick up the proofsheets "because it was too precious to mail or ship." Too many things could happen to it in transit, and Hines was not about to leave his fate to chance. Therefore, three or four times a year Moore drove to Bowling Green to pick them up. Since Nashville was only an hour's drive away, it was no trouble for Moore to drive north, cross the Kentucky state line, and arrive in Bowling Green. When he sat down before Hines and his staff, he spent two or three hours examining in detail the necessary changes and revisions their next publication would have to undergo.[352] Moore consulted with them not only on revisions but on design improvements and production schedules. "Before they did the actual printing," said one of Hines's secretaries, "they would send us a copy and [two of us] would have to proofread that thing from beginning to end" which took "a long time! Several weeks!"[353] When the books were printed and deposited at the office, they were carried to the storage room. When orders came in, Hines's staff boxed and packaged them in a second room off to the entrance and sent them to the post office immediately.[354] It was an efficient system for the country's best-selling author-publisher.

11

A FEW PET PEEVES

The nation's media organs continued to give Hines's restaurant guide very favorable reviews. One Chicago columnist wrote that he had seen a "notable change" in American restaurants—for the better. Some of this, he believed, "must be credited to Mr. Duncan Hines, whose book *Adventures in Good Eating* seems to be carried by an astonishing number of tourists."[355] A reviewer in the Nashville *Banner* examined Hines's eating and lodging guides and closed her appraisal with the question, "What did people do before Duncan Hines made motoring easy and pleasant?"[356]

In January 1940, Hines and Emelie moved from their cramped, downtown Bowling Green apartment into their brand new white, Colonial-style home; two miles north of Bowling Green. Many of those who laid eyes on it said the structure reminded them of George Washington's Mount Vernon. And like Mount Vernon, Hines's new home and office was surrounded by nothing but farmland for as far as the eye could see. Hines only wanted a few acres, not a farm because, due to his frequent absences, he would not be home long enough to give it the attention it deserved. His new home was small, and he built it with "apartment house compactness" for a good reason: to prevent his many acquaintances from dropping in on him unannounced and prevailing upon his Southern hospitality. There was no place for guests to spend the night—unless they wanted to sleep on the floor. In fact, one of its curiosities was that it did not even have a bedroom, let alone a spare one. When it was time to turn in for the night, he and Emelie went to the living room and pulled out a bed that folded out from a closet.[357] Besides, after traveling three weeks out of every four, Hines did not have time to entertain guests; he had oceans of paperwork that needed his attention. When a friend arrived at his doorstep, Hines usually directed him to the local Bowling Green hotel.[358] One of his secretaries, describing the home's interior, said it consisted of a living room/bedroom, a kitchen, a library, and a bathroom. "It was furnished beautifully. It had antique furniture. I just thought it was the prettiest thing I had ever seen."[359] Although Hines wanted a larger office, what he built was one scarcely more spacious than the last; it is unknown why this happened, since he built it. Nevertheless, he and his staff managed affairs out of two rooms: a main office for his secretaries and a storeroom for his file cabinets.[360] Behind the structure, on the far right-hand section of his property, Hines constructed two additional buildings: a smokehouse for his country hams and a house for the groundskeeper who took care of his property.[361]

Duncan Hines employed many people over the years. One was Paul Davis. In November 1940 Davis went to work for him and remained his employee until the following April, when he joined the US Marine Corps.[362] Davis was hired because Hines needed a shipping clerk and office boy. Although he had no credentials or experience for the job, Hines hired him anyway. At $25 a week Davis "was very happy to have it," because his father was ill and was dependent on the boy for the family's livelihood. His job was twofold. When he came to work each morning, the first thing he had to do was process the book orders that had arrived in that morning's mail and ship them to Hines's customers. In addition to moving his home and office into the country, Hines had also relocated his fledgling country ham business to the little building behind his home. When Davis had packaged all the book orders and taken them to the post office for shipping, he returned and began filling the profusion of country ham orders that had piled up during the previous twenty-four hours. When he completed boxing and addressing those, he made another trip to the post office.

When he returned from town, Hines had yet another chore for the boy: assisting him in the revisions of his guidebooks. Regardless of which one he was working on, Davis's job was to mount hundreds of listings on 8" x 11" sheets of paper and organize them into a state-by-state alphabetical scheme, so that the first page began with Alabama and the last ended with Wyoming. He then compared information of previous listings with the current ones, writing down any needed changes. When he was through, he gave his revisions to one of Hines's secretaries, who typed them and shaped the manuscript into its final form.[363]

To the outside observer, it may be hard to understand why compiling one of Hines's books took so long. The answer was that editing approximately 2,000 entries per book per year was a considerable project that exacted a substantial amount of time.[364] To keep up with each restaurant and lodging listed, Hines assigned a file to every establishment; without them, Hines's business would have been sheer chaos. Depending on the type of establishment, these files contained data such as hotel and motel rate cards, copies of menus, figures on the number of people it could serve, and other assorted data.[365]

Hines's country ham business was a small operation. He hired several local men to buy his hams for him, who hickory-smoked them in several Warren County barns and let them age for two years. When they were ready for sale, they were moved to the ham house behind Hines's home, and they remained there until they were sold either through the mail or to visitors. The hams had a good flavor and reputation for quality. Hines sold them for a dollar a pound; in 1940 a ham sold at that weight for that price was considered a premium cut.[366] Hines, however, did not sell hundreds of hams a day, nor did he want to. He cured and sold country hams for the fun of it; it was his hobby. "Money was not his big thing," a relative remembered. He did not need much. In fact, Hines did not seem to be interested in money at all. He was very secure with himself and never felt the need to impress others with the size of his income. His wants were quaint. Aside from a nice suit of clothes, his extravagances were few. The only luxury he ever showered on himself was a weekly order of fresh flowers from Deemer's Flower Shop in Bowling Green, which they delivered to his home once a week. His motto was: "Have what you want, but want what you have."[367]

Davis admired the way Hines conducted his business and thought him to be a good role model. Davis saw him as a highly ethical man who set both moral and work standards for him to follow. Hines became quite displeased with his employees if he thought they did not display the ideals he evinced. His sense of business ethics, in Davis' eyes, was unimpeachable. Right was right and wrong was wrong, pure and simple. There were no shades of gray.[368] Another who worked for Hines in the 1950s, said Hines "espoused utter honesty." He was quite loyal and expected equivocal treatment. If he doubted the honesty of those in his company for a moment, "you were through. He didn't want a thing to do with you."[369]

Hines was something of a boy scout, in the most honorable use of that phrase. Consider bribery for example. Many people would have sold their souls to get their establishments into his guidebooks. Those who attempted to bribe him did so in vain. From Hines's point of view, taking a bribe was nonsensical. It would destroy his credibility. If he took one, how could anyone trust anything he ever said again?

In Davis' eyes, Hines was a rather egotistical figure. Many others saw him this way, too. In his defense, however, Davis made the observation "that any man as successful as Duncan Hines must be somewhat egotistical, must have a large ego," and he added that "I don't think it got in his way. I don't think he became any less attractive or interesting because of that" quality. In Davis' eyes, Hines was a secure man with an outsized personality. He was a man of his times. He was a Victorian, who dressed conservatively, was always clean shaven and had a conservative philosophy toward life. He had little patience with individuals who would not work.

He respected people who had made something of themselves. He had very little patience with those who were unsuccessful and lacked self-discipline. He believed it was one's mission in life to strive to do his best, to conduct himself in the most ethical, most honorable manner possible. He "was very honest, very ethical, very fair," said Davis, and he expected nothing less from others.[370]

Due to the nature of his business, Hines developed few deep friendships in the Bowling Green area outside of his family; very few local people came by to visit him. One person who got to know Hines well, though, was Aubrey C. Roberts of nearby Scottsville, Kentucky. One year Hines sent Roberts a letter thanking him for a Christmas calendar, adding, with much wry humor, that he had been hoping to travel to Scottsville, but that, unfortunately, he had "been too busy standing on the front porch with my shotgun looking for Santa Claus, but he came last night and I held up the sleigh, and we got all kinds of junk for Christmas."[371] Although his Bowling Green acquaintances were few, there were always the tourists, and, increasingly, they kept him occupied and happy—if, at times, a bit busy. His house was located on a major highway and many travelers dropped by unannounced to see him. They stopped, though, not because they knew his address but because of the advertising: He had erected an enormous sign on his front lawn that announced to all passing motorists that this was where he lived. Most people regarded the sign's erection to be an invitation to visit him. He was probably the nation's only celebrity who craved this kind of attention, before or since. To the disappointment of many, most of the time he was away, but when he was there, Hines was cordial and gracious with his visitors, acknowledging how thankful and pleased he was they had taken the time to stop by.[372]

Sometime around 1940 Hines began a personal crusade to clean up America's restaurants. As the decade unfolded, his stratagem for accomplishing this goal became more apparent. Taking advantage of the respect his name commanded, he told Americans they should demand that restaurants either clean up or close up. He knew if he kept harping on the subject at every opportunity, restaurateurs would eventually have to give the public what *he* wanted.

By 1941 Hines had attended several conventions organized by the National Restaurant Association. He was repeatedly invited to speak at the organization's annual gathering because he had drawn so much attention to their industry. And he never missed an opportunity.[373] So popular was he at these functions that beginning in 1941 he inaugurated, with the convention's permission, a separate function of his own: the Annual Duncan Hines Family Dinner, a meeting and banquet that united the restaurateurs and innkeepers fortunate enough to be listed in his books. Through 1958 Hines told his "family" members at these meetings how wonderful they were—after he lightly chastised their imperfections and offered suggestions for improvement.[374] When Hines addressed his audience, he enumerated a long list of complaints, told them of his recent activities, and exhorted them to continue their good work. He concluded his criticisms and remarks by promising that he and Emelie would try to visit their respective restaurants during the coming year, which was a likely prospect since each day, he said, they usually ate "two breakfasts and lunches and sometimes have as many as seven or eight meals a day." But, he cautioned, "We merely taste, and don't eat all the food that is set before us." If they did, he said, they "would, no doubt, spend most of [their] time in a hospital."

At this same function, Hines observed that for every 100 copies of *Adventures in Good Eating* sold, the public bought seventy copies of *Lodging for a Night* and 40 copies of *Adventures in Good Cooking*. His cookbook, he said, was selling "far more copies than I ever expected."[375] And because he was selling more copies, he could employ more people. In addition to his secretaries, Hines said, he now employed five salesmen to call on bookstores across the country. Things, overall, were looking pretty rosy. But, as with any business, there were some problems.

First of all, his books were not distributed adequately. Not all his listed restaurants bought them. In his eyes, those restaurant owners in his book who refused to help him in this small matter were nothing but ingrates. As far as he was concerned, should a contest ever be held for those who turned white as a sheet when asked to spend a penny more than they had to, hundreds in the restaurant industry would vie for first place. Hines found their penury frustrating. He was trying to improve their industry and the public's perception of it, but those in whose interest he was working frequently could not see past the day's receipts. At one of his annual meetings, he noted that only half the places listed in *Adventures in Good Eating* had ever bothered to order a single copy. This type of proprietor was a mystery to him. Though they were successful, they were narrow-minded, paranoid and consumed with the unadulterated conviction that their next meal would be their last. In their eyes, nothing was ever good enough. Something was always wrong. Not even a much sought after recommendation by him mollified them. When Hines met with these types, he often had to endure their ungrateful, petty, insignificant gripes. Once, while speaking to an audience, Hines expressed his annoyance with these individuals. He shook his head and rolled his eyes heavenward when speaking of them. "Many places complain that their listing is not larger than their competitors, or that the description should say theirs is the BEST PLACE. Lengthy descriptions do not necessarily mean that any place is superior to all others. THERE IS NO ONE SUPERIOR PLACE. If all descriptions were about the same, the book would not carry the reader interest it does, and this applies to the use of photographs as well." If some owners of restaurants and inns refused to sell his guidebooks because of base selfishness, there were others who insisted on selling only the volumes that featured their listing, conveniently ignoring the fact that the public might possibly desire additional information about other places to eat and sleep. Then there were those establishments that ordered books—and then refused to pay for them. This always called for a bottle of aspirin.

Yet another needless irritant were those establishments that
changed locations but had not the courtesy to inform him.[376]

When a restaurant or inn was included in Hines's guidebooks,
the establishment's owner often wanted to capitalize on it. Since
they could not advertise in his books, Hines provided them with an
inexpensive, yet ingenious service. For an annual rental fee of about
ten dollars, he let them display the soon-to-be famous Duncan
Hines Seal of Approval. The sign stated, in a facsimile of his
signature: "Recommended by Duncan Hines." The idea was that
renters could place it in front of their establishments for passing
motorists to see. For those intelligent enough to rent one, a
Duncan Hines sign meant financial salvation. And yet, once in
place, for some the sign was both a blessing and a curse. If the sign
was removed, for whatever reason, financial doom sometimes
ensued. Potential guests, if they discovered the removal, sometimes
suspected something was wrong and avoided it. Word-of-mouth
spread quickly, and it soon closed.[377]

At Hines's insistence, the signs were uniform in design so they
would be instantly recognizable. They were also color-coordinated.
Like the books, restaurant signs were red, lodging signs were
blue.[378] When a red sign was posted in front of a restaurant, its
owner never worried about having a full dining room for breakfast,
lunch, or dinner. Likewise, when a blue sign was displayed in front
of a motel, hotel, or guest house, the innkeeper usually filled every
room by eight that evening.

His sign business presented its own set of problems, ones which
irritated him endlessly. When a restaurant or motel was dropped
from the book, Hines made arrangements with the Staley Sign
Company in Indianapolis, who manufactured his signs, to have one
of its representatives drive to the scene and reclaim it. When Hines
was alerted to a restaurant or inn performing poorly, he would
sometimes travel to the offending location and haul the sign away
himself. After all, it was his. Some restaurants painted Hines's
famous slogan on the side of their buildings—with a twist. They
proclaimed their establishment was "NOT Recommended by
Duncan Hines."[379] After they had been dropped from the

guidebook the perpetrators who used his signs illegally usually desisted after Hines wrote them a direct, curt letter, telling them in no uncertain terms to remove his sign from their premises and return it to him or else he would settle the matter in court. When the violators returned his signs, Hines did not reuse them; instead he ordered his handyman to throw them into the trash.[380]

Due to his influence in the restaurant industry, Hines criticized it and its practitioners more than ever. Now that he increasingly had the public's ear, he made plenty of noise over a host of matters, the repetition of which, he believed, would force the industry to abandon some of its abominable practices, particularly those found in low-grade restaurants. In a profile in a Kentucky newspaper, Hines discoursed on the condition of dirty lunch-counters. He asked his interviewer, "Have you ever looked at the water in which they wash the dishes? Or the color of the towels they use?" In his mind, lunch-counters were just "plain filthy." And so was their food. When Hines spoke of such places, he grew "quite red in the face, as he graduate[d] from one pet hate to the next." When he mentioned steam tables, for example, Hines thundered that it was, "a perfect device to take all the flavor—and, incidentally, most of the vitamins—out of the best vegetables. Steam table spinach. Can't you see it? Green and slimy, dripping off the end of a tarnished fork." The proprietors of lunch counters, he declared, could learn a thing or two from their competitors. "There is a place in Chicago," Hines said, "where your vegetables are cooked to order.... Your vegetables are cooked under pressure—and are served up after five minutes of cooking—succulent and fresh. That," he stated flatly, "is how vegetables *should* be prepared."

Hines theorized that many of the coarse public troughs he spoke of were not really restaurants at all. These "roadside eating-houses—barbecue depots and short order places," he said, shaking his head sadly, were "not run by chefs—some not even by cooks." Instead they were operated "by men who have decided to try to pull a few chestnuts out of the fire by the old procedure of feeding the weary traveler." He offered as an example the "farmer whose farm isn't doing so well—and who happens to own a few hundred feet on the pike." That person, he said, "will put up an eating joint," and the innocent traveler has no way of knowing if the man behind the counter can cook until he sinks his teeth into his meal.

He gave another example: "A gas station, trying to make a little more money, will advertise short orders.... Well," he snorted in a tone of exasperation, "these fellows aren't cooks." Such places, in his estimation, were better left boarded up. He was not alone in his opinion. His experience with these roadside hellholes was duplicated every day by millions of Americans, and the widespread contempt these amateur chefs generated no doubt explained the popularity of *Adventures in Good Eating*. The hundreds of dreadful little roadside restaurants that littered the American landscape reminded Hines of his early years on the road. Recalling those days, when he wished he had had his own guidebook to help him detour around these culinary armpits, Hines said, "I'd eat a terrible meal, and then discover that perhaps twenty miles farther I could have stopped at an excellent restaurant. If I'd only known about it. And it's worth traveling twenty miles or even 200 miles to get the food you want. At least it is to me. I'd rather spend my money on gasoline and food than on doctor's bills."[381]

In June 1941 Frank J. Taylor profiled Hines in a magazine article for *Scribner's Commentator*. That same month, the article was reprinted in *Reader's Digest*. Taylor's article was entitled "America's Where-To-Eat Expert." What the *Saturday Evening Post* initiated in December 1938, Taylor's article solidified. The *Digest* had a vast readership, which stretched into the tens of millions, if there were Americans who had never heard of Duncan Hines before, there was no excuse now.

In the piece, Taylor quoted a famous chef who said Duncan Hines had "done more in four years to lift the standard of the American cuisine than all the cooks had done in the previous forty." The *Digest*'s readers learned how he had accomplished this impressive feat. He had essentially rigged the industry to satisfy not only his wishes but the patron's, too—and had done it all with a book. Taylor explained, in a nutshell, that because Hines's restaurant guide had become the most trusted book in America on where to dine, any supposedly good restaurant not listed in its pages aroused public suspicion or skepticism concerning its cleanliness and worthiness. Because of this reaction, restauranteurs who wanted his approval were forced to keep their kitchens extraordinarily clean. When they kept their kitchens clean and served excellently-prepared meals, they generated public attention. If they generated enough attention they were inspected by Hines's dinner detectives or Hines himself. If they met his criteria, they were awarded with a listing in *Adventures in Good Eating*. To restaurateurs, a listing in its pages meant more customers, and more customers meant more profits. Restaurateurs wanted higher profits so they kept their restaurants clean. They kept their establishments in pristine condition because some restaurateurs feared Hines—not for what he would say, but for what he would not. They never knew when he might seat himself in their dining room or ask to inspect their kitchen. And they knew the consequences of refusing to show him around. So it paid greater dividends to keep their kitchens well-scrubbed, uncontaminated, and modernized than to keep things as they were. In short, Hines pushed them into excellence.

Soon after the *Reader's Digest* article came out, nearly every diner in America knew that when a restaurant proclaimed itself to be "recommended by Duncan Hines," the meal served there was not only one to savor and long remember, it was also prepared in one of the cleanest kitchens in the country. Therefore, most travelers who knew of *Adventures in Good Eating* and understood its value patronized only the places he recommended. "His word is gospel," wrote Taylor. And so it was.[382]

The publication of the *Digest* article had one additional benefit: it secured Hines's fame and influence. The article also benefitted Hines financially. Sales for his books rose to an unprecedented level. Requests for him to speak, requests for him to investigate restaurants and hotels, requests for country hams, all flooded into his Bowling Green office like a torrential rain. Hines could not have been happier.

By 1941 Hines was dropping scores of restaurants and lodgings from his guidebooks, particularly the former. Again, cleanliness was the determining factor. One that was eliminated from its pages was "one of the country's famous, century-old restaurants" in Washington, D.C. Hines walked in one day, discovered a dirty kitchen, walked out, and removed it from the book's next edition. Whether the restaurant later took Hines's suggestion—that all restaurants install a glass partition between the kitchen and the dining room so that diners could watch their food being prepared—is unknown. But other restaurants previously listed in his guidebook instituted this recommended design change so they could work their way back into his good graces. Hines liked the idea of the glass partition because, he said, it put "the kitchen staff on its mettle."[383]

Shortly after the *Reader's Digest* article was published, Hines armed himself with scores of new wisecracks contrived to shame restaurants who not only operated on the cheap but who surrounded their premises with fads and gimmicks instead of good food. One of the fads circulating in the early 1940s that drew his ire was the practice of lavishly decorating establishments to impart an air of "atmosphere." Under the delusion that "atmosphere" would lure in more customers, some places covered their dining rooms with expensive drapes, slung impressive-looking white linen table-cloths across their scarred-up tables, and placed flowers and candlesticks between their guests to impart a sense of "romance." Yet, despite their expensive efforts to dress up their businesses, they did not make the one necessary change that guaranteed them a continuing clientele: serving good food. Instead, serving high quality, sanitary meals never crossed their minds. Hines scoffed at their laughable endeavors: "Candlesticks and decorations don't make a restaurant." And why should they? After all, they were not on the menu.[384]

An emphasis on flowers and candlesticks were not the only thing that drew his contempt. He had a host of pet hatreds, and he volubly aired them as frequently as possible. He told Frank Taylor that veal listed on a menu as "baby beef" made him see red. Said

Hines, "There's too much baby on the menu. Baby beef, baby lamb, baby lobster, baby chicken, baby this, baby that. Who wants to eat babies, anyway?" Another pet peeve that made him develop a coat of froth around his mouth was when a restaurant seated him at a table that had not yet been "cleared of the last patron's dishes." This practice, he said, had to stop. He also wanted restaurants to stop packing its patrons within its walls "like sardines." This policy, he said, induced even mildly claustrophobic people to go mad. Lastly, he insisted he would not list—let alone eat in—a restaurant "where chefs smoke while they are cooking." The practice was barbaric. Who wanted to eat someone else's cigarette ashes?, he asked.[385]

In the dining room, he had certain culinary predilections. His face clouded over with intense annoyance when he swallowed a mouthful of soggy mashed potatoes or tried to chew a portion of ham that tasted like veal, or sipped muddy-looking coffee.[386] However, what particularly vexed him were those restaurants that "denied their geography." These he disliked passionately. Hines had no time for seafood in Nebraska or Mexican cuisine in Maine. A restaurant, Hines fervently believed, should serve the cuisine popular to the people who inhabited the area. He believed the best American cooking was regional cooking.[387] Lobster in Iowa was simply not as genuine as lobster in Maine. A Kentucky hot brown served in North Dakota was simply a denial of the Midwestern state's German culinary heritage.[388]

When asked about the worst place to eat in America, Hines wouldn't name a candidate, but offered that "the most barren" stretch of good restaurants in America was "the region between Chicago and Indianapolis." Between those two cities, he said, there was not one restaurant on the main highway that he could recommend.[389] However, his focus was usually on good restaurants—particularly those that served regional specialties, which he urged all his readers to indulge in for a bit of roadside culinary adventure. He urged them to "insist upon fresh chowder in New England, freshwater fish in the Great Lakes region, soft-shelled crabs in Maryland, shrimp in the Southeast [and] Spanish dishes in the Southwest."[390] Massachusetts may have been his favorite New England state when it came to food, but Maine was close behind. When he thought of the Pine Tree State, he thought of the clam chowder served in Portland. Said Hines: "It's a chowder thick with clams fresh from the sea, free of tomato. It carries the sweet breath of onion, it's enriched with salt pork." Asked to describe a single word for it, he replied, "rib-comforting."

Despite his acidic remarks about Southern restaurant cooking, Hines had more than a few favorite restaurants there. Maryland, he said, was the place to go if one wanted crabs. South Carolina was the destination for the palate that longed for okra and "corpulent" shrimp. Florida was the place to go if one wanted to indulge in devouring "giant stone crabs." Florida also was home of the pompano, he said, "but cooks there invariably ruin it in preparation by adding a spicy sauce which muffles the delicate flavor."[391]

The upper Midwest was full of surprises, too. The area comprising the Great Lakes states, he stated, was the best place to go if one wanted to dine on inland seafood. One of his favorite places in that area was the Fish Shanty restaurant in Port Washington, Wisconsin. Hines wrote that it had "long been a famous place for those who enjoy fresh fish caught right out of Lake Michigan by their own flotilla of troller boats."[392] Pennsylvania was the destination for travelers who drooled for the cuisine of the Pennsylvania Dutch. In 1938, noted Hines, one could still find places that served *schnitz und knepp*. Hines often spoke and wrote of the region's food, especially its "shoofly pie, that molasses crumb pie, so perfect for Sunday breakfast with salt mackerel and coffee. But try to find it in a restaurant!" The search was difficult. Ohio was the place to go if one wanted good average American cooking, like old-fashioned chicken with dumplings. "I don't mean that disgraceful travesty you get along with two leathery waffles," he said. "I mean stewed chicken [that] is delicate in flavor, tender, the dumplings light as thistledown, cooked in...rich creamy gravy."

When Hines thought of the South, New Orleans often came to mind. Perhaps that city's top rated dish in his estimation was the Oysters a la Carnival. Describing the process by which the dish is prepared, Hines said "the oysters are chopped,...mixed with sauteed onion, garlic and herbs, blended with bread crumbs, heaped into half shells, crumbs over the top, butter dotted on, and baked." When Oklahoma was mentioned, Hines thought of "black-bottom pie with crumb crust, a chocolate-custard base topped with a gelatin meringue," topped with whipped cream, and sweet chocolate shaved over it.

When he traveled to Los Angeles, Hines could never stifle the urge to pay a visit to the Melody Lane restaurant and sample their tamale pie. "This," he said, "has a delectable filling of ground steak and green peppers, of ripe pitted olives with grated cheese and corn meal [and] hot peppers, but not hot enough to make the mouth smoke." Another dish that brought Hines to California was the crab custard served at the Valley Green Lodge in Orick. He described the dish as "sweet lumps of crab meat...baked in a rich sauce, scented with onion, zested with tabasco, bedded under a blanket of buttered crumbs."[393] He was full of regional culinary knowledge; all anyone had to do to unearth it was ask him a question and he would empty his head.

Although Hines enjoyed foreign food, it was hearty regional American food—victuals prepared over a hot stove all afternoon—that most gained his admiration and affection.[394] Escargot did not make him salivate, but sliced hickory-smoked country ham did. His penchant for regional food items occasionally resulted in a preference for oddball food items—such as maple syrup salad dressing, a delicacy he could find nowhere else but in Vermont. As stated earlier, his favorite culinary region was New England; by contrast, his least favorite area was the American South. Good Southern cooking he said, was a myth. Except in private homes, there was not any. "Why, most of the people who hang out [restaurant] signs" there, Hines thundered, "have been raised on side meat and dirty, greasy beans. They've never tasted good food." Speaking his mind about the South's turnip greens and "pot likker," Hines remarked that it tasted like "like broiled crow with tobacco dressing. I can eat it, but I don't hanker for it." And when he spoke of Maryland's fried chicken, he informed all who would listen that "it can be good, but too often it conceals a multitude of sins. Instead of fine young chickens, the cook has killed a few old roosters or tired arthritic hens, parboiled them and embalmed them in the icebox. Later they are warmed, covered with hot batter and served up unctuous and sizzling."

Another subject that raised his ire was the food served in hotel restaurants. Hines's frequent public denunciations of the hotel industry's kitchen practices had by 1939 led to his being invited by hotel owners "to appear at their conventions and give them straight-from-the-shoulder advice." Hines took advantage of these invitations so he could have a forum to address his concerns. His biggest complaint concerned the hotels' managers, claiming they were foolish to let their guests take their meals a block or two away when all they had to do was institute a few simple reforms. They were insulated from the real world, said Hines, "they never get around except to other hotels like their own. They spend a lot of effort on efficiency and checking little items [for] waste," but they "never find out what average people are eating."[395]

As early as the 1920s, Americans were beginning to forsake hotel food for that served in the roadhouse and highway inn, despite the potential dangers they posed. The main reason for this trend, Hines said, was because big hotels prepared their meals "without imagination." And he had a villain in mind whom the industry could blame for all its economic woes: the efficiency man. This individual, he griped, was the person who told them how to save money—usually at the diner's expense. "The efficiency man has discovered," he said with contempt, "that pork shrinks with proper cooking. Pork should be well done...but in a large enterprise underdone pork will serve a great many more portions than well-done pork. The same thing holds true with turkey. Boiled turkey will provide more portions per pound than roast turkey, but good turkey is roast turkey."[396] And the best way to serve roast turkey, Hines thundered, was when it was basted with wine and butter.[397]

Exposing the efficiency man's crimes against hotel food was yet another reason why Hines caught on with the public. They liked what he had to say, and the way he said it. And newspaper and magazine editors did not ignore their readers' desires. Therefore, in scores of articles, Hines gave the public plenty of tips as to what motorists who wanted to eat well when traveling should look for. In one article he stated that "the highway inn which serves no liquor is likely to be more painstaking about its food than the more exciting place which does." Hines liked Scotch and soda, and he listed many places in his guidebooks which served liquor, but he noted that while "liquor may attract a crowd," after a few cocktails or highballs, *any* restaurant patron would find the food good.[398]

Good restaurants were not his only concern. Within a few months Hines also came to believe he could help change Americans' eating habits. His agenda changed as his fame grew. His philosophy in this regard evolved slowly over the next few years in piecemeal fashion. But when he formed an opinion and chanted it incessantly through the many organs of that day's media, Americans read and listened to what he had to say—and assented their approval. An example can be found in his fellow Americans' eating habits, which he deplored. Hines believed the remedy for this deficiency lay in education, and he thought himself to be the perfect teacher. As the 1930s gave way to the 1940s, he became more vocal on this subject. He believed the more the public knew about proper diet, the more rapidly they would change their ways. He observed the average American "wants his food in a hurry. He likes it well prepared, but he is unwilling to wait while it's cooked to order." To Hines's mind, the most "sinister" influence "in the modern social order" was the drugstore lunch counter. "In the Middle West, the younger generation is being raised at the lunch counter. How in God's name can anyone who regularly eats drugstore snacks ever be expected to recognize a good meal when it's served?"[399]

The drug store lunch counter fostered two more of his "pet peeves," one of which was the penchant to overeat, which he scorned and found repulsive, for it contradicted his philosophy that one should eat in moderation. The other irritant was Americans' tendency to "bolt it and beat it," believing the consumption of a meal should be undertaken slowly, leisurely. A meal was something to savor—not wolf down. Finally, he did not believe in dining at bargain-basement prices, stating once that "usually the difference between a low-priced meal and one that costs more is the amount you pay the doctor or the undertaker."[400]

12

THE WAR YEARS

As Americans adjusted to a war economy a few short months after the attack on Pearl Harbor in December 1941, Hines published the 1942 edition of *Adventures in Good Eating*. With the nation in domestic chaos, he was not sure how well the book would do financially. He expected the worst. What happened at first, however, surprised him. All three books sold more copies during April and May 1942 than they had the entire previous year. "No doubt," Hines observed, this was "brought about by the fact that defense workers and their families are now using my books when they are on the move from one part of the country to the other." More interestingly, for the first time *Adventures in Good Cooking* was outselling *Lodging for a Night*.[401]

Nevertheless, the Second World War made matters difficult for Hines's business, but not in the way one might expect. Between 1942 and 1944 America had to cope with gas and tire rationing, a move which curtailed all nonessential automobile driving. However, Americans could accumulate rationed gasoline coupons. If they saved enough of them, they could take a trip to a nearby city or across the continent. While Hines's business suffered during this time, it did not fare as poorly as he initially feared; people had to travel, and therefore they continued to buy his books. As the nation mobilized for war, millions of Americans were transported back and forth across the country, usually via train. During the course of their travels many transients found themselves in unfamiliar cities. Because they often found themselves in strange locales and were thus unaware of good places to eat and sleep, many men and women bought his guidebooks to locate them.[402] Indeed, for many servicemen a Duncan Hines guidebook was a required possession, particularly when they were on leave. Likewise, Americans not in uniform also found the books useful, particularly on those occasions when they visited their loved ones in the armed services.[403]

Although gasoline rationing hampered Hines's ability to investigate potential dining and lodging facilities, which annoyed him, he nevertheless tried to travel as much as he could. But in the early days of the war, most of his time was spent dealing with a restaurant industry thrown into confusion. Confident that America would win the war, even early on, he saw it as his mission to raise the morale of the nation's restaurateurs until the storm passed. He dealt with all sorts. Some restaurant owners were nervous over the uncertain turmoil that gas and food rationing would have on their businesses. Some restaurants had more business than they could handle; others had virtually no customers at all, particularly if they were located miles from a metropolitan area, where most soldiers tended to be stationed. To boost their confidence and to help them analyze the current state of affairs, Hines held several regional meetings for his "family" members.[404]

It was during this time that politicians began to seek his advice. Before the Ohio State Health Commissioners' Conference in September 1942, Hines testified he would grade restaurants, scoring them according to cleanliness. "I'd like to see letters six inches high on the entrance door," he told them, "and front display windows showing the grade of the restaurant, and if I operated a restaurant, I would add under the grade *Our Kitchen Is Open For Inspection By Our Guests.* And then I would add another sign: *No Pets Allowed In Kitchens Or Dining Rooms Regardless Of Who They Belong To.*"

As noted earlier, Hines had no patience with people who had failed in life. If they failed at one career, they would probably fail at another; he told the commission he did not want these individuals to enter the restaurant profession, because they would undoubtedly fail again—and at the customer's expense:

> It seems to me that the American public has suffered enough from food being prepared by people who have failed in previous occupations and possess no knowledge of the proper preparation of food, its cooking or the importance of maintaining cleanliness in all departments. I believe there isn't any profession that requires more artistry and talent than the careful preparation and cooking of good food. I believe no license or permit for operating a public eating place should be issued unless the owner can pass an examination which would prove his knowledge and ability in the proper preparation and correct cooking of wholesome, appetizing food.

As to his well-known pet peeve, restaurant cleanliness, Hines testified that "it has been found that silverware and dishes become carriers of disease if they are not thoroughly rinsed in 180-degree water after washing....30 percent to 45percent of the deaths in the United States are caused by diseases in this way. So when a place does not look or smell clean in the kitchen and in the back end, all their chromium fronts won't inveigle me to eat in their dining room." He added that it "seems that many owners of eating places compete with others to see which can raise the largest and most cockroaches. Many of them apparently look upon roaches as friendly pets."

Turning to another topic, Hines told the commissioners he did not have much faith in State Boards of Health. While their efforts were welcome, in his view, they were usually ineffectual. Hines said he had recently, received a letter from a State Board of Health reporting to me on eating places. They thought these places were clean because the State Board of Health inspected them. Once a year might be better than never, but not much. A place may go to the dogs almost overnight. In my opinion, it is first a matter of education to the owners, managers and employees of public eating places…. There should be frequent and adequate inspection. For first violations[,] a written warning; the second violation, [a written warning and] a stiff fine, and for the third violation, a permanent revocation of license.

When the government penalized a restaurant with a fine, he said, horselaughs ensued; what the government did was a joke. He cited one recent government report which detailed over 250 restaurants which had violated the health laws. "A little over 8 percent were fined," he said, and of that remaining percentage, the transgressors were punished with a hefty fine, usually a whole dollar. "Imagine," exclaimed Hines, "a fine of only one dollar."[405]

At a Rotary Club meeting in Cave City, Kentucky, Hines told his audience of how his publishing operation was coping during the global conflict. "I am very happy to report that my books have found a place in the war effort," he told them.

Millions…have been transformed from civilian to military life. They are taxing our transportation facilities to the limit, traveling all over the nation. My travel books…are going with many of them—guiding them to the best in unfamiliar places throughout America. I wish you could read the enthusiastic letters I receive from men in the service who are using the books. The government has placed the travel books in the libraries of many camps, also in large deluxe transport planes for the use of navy personnel.[406]

Despite the limitations the worldwide discord had placed on his ability to conduct business, Hines managed to earn enough profit to avoid a temporary shutdown. One newspaper revealed that his

books had "been reprinted [at least] 10 times in one year," and that
the accumulated sales of all three of his volumes now exceeded over
a million.[407] After a burst of extremely robust sales for the
guidebooks during the war's early days, by 1943 activity had
tapered off. In a letter Hines sent to his Duncan Hines Family
members, he wrote, "The sale of my travel books naturally has
slumped," but sales for his recipe book, *Adventures in Good
Cooking*, had picked up. "I hope the sale of this book will help meet
our office expenses for the duration."[408]

Sometime that year Hines established the Duncan Hines
Foundation, the purpose of which was to promote restaurant
sanitation. The Duncan Hines Foundation was established to
provide scholarships to students in hotel and restaurant management schools of both Cornell University and Michigan State University. "He was very proud of that," his secretary remembered.[409]
Hines also chose to create a scholarship fund at Cornell University
because it was the best hotel management school in the country.[410]
Hines was one more name in a long line of individuals who
contributed to the school's fortunes.[411]

A month after the D-Day invasion of 6 June 1944, the pivotal
event for the Allied involvement in the Second World War, Duncan Hines published a short piece in *Table Topics*, a trade publication for wholesale food distributors. The war, he wrote, had kept
him quite busy. Since it began, his dining guides had undergone
fourteen printings. He knew they would cease being authoritative
sources if they remained out of date and the numerous printings
were the result of his attempt to remain current with the frequent
changes in the restaurant industry. Hines reported that many
places either in the country or on the outskirts of cities that were
dependent on transients for their business had been forced to close
their doors. As many as 500 deletions and additions were made to
the guidebook's pages to keep it as current as possible. Hines said,
"If I had foreseen the enormous amount of work it was going to
involve to maintain my books on an unbiased basis, perhaps I
never would have started it as a hobby." Still, he reflected, "It has
now become a serious business and, although there is hardly

enough profit in it to justify the time and work involved, I am
rewarded to some extent by hundreds of letters of appreciation
from [its] users."[412]

The guidebooks underwent so many changes that by 1945 Hines
had sent revisions to the Williams Printing Company twenty-eight
times. Restaurant and lodging circumstances could change every
few months and Hines could not afford to print large quantities of
each edition. If he did, he could very easily be stuck with thousands
of out-dated copies. Therefore, he managed to solve his problem by
printing small quantities of corrected editions every few months.
This business decision was still not profitable for Hines because,
then as now, it cost more to print small quantities than large
ones.[413] By the time the war came to its cataclysmic close, the task
of keeping the guidebooks updated was becoming horribly difficult. So much was happening so fast. Hines said it was as bad as
keeping track of railroad timetables. "Divorce, change of ownership, death, fire, and war shortages are the background for most of
the listing changes."[414]

One day toward the end of 1944, Bowling Green's newspaper
reported that Marion Edwards, a staff writer for *Better Homes and
Gardens* magazine, had recently visited the Duncan Hines home
and advised readers to look for an article about him in its upcoming pages.[415] The article was published in May 1945. In her
article, Edwards revealed that Hines's restaurant guide was now in
its sixteenth printing since Pearl Harbor and the public was buying
it at the rate of 3,500 copies per month. In fact, so many were being
sold that she noted it was a common sight to find a copy of
Adventures in Good Eating peeking "out of the back pocket of dusty
G. I. trousers" as well as from "the crowded traveling cases of
tagalong brides and wartime businessmen." Everyone, it seemed,
was using it.

Because the public was using it, the book was gradually helping
change American attitudes. Based on his travels and conversations
with thousands of individuals, Hines could see the beginnings of
several trends that boded well for the future. When Edwards visited
him in Bowling Green, he explained how the war was changing the

eating habits of millions of American soldiers. "Let men loose in a restaurant before the war," he thundered, "and what did they order? Steak, French fries, iron-crusted rolls, pie! They drowned the steak in hot sauce so they couldn't tell whether they were eating meat or ground rubber bands." Hines found their habit of dousing sauce on top of their meat to be an insult to the beef. Pointing a finger at himself, he exclaimed, "When a waiter comes up to *me* with a lot of condiments, I ask him, 'What's wrong with the meat?'" Nevertheless, he continued, wartime rationing and mess halls had combined to bring about a changed attitude toward food among the American public, especially men. Before the war they cared little for what they swallowed. So long as their stomachs were filled, they were satisfied. But during the war men found opportunities to experience new types of food. Much of this changed attitude, Hines explained, came about because of the shortage of meat. Searching for a substitute, mess halls on military bases began experimenting with and serving such items as "an appetizer, soup, and salad before the entree.... Men liked it. And the boys in the mess halls got balanced meals—often for the first time in their lives." Hines predicted that "when these fellows come back, they'll surprise people with the way they eat. They won't be satisfied with leathery eggs or vegetables in billboard paste or dishwater soup. They'll have sampled meals around the world, and they'll expect [the cooks in their] home to produce the best." He was not far off the mark. At war's end, this changed attitude created not only a demand for better food, it also created a parallel attitude for better food in restaurants. This development could not have pleased Hines more.[416]

In this vein, Hines had some other thoughts which had ripened within his mind concerning the effect the war was going to have on restaurants. "The wartime family habit of going to the restaurant once a week to save rationing points," he said, was going to carry over long after the war ended, mainly because wives across America had enjoyed the liberating experience of not having to cook every single day. Wives would be demanding a day off from "kitchen duty" once a week, and their husbands would acquiesce, if only to preserve domestic tranquility.

While no definite cause and effect can ever be shown—because human experience is so varied—an outline began to take shape. Americans, regardless of their income level, began to expect more from life. They had suffered through the Great Depression. They had endured the Second World War. When the global bloodbath had finally ended, they had survived both calamities to find themselves citizens of the greatest nation on earth—and they knew it. With this knowledge came an expectation to be treated better in all realms of life—and, though it was small in the wider perspective of historic change—their expectations included eating a well-prepared, sanitary meal at a public restaurant at a reasonable price. After what they had been through, Americans felt entitled to expect as much. Thrown into this human calculus was the renewed strength of the American economy, a factor that had been building since 1940 but which had taken on strengthened vigor by 1945. In the spring of that year, with the war in the European theater nearly over and with a domestic economy improving daily—particularly after the government lifted tire and gasoline rationing—there came the desire and the opportunity among Americans to spend the discretionary dollars they had saved throughout the conflict. The collective release of this pent-up desire produced a surge in travel by Americans. They used any mode of transportation available to them, whether it be automobile, truck, train or plane. Regardless of how they reached their destinations, more Americans than ever before were soon in some sort of transit from one location to another, often traveling to places they never expected to visit.

With this development came another expectation. Whether those in transit be military personnel or civilian populace, whether they ate on a train or on a plane or in a roadside inn in the middle of nowhere, they insisted that what they put in their mouths be of high quality. In addition, the military had taught hundreds of soldiers how to cook for large numbers of people, unintentionally creating a whole new generation of chefs. Hines had predicted as much, forecasting that many new restaurants would open in the near future, "operated by G. I. cooks, whose culinary" abilities would be highly regarded by the public.[417]

Meanwhile, Hines began taking an enthusiastic interest in the new technological kitchen innovations that were becoming available. He began insisting that to get his approval "every restaurant should install electric dishwashers and as much automatic equipment as they can once it's available." To push restaurants along in this progressive direction, he began to examine other factors in restaurants, such as "acoustics, design, air conditioning, dishes, and furniture." Hines said, "restaurants will have to throw out juke boxes and chipped dishes and buy comfortable chairs. They'll have to get modern." Little by little, he pushed the industry into the modern era.

Due to wartime gas rationing, the war slowed the activities of Hines's dinner detectives. While many chose not to travel as frequently, Hines was grateful for those who gave him any information. However, he did make one significant change with respect to their activities. During the conflict he instituted among them a system whereby they were to "carry little cards identifying them as his representatives, to be presented after they [had] paid their bills. The cards request[ed] the privilege of inspecting the kitchen and sleeping quarters" of either those establishments already in his guidebooks or ones under consideration. Sometimes these "checkers" sent in "voluminous reports, sometimes a cursory note." One note that came into his office during 1944 read: "The dump you recommend here is lousy, but it's the best place within 150 miles." As in the past, if there was no better alternative, the recommendation went into his book until a more suitable substitute could be found. As always, the dinner detectives refused any payment for their recommendations. Any proprietor, whether he be a restaurateur or an innkeeper, could easily spot a phony Hines representative, and he knew what to do if one showed up and requested payment for a listing: point the imposter toward the door.[418]

With the surrender of the Japanese in late summer 1945, many soldiers dreamed of returning to the United States, sitting down in a nice restaurant, and eating a big, juicy steak. However, they did not want just any steak; they wanted the best money could buy. The result of this desire soon manifested itself in bookstores throughout the country. Soon after V-J Day, reported *Publishers' Weekly*, booksellers across the country were deluged with requests for *Adventures in Good Eating*; over 500,000 copies were sold within a few weeks of the war's conclusion. Another indication that the war had ended were the numerous tourists who began criss-crossing the countryside, many of whom found time to visit Bowling Green. Marion Edwards was amazed to find the number of tourists who came by just to see Duncan Hines. "Visitors come in droves in normal times. On a good day," as many as twenty-five cars were "parked around his gravel drive at one time." Sometimes, they mistook his unusual-looking Colonial-styled home for a restaurant. While Hines was resting in his living room chair early one morning, he was surprised to hear the footsteps of a large family walk into his office; they barged through the front door as if it were a public facility. They had, in fact, thought it was. They had seen the huge Duncan Hines sign in front and assumed it was a restaurant approved by him. When Hines came into the office to see who had walked in, a young woman, not knowing to whom she was speaking, thrust a baby bottle into his hands and said, "Here warm this. Then we'd like breakfast for five right away."[419]

The most significant recent change in his life was that Emelie was no longer there. There were several reasons why she left him sometime in 1943. Life was not as glamorous as she had hoped. When they were not traveling, "their social life was restricted almost entirely to playing cards, rummy, or something with Clara and Clarence Nahm. They were a foursome."[420] It has been plausibly conjectured that, over the years, Emelie grew to detest living in the country, 2 miles from town. She also eventually grew weary of Bowling Green. Although Hines had built for them a Colonial cottage, and although they traveled a great deal and shared an interesting life that was the envy of many, she was dissatisfied. Traveling around the country with her husband was a lot of fun, but she was always a little dismayed when they returned home. It is likely that she longed to return to Chicago to get away from the small Kentucky town. In her eyes, Bowling Green simply could not compare with the cosmopolitan excitement that Chicago offered. She grew bored with Bowling Green and the people in it. She was homesick for her native city. Besides, she had family and friends there, and although she and her husband visited them often, she missed them as soon as she left. No sooner had the two returned to Bowling Green than she was pining for a return trip. No doubt this agitated Hines and led to some domestic friction, but there was nothing he could do about it. He was now known across America as a resident of Bowling Green, Kentucky. And he made it clear that he was not going to forsake his home for the Windy City. Besides, he had grown accustomed to living in the country. His family lived nearby; he enjoyed their company; he liked things as they were. They were not going to move to Chicago.

Another source of conflict between the two, one that steadily grew worse, was that instead of going out on the town when the sun set, as perhaps she had done in Chicago, Hines was an early riser who was ready to go to bed by nine that evening. Also, when he ate his meals at home, she discovered he did not want to ingest sizable portions of complex, sophisticated food; instead he wanted to eat something simple, like ham and eggs. A final contributing factor was that they had few friends in Bowling Green. Those they dined with and visited from time to time, she eventually grew tired of. Besides, playing cards with another couple until bedtime was not the sort of life she had imagined—or wanted—when she married him.[421]

It is within this context that Emelie left him and moved back to Chicago. More than two years later, on Wednesday, 5 December 1945, the Warren County, Kentucky circuit court granted her a divorce on the grounds of "cruelty." So bitter was she at the time that she threatened to restore her name to Tolman.[422] While the divorce was by several accounts, an "unpleasant" affair, after her unhappiness subsided, Emelie often spoke favorably of her former husband and their years together. While cultural differences were probably the main ingredient at work in their separation, over the years she repeatedly cited Hines's family for the breakup, rather than him. After her return to Chicago, she spent the rest of her working years as a secretary. In 1964, at age 68, she retired, and moved into a condominium she owned in Palm Beach County, Florida, where she lived for the next twenty-two years. She never married again.[423] When she died on 9 November 1986, her death certificate listed her as the widow of Duncan Hines.[424]

13

CLARA

When Emelie left Hines, she let him fend for himself. As had been the case after Florence's death, without a woman about the house he was rendered somewhat helpless, and his family knew it. To compensate for his loss, someone from his family—Porter or his children—went to his house almost every evening he was in town to cook supper for him. He did not like to drive after dark, so it was more convenient for him to stay home and have his family keep him company than to drive into town toward dusk and risk a traffic accident. When someone came to look after him, they usually played checkers or Utica or whisk—a short form of bridge—or rummy. If someone mentioned an old forgotten card game, they spent the rest of the evening trying to remember the rules as they played a round. Playing cards came naturally to him. When he couldn't sleep, he usually idled the night away playing solitaire.[425] When Hines became bored with this form of relaxation, he listened to the radio. One of his favorite programs was "Amos and Andy." He would not, however, listen for more than an hour; remaining immobile for long periods made Hines restless. He needed something to occupy his hands and his mind. Quite often he simultaneously played solitaire while listening to the radio.[426]

It was believed he needed a female companion and early in 1946 his family suggested that Hines date his recently-widowed friend, Clara Nahm. During the years that he and Emelie were married, they frequently dined with Clarence and Clara Nahm; afterward the foursome usually retired to a long evening of card games. The two couples were probably attracted to one another because they were both nearly the same age and had similar interests. Another factor cementing their friendship was that neither were burdened with children to raise.[427] The Nahms lived just two doors away from Annie's residence at 615 East Main Street, so it was relatively easy for the two couples to be introduced. Clarence Nahm and Hines became such good friends that Nahm even let him store country hams in his garage.[428]

Mose and Adelia Rosenthal Nahm came to Bowling Green from Jeffersonville, Indiana in 1863 during the Civil War. Along with John W. Jackson, he began operating a dry goods store in 1871. In 1873 his brother, Ben Nahm, bought Jackson's interest and renamed the firm Nahm Brothers. Clarence Nahm was born on 21 March 1874. Nahm Brothers was a great success, and it afforded the couple to make ample financial provisions for their son's education. After graduating from Vanderbilt University Dental School in the mid-1890s, Clarence established a practice in Bowling Green. Soon afterward, however, he and his brother, Floyd, entered their father's business. From then until 1932, when the Depression brought about the firm's end, Nahm Brothers remained Bowling Green's most popular dry goods and ready-to-wear store. Clarence and Floyd Nahm then established Nahm Brothers Insurance Agency, which operated successfully until Floyd's death on 11 May 1939, after which Clarence went into semi-retirement.[429]

Clara Wright was born on 26 July 1904 in Port Royal, Virginia. Her father, Arkley Wright, was a teacher in the northeastern Kentucky town of Carrollton. She was the only girl. Her mother, Anna (nee Mattick) died in 1905,[430] and her father soon remarried, and in time Clara had five step-brothers. At some point Clara was sent to live with an aunt and uncle in Prestonville, Kentucky, a town across the river from Carrollton. Her relatives raised her along with their own child who was close to Clara's age.[431]

Upon graduation from high school in about 1919, Clara went to Cumberland College, a small, four-year college in Williamsburg, Kentucky, in the southeastern part of the state.[432] Following graduation in 1923,[433] she became a teacher in the Carroll and Harlan County school systems.[434] In 1929 she moved to Bowling Green and found steady employment as a recorder in the admissions office of Western Kentucky State Teachers College. She remained a member of the administration until 1932,[435] when she left the college to become a secretary for Clarence Nahm. One year later, on 27 December 1933, they were married.[436]

A few days before his death, Clarence Nahm suffered a heart attack at his downtown office. He was moved to his home and shortly thereafter suffered a second attack which took his life. On 4 October 1944, Clarence Nahm died at age 70, leaving a 40-year-old widow.[437] It was not too long afterward that Hines came around offering her first friendship and then a marriage proposal. Clara was lonely and no doubt wanted another husband to keep her company. Hines was lonely and desperately needed someone to run his household. Since both offered the other qualities their lives were lacking, Clara accepted his proposal. On 22 March 1946,[438] on a very warm day for that time of year,[439] Duncan Hines married Clara Wright Nahm at a private wedding ceremony in Annie's home.[440]

For the next thirteen years Clara remained his constant companion and best friend as they traveled throughout the country, sampling the best in food and life.[441] Theirs was a mature love. They were dependent and respectful of one another. Clara loved to travel as much as he did; she also enjoyed returning to Bowling Green after a long trip—an attitude which pleased Hines immensely after his experience with Emelie. Hines loved to kid Clara, and she loved to be kidded. Clara also loved to buy beautiful clothes, and she returned from their trips with one hat box after another. One day in the mid-1950s, Clara came home with a hat which looked as if it had sprouted little ears of corn from its corners. It amused Hines. Remembering a character he had seen on the "Captain Kangaroo" television program, he told everyone that she had purchased "Mr. Green Jeans hat." He kidded her, saying, "Clara, here's a dime. Now get your Captain Kangaroo hat and let's go to town." Upon which, she smiled, quickly retrieved it, and within moments was scampering toward the car. She never minded his kidding, and she did not try to kid him back. She let him be the show because he *was* the show. Always the entertainer, he liked being the center of attention, performing for everyone around him.[442]

When they were home, Clara usually cooked their meals, but she delegated the two duties he was most capable of: making coffee and the salad. While in Bowling Green, they used "their three-month rest period to take off the pounds they [had added while] on the road." During their months at home, "instead of eating a lot," they just talked about it.[443] One caloric indulgence Hines allowed himself during these rest periods, however, was a cocktail Clara dreamed up. This unorthodox concoction contained "the juice of watermelon pickle, a whole egg, cream, gin, grenadine, orange-blossom honey and lime juice." Hines stated with gusto that he could "drink a dozen of them" without any ill effects.[444]

His love and appreciation for Clara increased as each year passed. So thankful was he for filling the void in his life that he began working her into his business. Almost immediately, he made her the chairman of the Duncan Hines Foundation;[445] he later made her the *de facto* editor of *Adventures in Good Cooking*.[446]

By January 1946 America's restaurant industry was booming and so was Hines's bustling little business. Bookstores across the country were deluged with requests for the latest edition of *Adventures in Good Eating*, which now listed over 5,000 places in which discriminating motorists could dine and sleep.[447] There was one significant change in his life. He was so busy that he no longer had time to pursue his hobbies. Due to restrictions imposed on his country ham business during the war, he was forced to terminate it; when the war ended, he had no interest in reviving it. A few years earlier it had been possible for him to cure and sell hams on the side for amusement, but this was no longer the case. When thousands wanted a Duncan Hines country ham, the fun of providing them vanished. Continuing his hobby would have only complicated his life. Besides, after the war the last thing he needed was a hobby.[448]

By 1945 *Adventures in Good Eating* had metamorphosed into an icon symbolizing the best in life's culinary pleasures. Hines was gratified so many people were relying on it, but he was also highly amused by the increased interest in his person and how much people trusted him. He said in a speech he gave in March 1946:

> it seems ridiculous, but it is true, that I receive a number of letters which do not pertain to my books. For instance, I received a [signed] blank check from a New Zealander asking me to buy him a forty-acre farm in Kentucky. And I have received many letters requesting me to purchase other things; or asking me just where they should settle down when they retire from business or asking me to send them a chef or a hostess. It may sound even more ridiculous, but they even ask me what to name their babies. I receive a number of letters from ex-servicemen and also from the Small Business Bureau in Washington, asking me to advise them in what locality this or that person should locate in order to open up a restaurant, what he should serve and what he should charge.

He referred such queries to parties more capable of giving a proper answer than he could. That he received many more letters like these, however, is demonstration enough that people did not care if Duncan Hines was an expert in a particular subject; all they knew is that he was not a phony and would give them a straight answer.[449]

If Hines had worked hard during the war, the post-war years taxed his physical and mental abilities to the limit. By the summer of 1946 his publishing venture had mushroomed into such a large enterprise that it was consuming all his time. New copies for all three books came out in June and had by then sold over 900,000 copies.[450]

For some proprietors a Duncan Hines recommendation was enthusiastically welcomed but, because of the heavy traffic his endorsement carried, they sometimes wished he had never discovered them. For others, however, his approval was a godsend. For example, Mary N. McKay, an elderly woman who ran the Old Southern Tea Room in Vicksburg, Mississippi, told a reporter for *Life* magazine that if her restaurant were dropped from the Duncan Hines books, she would be forced to close her doors.[451] Wrote the *Life* reporter, "For many small restaurateurs, being a member of the Duncan Hines Family means a chance to stay in business, thanks to the customers who place an almost blind faith in the Duncan Hines endorsement sign."[452] The public who possessed this blind trust, she wrote, consisted chiefly of those who were "middle aged, of substantial income, [and] travel for pleasure." They were "accustomed to certain comforts." Hines made their travels more enjoyable; but, of course, he did not stop with restaurants. Places to sleep were just as important as places to eat. It was the quality of the place that counted with travelers, Hines said, not its historical significance or some other balderdash. In exasperation with the literally thousands of wayside inns proclaiming to be places where George Washington spent the night, Hines exclaimed, "What do I care if Washington slept there? Do they have a nice, clean bathroom and do the beds have box springs—that's what I want to know."[453]

During 19-21 September 1946, columnist and food editor for the New York *Herald-Tribune* and *Gourmet* magazine, Clementine Paddleford, was Hines's guest in Bowling Green. The two had become acquainted while attending food writers conventions, and he invited her to visit him.[454] After her three-day visit, Hines and Clara had no idea what shape her article would take. So many questions were asked that Clara said, "she didn't know whether the article…would deal with [Hines's] private life, home, menu experiments or his writings, because all were well covered."[455] When Paddleford's piece was published, everyone liked it. The 12

January 1947 article appeared in the widely-read weekly Sunday newspaper supplement, *This Week.*[456] So popular was it that *This Week* was deluged with reprint requests. The article not only gave readers tips on how to be better cooks, it also let Hines ruminate on the many things that annoyed him about restaurants. His most popular suggestion, of course, was that diners should enter a restaurant's back door before entering its dining room; if they did not find the kitchen's appearance appealing, they should leave through the front door and never return. "Hines himself," wrote Paddleford, "after a look at the kitchen, refused to eat in 7,000 of the 9,000 restaurants" he visited.[457] He said if patrons duplicated his practices, practically all of America's bad restaurants would vanish within a few months.

Poor kitchen conditions, Paddleford reported, were not the only thing that tried his patience. Hines never failed to fume when he discovered his menu contained misnamed foods. To put it mildly, he was not especially appreciative when the "baby lamb" turned out to be "a grown sheep." Roared Hines, "Fancy names don't make food taste any better. Call it Terrestrial Cake—but it remains a mud pie."[458] A dish with dressed-up sobriquets was his personal *bete-noire;* it amounted to false advertising. "I steer clear of hashes and meat loaves with fancy names," he said, "and from dishes disguised with French names that don't mean anything in a Midwest hotel. I always dodge chicken a la king, if it is offered at bargain prices...because that is a sure sign it is leftover or second-rate chicken, whereas real chicken a la king is expensive, being carefully selected cuts of the best-grade fowls."[459]

During the course of her visit, Paddleford noticed Clara was not at all intimidated by her husband. She did not have to be. When she was around, Hines was an obedient boy. When asked if her famous mate was hard to please at dinner, she put the notion to rest with a nonchalant wave of her hand, "No, he's easy to please." She turned to him, and asked, "Dunc, what's for dinner today?" After a moment's hesitation, he shrugged his shoulders and said, "Oh, just anything." Then, after a moment, quickly interjected, "hot biscuits, of course." Hines told Paddleford, "Clara's biscuits

are the best I ever tasted. That goes for her fried chicken, too."
Clara took the hint; that evening she served a salad, squash, and a
plate-load of fried chicken accompanied with hot rolls that were
"wading in gravy." The salad, wrote Paddleford, "was a tomato
stuffed with cottage cheese, blended with grated onion and
cucumber." Hines eyed the tomato icily for a moment, then said
with a twinkle of a smile, "I like a plain crisp green salad with a
French dressing.... This sort of tomato thing I call woman's club
chow." He ate it anyway. Rounding out the dinner was his sister's
recipe for apple pie.[460] Paddleford was so impressed with the repast
and other items made by Clara's skilled hands that she invited her
to visit New York for the purpose of sharing her recipes with the
Herald-Tribune's readers.[461]

Three months later, Hines and Frank J. Taylor collaborated on
an article that was published in the 26 April 1947 edition of *The
Saturday Evening Post*. Hines wrote that the "game" of finding a
good restaurant was well worth the hunt. He and Clara found it
worth their while, he wrote, "not only for the sheer thrill of hitting
the jackpot every so often but" also because their "comfort and
health" was important to them. He admitted, however, that
sometimes their luck in finding good restaurants was still no better
than that of other restaurant scouts: "We've found prospecting for
good meals great adventure. Often, [however,] we don't hit a vein
of good eating until after several tries, even in territory we know."

In the *Post* article, Hines recounted his misadventures, some of
which were ones he had been telling for years—such as the
snoozing cat stretched out on the warm bread dough. That there
was a gap—sometimes several decades—between the actual
occurrence of his many tales and their publication was immaterial;
he was not about to let that inconvenient fact get in his way.
Besides, since his yarns were, even in 1947, within the realm of
possibility, no harm was done. What was important to him was not
the exactitude of his stories but the lasting effect they had on the
public. If they caused people to question the cleanliness of
restaurants, if his anecdotes compelled Americans to demand they
remain spotless at all times, they served their intended purpose. His

design was to stir up the public, to agitate them, to motivate them into pressuring restaurants to clean up their act. To a large degree, his article was successful in this objective. In an age when the written word was more respected, an engaging article that reached twenty million readers was impossible to ignore.

In the article, Hines instructed the public to follow his lead. Do as he did when visiting a restaurant and they would rarely go wrong. As a model example, he offered the following story. Once he and Clara were heading north from Bowling Green when they stopped "at a Louisville hotel for lunch. We ordered hot-roast-beef sandwiches, usually a safe choice. When these came, I looked at the unappetizing, razor-thin slices of cold beef on soggy, untoasted bread, smeared with gravy that looked like misplaced billboard paste, and asked the waiter if he ate the hotel food. 'No, suh,' he replied emphatically. 'Ah eats down the street.' Hines said, 'We'll do that too. Bring me the check.'" They "left the food untouched," and tried another hotel dining room, "where the most promising item on the menu was pork tenderloin." When the meal was served, Hines immediately noticed "the pork smelled like catfish." He inquired how this came to be and "learned that it had been fried in a pan in which catfish had been cooked, after which the stale grease had not been cleaned out." Hines paid the bill without eating it and, once again, they searched for another place to have lunch. This sequence continued until they found a satisfactory place.[462]

Hines unabashedly proffered a remedy for America's restaurant ills. "I would like to be food dictator of the USA just long enough to padlock two-thirds of the places that call themselves cafes or restaurants," he exclaimed, adding that about half of those he had in mind also doubled as places of lodging.[463] But since he knew he would never be America's food dictator, he hoped his "pet peeves" would become the public's. "Mine is a private crusade," he proclaimed, but "if I can induce a million [of you] to work with me, we can make America a safe place to eat, quicker than it can be done by laws." In his *Post* article, Hines suggested that all his readers had to do was "stroll around to the back door of an eating place before" going through the front entrance, "even if [you] have to walk halfway around the block. A glance and a whiff at the back door tells you in nothing flat whether or not you want to go" inside. "When I go into the front door," he said, "I look around to see if there is a 'Keep Out' sign over the door leading to the kitchen. If there is, I keep out of the dining room as well as the kitchen."

Defending his practices, he said, "they may put me down for a fussy busybody, but I know that if enough customers do that, they will scrub up the kitchen, so that they are not afraid to have it seen." He understood that some Americans were not brave enough to embrace his suggestions, that they would forever remain passive eaters. But he had some advice for these submissive individuals. "It calls for some nerve to ask to see the kitchen of public eating places," he said, "but after you have seen one littered with filth, food and garbage exposed to flies, and sloppy cooks dropping cigarette ashes into whatever they are cooking, you find it easy to screw up your courage.... I still have my appetite and health, but it is only because I have been a fussy busybody and have walked out on thousands of places whose kitchens were dirty or emitted rancid odors."[464]

Even before 1947 hundreds of thousands had already taken his advice with respect to inspecting restaurant kitchens. The Maramor, a restaurant in Columbus, Ohio, Hines had recommended for years, received so many requests to inspect its kitchen that scheduled tours were "stacked up eight weeks ahead" of time, with a limit of five customers allowed on the premises during the busiest hours. After the *Post* article appeared, those numbers seemed quaint; everyone, it seemed, was asking to inspect restaurant kitchens. The requests became so numerous that the owners of the Rathskeller, in Rockford, Illinois, looked for a way to slow the demand for kitchen tours by "self-appointed kitchen inspectors." They found their solution by taking one of Hines's repeated suggestions: installing a huge plate-glass window on its premises, one so large it completely separated "the dining room from the kitchen," enabling their customers to easily "see the chefs and cooks at work."

Not content to lead the charge for cleaner kitchens, Hines sought other restaurant reforms. Many of his "pet peeves" were still being practiced throughout American restaurants, and he was determined to eliminate as many of them as possible. One annoyance that vexed him endlessly concerned the "oversized portions of poorly prepared and badly served food at low prices." Whenever Hines discovered a so-called restaurant "bargain," for example, he instantly became "wary." His first reaction was characteristically typical: "I want to check the kitchen to see that they are not salvage leftovers from the plates of earlier customers," of what he was sure was "second-rate food." He felt justified in having such suspicions. "It isn't in the cards," he said, "for one restaurateur to be so much smarter than his competitors that he can give twice as much for less money and survive."[465] It also irked him that the large portions he railed against were far more than most customers could possibly eat and, as leftovers, were later thrown away. Exclaimed Hines, "The American people waste enough food every day to feed all of Europe. Just the other day I read about the garbage collector in some Ohio city finding a twenty-four pound unopened sack of flour and half a ham among other discarded foods. Whoever threw away such foods should be compelled to do without any food for a reasonable length of time as a punishment for such wastefulness." The reckless squandering of foodstuffs horrified him. He pointed out that the sanitation department of New York City carted away an average of 476 tons of edible food each day, an amount equaling one-eighth of a pound per resident, and that the New York Trust Company estimated that Americans wasted food at the annual rate of a billion dollars.[466]

Much as Hines enjoyed the company of his countrymen, there was one irritating habit they practiced that really provoked his wrath. He was aghast at the rapidity with which they consumed their meals. They could not seem to eat fast enough. No doubt, he was sure, that if the average American could, he would lift his plate above his face, tilt it as he opened his mouth, and swallow it whole as it fell into his ravenous cavity. He had no use for the restaurant patron "who gobbles his food so fast that he scarcely has time to taste it as it zooms past his tongue." It alarmed him that many Americans wanted their food served quickly. "We need more dining rooms with the leisurely tempo of California's Santa Maria Inn" or the various New England inns, "where your order is taken in the lounge, and where the table is set with the first course upon it before you are invited to sit down." In this respect, however, he never got his wish. It was one reform Americans conveniently ignored.[467]

14

LET'S WATCH HIM EAT

Hines had a considerable influence on the fortunes of many establishments offering lodging to travelers. His files contained many letters from proprietors whose businesses had literally been saved from bankruptcy thanks to a listing in *Lodging for a Night*. One elderly architect who invested his life's savings in a Massachusetts lodge known as the Cape Cod Inn wrote Hines, "I was about to close my doors when a stream of guests appeared like the robins. They all carried the Duncan Hines books under their arms. You certainly saved our lives." Had it not been for his penchant for "exceptional inns tucked away in mills or barns or distinctive old homes" many of which were located off the main highways, no one would have ever found them.[468]

By 1947, *Lodging for a Night* had undergone a few changes. The introduction had been substantially shortened, and his voluble comments about motels had been reduced to two paragraphs. The motel industry had undergone significant changes since 1941; they were no longer little better than comfortable shacks.[469] In his update on motels, Hines said "the modern motor court, when under competent management, offers the motorist the maximum convenience in pleasant and comfortable lodging accommodations. More and more of the deluxe type are being built throughout the country, having such conveniences as telephones, radios, electric razor outlets, air conditioning, carpeted floors, tile baths, etc., also private locked garages." In short, they were far and away better than the prevailing norm when Hines began to compile his first volume. The increased trade that motels experienced during and after the war made it financially possible for their owners to offer an ever expanding number of luxuries.[470]

The war brought about this change. After America's entry into the Second World War, motels began receiving a class of Americans who, beforehand, had never entered one. Up until that time the public had, by and large, stayed away in droves because they did not want to be associated with the "bounce-on-the-bed" trade, i.e., the type of people who kept many motels financially afloat. They also did not want to be identified entering what were sometimes viewed as legitimized houses of prostitution or convenient places to dump murder victims. Despite this aura that hung over the industry, during the war newer customers began to patronize motels in increasing numbers because, quite often, they had no choice; a motel was frequently the only place available to spend the night. More often than not, the newer customers came from a different economic and social class; and since they were from a more prestigious social milieu with more money to spend, motel owners began to take measures to ensure they would return as well as hope they would recommend it to their friends, who were, undoubtedly, also from similar economic and social circles. Assessing the type of trade that had been keeping their industry alive and deciding it was no longer economically healthy for them, motel owners began to screen the patronage of those they served. The strategy was effective. By the end of 1940s this newer class of customer had, more or less, driven out the "no tell" motel image. The widespread patronage of this newer type of customer enabled the industry to financially improve its image at an astonishing pace; within a few years after the war, motels had displaced hotels as Americans' favorite place to sleep. "By 1948 there were over 26,000 [motel] courts—twice the [number found in the] 1939 census. Another 15,000 were built between 1949 and 1952."[471]

When a motel provided its customers with luxuries that only a few years ago seemed unimaginable, Hines noticed. If the establishment was of exceptionally fine quality in all respects, he included it in his lodging guide. Well, almost. After the war, the motel also had to offer one other important item to receive his recommendation: a good dining facility. He only gave his blessing to motels with high quality dining rooms and coffee shops, and he believed his reasoning was justified. People were tired upon their arrival and they did not want to leave the motel to find a place to dine. Besides, when a motel offered both a place to sleep and eat, each feature simultaneously promoted the other. His insistence on this feature therefore, is why almost all good motels of the day began to have dining facilities.[472]

Craving anonymity when he could find it, Hines did not advertise his arrival when he slept somewhere. As with restaurants, he believed his readers would be badly served if he alerted an innkeeper he was planning to spend the night there. Why give a proprietor the whole day to create for him a false impression? It was either a good place to sleep or it was not. To avoid this potential travesty, he made his reservation under another name. Once ensconced in the lodging of his choice, he walked around the premises to "scrape up conversations with other travelers...[to discover] what places they liked along the highway...." In this way he usually learned of even better lodgings elsewhere. When he arrived at one of them a day or so later, instead of checking in for the evening, he first asked to see an unoccupied room. After being shown one, he performed a routine yet thorough inspection in an effort to see just how clean and comfortable it really was. First he "would thump the beds to see if they [had] springs," then he would "count the blankets, try the plumbing," and "turn on the lights to see if" he was "paying for burned-out or thirty-watt bulbs." If anything fell below his standards, he asked to see another room. If he could not find a room to meet his specifications, he left.[473]

As in any hotel or motel, there are better rooms than others. Hines had a stratagem for getting a good one. "The way I make sure the room is the one [I] want is by asking, after I register, 'May

I see the rooms you have available?' If I'm an early bird, I know there is some choice. It takes some nerve to do that…but in these times the timid traveler gets the leftovers." He noticed that unlike hoteliers in the cities, "motor court and tourist-home operators are invariably gracious about showing rooms; that is one reason why they are luring business away from the hotels." But he had another theory as to why motels were increasingly attracting business away from those polished palaces: the "convenience of having your car near your room, and the ease of getting away without a spasm of tipping." Tipping. Hines was sure this was why so many people hated hotels, and it was his biggest pet peeve about them. "Lodging the customer for the night has become a racket," Hines said, "particularly in some of the big hotels, the object of which is to separate him from as much cash as possible, and as fast as possible." He grew exasperated every time he mentioned the subject. He wrote that "the tipping racket is driving customers out of the hotels" and "into the motor courts and tourist homes. It begins with the doorman and the bellboys. You drive up to a hotel, the doorman unloads your baggage; he has a smile, is very courteous, and you tip him. He proceeds to set the bags inside the door and go back on the street to wait for the next customer. Then comes the bellboy, and he carries the bags into the lobby and stands by your side while you register, and says, 'Yes, sir, your bags are right here and I am watching them.' So you tip him, thinking he is the boy who is going to escort you to your room. But as soon as you give him a tip he disappears. Then another boy comes along and carries your bags up, opens the door and the window, turns on the lights, and asks you if there is anything else. There being none, you tip him and he is gone. Then, inside of ten minutes, along comes the maid, and she says, 'Yes, ma'am'—whether she is talking to me or my wife. 'I just want to inspect the beds and see if they have clean sheets on them, and see if you've got plenty of towels.' Just for the devilment, I say, 'If we haven't got all those things, why the heck will they rent me a room at eight bucks a day?' She says, 'I don't know. I just want to make sure you are comfortable.' So what? You give her fifty cents to get rid of her." Little wonder why Hines called tipping "a racket."

In the restaurant industry "another racket is headwaiter tipping," he said. When he and Clara arrived at a high-priced restaurant, they usually discovered that they had to wait in the lounge or bar until called. Hines noticed this never failed to happen despite the fact he had made reservations well in advance. When he spied several unoccupied tables and pointed them out to the management, it made no difference. On these occasions Hines sometimes slipped the waiter two dollars to get a seat, but only to prove to himself the "tipping racket" was alive and well. Usually when Hines dined he had a firm rule about tipping: "...twenty-five cents per person, when I am served with courtesy. If the waiter is surly, I give nothing."[474]

Hines and Clara developed a routine when on the road. Before starting out that morning they ate a light breakfast. Shortly before noon they dined on an equally light lunch. They ate just enough during these first two meals to taste and comment on them. Unless circumstances dictated otherwise, their big meal was reserved for that evening. Before going to a restaurant for their feast, however, they relaxed. They usually pulled into a hotel or motel around 3:00 or 4:00 P.M., stretched out on the bed after settling into their room, and took a nap. They had been driving for six or seven hours and relaxation before dinner was essential; they were always meeting people wherever they dined, often individuals of some importance; so Hines could ill-afford to be seen as tired and cranky. He wanted to feel fresh when he arrived at the restaurant. He also wanted to be seen as immaculately dressed. No one ever saw him in dirty clothes. Even when he attended family picnics in Bowling Green and wore work clothes, his garments were excessively clean.[475]

Clara traveled with Hines just as much as Florence did a decade earlier. An example of their extensive travels together was one that took place during July and August 1947. On 6 July they left Bowling Green shortly after noon and arrived in Evansville, Indiana three hours later, where they spent the night at the McCurdy Hotel, a large opulent structure about which Hines wrote: "Most hotel food is blah, but that is not true of this hotel."[476]

The following day they arrived at their destination, Urbana, Illinois, where Hines spoke at the Urbana-Lincoln Hotel to a group of students and faculty members from the University of Illinois on the importance of restaurant cleanliness and other related topics. From there he and Clara drove to Chicago. While in town they received a call from a friend in Negaunee, Michigan, located in Michigan's upper peninsula, who invited them to sample that area's local cuisine. Hines and Clara accepted the invitation and drove there a day or two later, where they were treated to dishes of Cornish pasty, venison steak, and partridge. The following day they visited another friend's lumber camp and ate flapjacks with the lumberjacks. The size of the flapjacks suited these men perfectly, being one quarter-inch thick and nine inches in diameter, twelve to fifteen of them piled high on each plate. Their table also included "17 varieties of sweets."

The next day Hines and Clara journeyed to Rochester, Minnesota, and visited the Mayo clinic for a thorough medical examination; said Hines afterward, doctors found both he and Clara "disgustingly healthy." From there they crossed the Wisconsin state line and headed for Mineral Point, the home of one of Hines's favorite restaurants, the Pendarvis House. Wrote Hines some years earlier,

Pendarvis House is one of the few places in this country where real Cornish meals are served, prepared from old authentic recipes, and where scalded cream (often called Devonshire or clotted cream) may be had. Their Cornish pasty, hearty and appetizing, is served for luncheon or dinner with homemade relishes and pickles, and green salads with fresh herbs. Wild plum, citron or gooseberry preserves with the scalded cream, tea and saffron cake, served as dessert, are delights which will thrill the most jaded gourmet's palate.[477]

As he had so many times before, Hines enjoyed his meal but was especially ecstatic over the Pendarvis House's cream of spinach soup.

The next day they drove southward to St. Charles, Illinois, to eat at the Thornapple Lodge. "Here you get a Swedish dinner," said Hines, "with loads of smorgasbord."[478] The following day was a long one, as they drove first through Indiana and then into the adjacent state before stopping, finally, in Ashland, Ohio, where they ate salad, T-Bone steak, chicken, and pie at the Cottage Restaurant on Main Street.[479] From there it was on to Wellsboro, Pennsylvania, not so much to eat at the Penn-Wells Hotel but to take advantage of the lovely, 50-mile drive through Penn's Grand Canyon, which was estimated to be 1,000 feet deep.[480] While traveling through this scenic landscape, they were forced to make a detour over an unpaved road, which resulted in a tire "blow out." After repairing it, they continued eastward until they stopped to eat and sleep at the Rip Van Winkle cottages, located at the foot of the Catskill Mountains.

After a night's rest, they traveled over the Mohawk trail through the Berkshires and on to Concord, Massachusetts to eat in the Old Mill Dam Tavern, a restaurant that was once the home of Ralph Waldo Emerson. There they dined on Vermont sausage and baked beans before heading for Boston where they stayed at the Parker House. Here, Hines let Clara loose upon the city for a day's worth of antique hunting. That night they ate swordfish steaks at Boston's Union Oyster House at 41 Union Street. The following evening they feasted on beef steaks at that city's famed restaurant, Durgin Park, located at 30 North Market Street, which was across the road from Faneuil Hall and was the home of 4,000-5,000 daily customers who gobbled down the New England fare that Hines proclaimed to be the best regional food in America.

They could not leave Massachusetts without walking through the doors of an old Hines favorite, the Toll House in Whitman, Massachusetts and tasting once again the magic of that restaurant's "lemon pie with four-inch-high meringue." So they made a side trip to visit Hines's old haunt, and the visit gave Hines a chance to introduce his friends, Kenneth and Ruth Wakefield, to his new wife. After their visit, Clara described the restaurant as the "most beautiful place in New England." From there the couple made their way to Kingston, Rhode Island, about 30 miles from Pawtucket, where they dined on chicken and lobster at the Crossways, a New England tea room, before driving over to Weston, Connecticut, to dine on home cooking at the Cobb Mill Inn, where they were waited on, to their delight, by "butlers in a barn." Late that afternoon they pulled into Norwalk, Connecticut, where they supped at the Silver Mine Tavern, a restaurant, "on a terrace overlooking an old mill pond."[481] There they spent the night.

Upon arising the following morning, they drove into New York City and checked into Hines's favorite hotel, the Waldorf-Astoria. Toward sunset they began a gourmet tour of the town that was to last for several days. To begin their journey into gastronomy, they first chose the restaurant Le Cremaillere, "where they had a leg of lamb for an entree and imported filet of sole cooked in white wine." For their next meal they entered Giovanni's to dine on "minced clams in aspic, breast of chicken with truffles, gnocchi (which is similar to fried mush) and, for dessert zabaglione." For their third restaurant, Hines and Clara chose Seman Brazilian Gardens where they sampled South American food. Their breakfasts, of course, were eaten at the Waldorf, delightful spreads which Hines could not stop praising. After three days of feasting on some of the finest cuisine in America, the couple elected to leave New York before they became permanently spoiled. Philadelphia was their next destination.

Once in the city of brotherly love, they sat down at the Bookbinders restaurant at 125 Walnut Street and ordered a sumptuous meal of red snapper chowder. It was so hot that day, though, that Hines decided to literally head for the hills—the Appalachian Mountains. While driving through the rich scenery the Pennsylvania mountains afforded, they stopped long enough to sample the culinary fare at the Harris Ferry Tavern and the Georgian Hall at Camp Hill. Toward sunset, they stopped in Cresson, Pennsylvania to sleep at the Lee Hoffman Hotel, which had long been another favorite Hines haunt. That evening they remarked to one another that although they had fled Philadelphia for the coolness of the mountains, they now had the opposite problem: it was too cold. In fact, the mountain air was so cold that evening that they could not sit outdoors on the hotel porch after dark; they had not thought to bring their overcoats with them in the middle of August. The next morning Hines and Clara feasted on buckwheat cakes, Loretta Farms sausage, and small green onions before heading down the road to Pittsburgh, where Hines was scheduled to attend an autograph party; that afternoon he signed 700 books in three hours.

Much of the next day was spent driving; Hines and Clara put 465 miles on the speedometer in eight or nine hours as they headed for Chicago; Hines wanted to visit friends there. Upon their arrival, however, they found the climate too hot and humid for their taste and, after a night's rest, headed for another old haunt, one that Hines and Florence had frequently visited years earlier: Arthur and Nelle Palmer's Lowell Inn in Stillwater, Minnesota. Continually filling their plates with fresh brook trout, they stayed there until the weather cooled a bit. Upon their departure, Hines and Clara set out again for Chicago. This time the city's humidity was bearable, and it afforded them a comfortable visit with several of Hines's friends.

Upon their departure a day or so later, they set off southward before coming to rest in Bedford, Indiana, where they retired for the evening. Early the next afternoon, after forty days of traveling, fifteen states, and about 6,500 miles, they pulled into the gravel driveway of their Bowling Green home. For dinner that evening, after gorging themselves on some of the nation's richest cuisine, they swallowed, in Hines's words, something simple: "ham hock, greasy beans, corn pones, and some of Clara's biscuits with new grape jelly—and," he said "that sounds good, too."[482]

The more Duncan Hines's recommendations were appreciated, the more an ever-growing cadre of admirers wanted to learn about him. In November 1947, he was featured in the widely-read general interest magazine *Coronet*. The article introduced him as the "gregarious Southerner" who, "through his lively interest in food and people[,]...has influenced the eating habits of a nation." The article's substance was drawn from an interview with him earlier that year in Tampa, Florida. On that occasion, the writer for *Coronet* witnessed a scene that was beginning to occur more frequently. Hines and Clara seated themselves at the table of an unnamed restaurant (most likely the Columbia, which was known for its Spanish and French dishes), ordered their dinner, and were quietly awaiting its arrival, when the house orchestra, a feature commonly found in the better restaurants of the day, struck up "My Old Kentucky Home." Said the writer, "Waiters appeared with huge platters of delicacies—far more than Hines had ordered. As he unfolded his napkin, the dining room was vibrant with suppressed excitement. Everyone was aware that they were about to witness a performance of major significance—like watching Bobby Feller pitch or Arturo Toscanini conduct. They were going to watch Duncan Hines *eat!*" The attention he received was on a par reserved for royalty. It is not known what he did on that particular occasion, but there can be no doubt he was highly embarrassed by the spectacle of having all eyes fixed upon him as he plunged a forkful of food in his mouth. He didn't realize he had been spotted by the management. Although he preferred to walk into restaurants unnoticed, eat his meal, pay his bill, and leave, as the post-war years rolled on, those days were becoming increasingly rare. He was a celebrity now and had to accept the trappings that came with it. Nevertheless, he was amazed that people could be so interested in what he did for a living. Said *Coronet*, "His name has become a national byword; as author, publisher and unofficial arbiter of the American tourist's eating habits, his fan mail rivals that of a movie star." Indeed, his mail by this time, if anything, was increasing in volume nearly every day. And there was no sign it would stop. The more people bought his books, the more mail his office received. By late 1947 Hines had sold nearly 2,000,000 copies of his books since 1936.[483] In 1947 alone sales of his books totaled around 225,000 copies.[484] He had become so popular he was now getting book orders from "people in India, China, South America, Australia, Europe—even Tahiti," who told him they were planning to make a trip to the United States and wanted to plan their vacations around the restaurants and inns he recommended.

By 1948 the postwar demand for his books had subsided to a manageable level. Although he still had representatives in the field selling them on a commission basis, business was steady enough to enable him to reduce his office overhead. By the end of that year, he employed only three full-time secretaries. He would, on occasion, hire two or three temporary workers for those occasions when things became hectic around the office, such as when the Williams Printing Company deposited a huge order of books at his doorstep, forcing his staff to quickly fill an enormous backlog of prepaid orders. But other than that, his office ran like clockwork. Hines's office manager, Edith Wilson, described him as "the perfect boss." Said Wilson, "If the outgoing mail stacks up faster than we can handle it, he'll pitch in and help us wrap packages and seal envelopes."[485]

After the war, so highly did the public come to regard anything Hines recommended that advertisers approached him to endorse nearly every product manufactured between the Atlantic and the Pacific Oceans. Market surveys demonstrated the sales power his recommendation would generate, and he was hounded daily by thousands of businessmen; they wanted—indeed, prayed for—his endorsement. Tempting offers came to him at every turn, many exceeded $1,000 just to say he *liked* a product. He turned them all down. Publishers for the last eleven years had regularly courted him, begging him to let them handle his books. They offered him generous contracts, one even offered to let him write his own contract, but Hines refused, saying that he feared "a publishing house would try to sell a million copies a year, thus glutting the market and killing future sales of new editions. So he refused all offers and kept the publishing ventures to himself." He also refused to star on radio shows of the day; his rationale being that, once he succumbed to a show with a sponsor, he would lose his most valuable asset—his independence.[486]

In interviews he seemed unaffected by his nationwide recognition. He remained, at bottom, an unpretentious native of the heartland who had just stumbled into a run of good luck. He was just being himself when he spoke with a reporter after sampling the food of a particular restaurant, cackling in his down-to-earth manner, "I ordered fried chicken and filet mignon.... You see, I was just sampling. I don't eat all the stuff, but honestly, this time I kinda stretched my belt because the stuff was mighty good. Then I filled up with coffee and apple pie, and while I think I could make a better pie myself, it was really quite satisfying."[487] Because of his folksy demeanor, his popularity continued to soar. His growing legion of fans continued to make pilgrimages to his Bowling Green home. So voluminous was this human traffic becoming that he was forced "to enlarge the parking space adjoining his home." Since he and Clara were on the road nearly eight months of each year, few visitors actually met him. While not many who made the pilgrimage knew it, if they came on a holiday, particularly Thanksgiving and Christmas, they were more likely to meet him.[488]

Many factors came into play after the war that contributed to the creation of the modern American tourism industry. Public roads improved. More automobiles were manufactured. Steel-belted tires replaced the inner-tube design. But the most important factor that energized it was the growing economy. When the war ended, America headed into a long stretch of domestic prosperity. Not only was the nation's economic health strong and vigorous, but as America advanced to become the greatest economic superpower in recorded history, its economic muscular might transformed the social status of its citizens. Thousands of families were unceremoniously swept into the American middle class. Wanting to validate, perhaps even celebrate, their new status, they indulged themselves in a variety of activities, one of which was popularly dubbed as "sightseeing." And Duncan Hines was there to take full advantage of it.[489]

In early 1949 Hines published *Duncan Hines Vacation Guide*, an annually revised, pine-green-colored guidebook for those who wanted to travel across America and see its myriad natural and man-made attractions.[490] The book's genesis originated from a suggestion by a long-forgotten person in Hines's employ who believed it would be universally beneficial to assemble a travel guide for families who wanted to know what attractions were available across the country; such a book would be especially useful for families who wanted to escape the trappings of domestic life for a week or two and enjoy themselves. Since Hines had already told travelers where they could eat when they were hungry and where they could sleep when they were tired, it seemed only natural to tell them where to go to amuse themselves.[491]

The official title of his new publication was *Duncan Hines Vacation Guide: Good Places to Spend an Enjoyable Vacation*. In its introduction he wrote that he had "selected places accommodating twenty-five people or more" and had limited his "descriptions to places where one is likely to spend a week or more, and where more than merely sleeping accommodations are offered." The book was intended for "those who want a comprehensive guide to places where people spend vacations." Following his introduction, he wrote a descriptive essay on each of the forty-eight states, detailing the regional characteristics and the vacation opportunities of each.[492]

The *Vacation Guide* was modestly popular with the public; it made money but was not a great seller. A year later, when establishments were asked to purchase the *Vacation Guide*'s second edition, many refused, because sales were slow and the public was not enthusiastic about them. "Why buy more?" they asked. It is easy to understand why they were unpopular. When potential book buyers examined a copy, the spirit of Duncan Hines was nowhere to be found. In fact, the book looked as if it was written by someone else—certainly not by Duncan Hines. Those reaching this conclusion were correct. Aside from the introduction, the *Vacation Guide* was not really written by Hines at all; its contents were put together by his office staff. They sent a questionnaire to selected parks and resorts and asked them to fill it out. When each was returned, the office staff copied the information it contained, and if it met certain criteria, the place in question received a listing. Said one secretary, since "it was [mainly] information about the location, about the place, the rates and the hours, any of us could write *that.*" The most glaring omission from the book's contents were Hines's quips of humor and old-fashioned homilies. Therefore, it was not surprising to discover that the final result looked as if it had been written by a committee. Perhaps Hines was simply ahead of his time. While American families in 1949 were eager to travel about America in their brand new automobiles on newly paved roads, for some reason they did not seem to be ready for a book listing what to do with their free time when not eating or sleeping. Whatever the reason for the book's very modest success, this was about the only time Duncan Hines misjudged what the public would lunge to buy.[493]

Late in 1948 Hines was on the promotion trail, traversing the nation's highways in his six-passenger Cadillac, extolling the virtues of his *Vacation Guide,* which was about to be published. When he reached New York City, reporters caught up with him at the Waldorf-Astoria Hotel. Hines, whom one of their number described as "a homey individual with thinning gray hair and glasses who looks like everybody's grandfather," told them "with a wisp of petulance," that he had spent all summer working on the *Vacation Guide* and that the effort had spoiled his summer. "I really had wanted to go to California," he said.[494] "If memory serves me," he continued, "there wasn't a completely-paved highway across the country the first time I drove to California. I know that in some places in the West I drove for miles in thick roily clouds of dust that liberally coated me and the car." On that first trip across the Western states, he said, the road was so rough that he "bumped and banged" his way across it until it almost dislodged his back teeth.[495]

As he held court while seated in a chair in one of the Waldorf's meeting rooms, the conversation turned to food and then to his "eatin' book," *Adventures in Good Eating.* He began to describe the food in some of the restaurants he and Clara had recently sampled. Earlier in the day they had tested the culinary fare at the popular restaurant known as Brussels, where they dined on *moules a la flamand,* and *lapin a la creme* along with a good wine. Most high-priced restaurant meals in 1949 cost $2-$5 or more; the bill for this particular meal totaled $48, with Hines remarking that this was an extravagance for them. "We save our nickels for months for this," he said. "'Course we manage to live nice just the same. I won't eat hamburger for anybody." Moments later, he leaned forward, put his elbows on his knees, and answered a variety of questions from reporters. The first one concerned methods for producing quality beef. "I don't like raw beef, see," said Hines. "But if you want the true flavor you mustn't cook it too long." He explained that grass-fed beef had an inferior flavor when compared to corn-fed beef. "It's easy to tell the difference.... The fat of grass-fed beef is yellow; on corn-fed beef it's white." He said the same was true with peanut-fed hams. "Know those peanut-fed hams?...Why those sweet little piggies never get to see very many peanuts. First place, the peanut crop is too valuable, so they get mostly corn. If they ate all peanuts you couldn't eat the pig. Its flesh would be too oily." The subject soon turned to a more prosaic matter: the best place to dine that evening. Hines told reporters he was debating with his stomach over whether or not he should visit his favorite New York restaurant, Voisin, on the east side of the city. "Mmmm—man, does it taste good!" he said, "If I hadn't had so much food this noon I'd be over there tonight. Come to think of it, I might go anyway."[496]

Hines, by this time, was quite content with the course his life had taken. He was the publisher of four successful books. The company he had organized in Bowling Green paid all his salary and traveling expenses. He could go where he wanted, when he wanted, and was treated royally everywhere he went. By way of the nation's media organs, he was influencing and changing the ways many restaurants and lodging facilities were being operated. His influence was everywhere to be seen. All things considered, he was a relatively happy man. What more could a human being ask for? One man found out.

15

ENTER ROY PARK

Over the years Hines had turned down hundreds of schemes promising to make him wealthy beyond his wildest dreams. If only he would willingly allow his name to be used to endorse this or that product, he was told, fabulous riches were his for the asking. He readily retorted to such blandishments that he was already rich—certainly wealthy enough to satisfy his needs. He had everything he could possibly want. And with those words he shooed them away with the back of his hand. Roy Park had better luck.

Roy Hampton Park was born on a large, family-owned farm outside of Dobson, North Carolina on 15 September 1910. An industrious youth, when he was twelve years old he became the correspondent for two weekly western North Carolina newspapers. Upon graduating from Dobson High School at fifteen and filled with dreams of financial success, he made preparations for a successful career in the world of commerce. A few days before his sixteenth birthday in 1926, he applied, was accepted and entered Duke University at Durham, North Carolina, with the intention of becoming a doctor. His dreams of practicing medicine, however, lasted only four days. He could not find a job in Durham that would support him during his quest for a medical degree, so he dropped the idea of becoming a physician and moved to Raleigh, North Carolina, where he enrolled in North Carolina State College, now North Carolina State University, to pursue a degree in journalism with a minor in business administration. To finance his education, his older brother secured for him "a job as a delivery boy for an afternoon newspaper." While enrolled, W. J. MacFarland, bureau chief of the Associated Press in Raleigh, "gave him a part-time job at $4.50 a week. The tasks he was asked to perform were menial ones. Eventually, though, he "taught himself to use a typewriter, operate a teletype machine" and soon he was writing news stories for the AP. By the summer of 1928 MacFarland put him to work as one of the Associated Press's two full-time staff reporters in their Raleigh bureau, paying him $15-a-week. Shortly afterward he received a $3-a-week raise.

During the 1928-1929 school year, Park was not only taking a full-load of college classes, he was also working full-time for the Associated Press and free-lancing feature articles for several North Carolina Sunday newspapers. He did not stop there. He also reported news and wrote a column for the college weekly newspaper, *The Technician.* He attributed his success in keeping up with his demanding schedule by adhering to a strict schedule of work, meals, sleep and rest.[497]

Park emerged from his three years at Raleigh in 1929 with a degree in Journalism.[498] That summer he began looking for work; surprisingly, he was unable to find it because, at nearly age nineteen, employers deemed him too young to hold down a mature adult job. He then discovered the editor of his college newspaper "was not only paid a salary, but reaped one-fourth of all advertising profits." In that light, editing the campus newspaper looked like a worthy goal. Shortly afterward he embarked on a year of post-graduate work in business administration and he became the newspaper's editor. As a result of his drive to succeed, the campus newspaper was transformed into a more professional-looking journal and, at the end of his tenure as editor, the paper had earned more money in one year than it had during the publication's entire history. At the very depths of the Depression, when dollars were scarce, this was no small feat.[499]

After he was granted a Masters degree in Business Administration from North Carolina State College in 1931, Park began looking for a job that challenged his considerable abilities. With his characteristic methodicalness, he kept a close eye on the want ads in the Raleigh *News & Observer* and wrote ten letters each day to those he considered leading prospects. One of the potential employers that interested him were the farm cooperatives; in the early 1930s they were touted as an exciting industry with which to become involved. Two of them were headquartered in the Raleigh, North Carolina area, one each for cotton and tobacco.[500]

One day the North Carolina Cotton Growers Association answered one of his letters and scheduled him to be interviewed. Confident of his abilities, Park put on his best black clothes, shined his best black shoes, and strode off to a job he was certain was his for the asking. But at the interview, he was disappointed when he was told by the interviewer, the head of the organization, Uriah Benton Blalock,[501] that the Association was looking for an older man, one with more experience.[502] This qualification did not deter him from his objective. He was determined to be hired, one way or another. Each day, he staked out the Growers Association's post office box (number 701) at the Raleigh post office, and each day, when Mr. Blalock arrived to pick up the association's mail, Park politely yet firmly hounded him for a job. Nevertheless, Blalock's answer was still "no." Park kept asking him every day anyway. One day he discovered Blalock's automobile had three flat tires and promptly changed them for him while wearing a white suit. Blalock was duly impressed by this act, but the answer was still "no."[503] Park then obtained a letter of introduction from the president of North Carolina State College and a family friend, Josephus Daniels; he also got letters of recommendation from several faculty members. He even wrangled a job recommendation from the Governor of North Carolina. But despite all his efforts, Blalock's answer was still "no." Undeterred by steady rejection, one day he confronted Blalock and offered to work for nothing. Blalock, who by this time was beginning to wear down, liked his spunk, and began talking to him at length. At one point in the conversation, Park requested a monthly salary of $250; Blalock hired him for $100 a month.[504] Elated, Park could not have been happier; he had secured his job over 800 applicants and had proved something to himself: anything is obtainable if one is never daunted by obstacles.

Park's official title was assistant to the general manager; in this capacity, he was given a number of things to do. One of his jobs was to edit and publish the cooperative's membership newspapers. As the association's publicity director, another of Park's jobs was to create publicity for them. Not long after he was hired, he did just that. One day at a meeting, Park suggested to the association's leaders that since their organization was in the business of promoting cotton, they should sponsor a "Cotton Ball." What Park had in mind, he told them, was a grandiose Southern reception that honored the daughters of the state's most prominent families. To draw a crowd, Park suggested the association hire a well-known dance orchestra for the occasion. The association's members were an extremely cautious coalition and did not like the idea. "It looked like a money loser to them." Park then offered to underwrite the cotton ball himself and pocket any profits that accrued. Since no money was to be extracted from their pockets, the association members agreed to Park's proposal. Park then hired the Kay Kyser Orchestra to play for the event and put his publicity skills into action. Subsequently, the event was a roaring success. When the festivities were over, Roy Park was several thousand dollars richer—much to the consternation of some of the association's members—but they did not argue with Park afterwards. The following year Park hired the Fred Waring Orchestra for $2,100 and earned the Grower's Association a tidy sum.

Park calculated that his regular duties for the Cotton Growers Association only took 25% of his time; because this inactivity left him restless, he became involved in more projects. He "persuaded the Cotton Growers Association to change the format of its trade journal and allow him 25% commission on all advertising." This move resulted in the publication of *The Carolina Cooperator*, the format of which Park modeled after *Time* magazine. *The Carolina Cooperator* eventually amassed a subscriber base of 100,000 readers. Park then "established and operated a printing plant" for his employers, of which he owned one-third.[505] In 1936 "the Carolina Cotton Growers Cooperative expanded its activities from the sale of cotton and set up a purchasing cooperative, the Farmers Cooperative Exchange, used by farmers to buy seed, fertilizers, and other farm supplies. Park remained with the two organizations as director of marketing and public relations." But even this level of activity did not satiate Park's restless nature.[506]

In 1937 Park took "a six-month leave of absence to travel over much of the country on an assignment out of Washington as a special assistant to do area surveys and publicity for the recently formed Rural Electrification Administration [REA], studying farm problems and rural electrification."[507] While with the REA, Park made the most of his publicity skills. Through newspaper supplements, he showed rural audiences the many ways in which electricity could benefit America's farmers. "The supplements carried advertising by merchants offering farmers everything from electric water systems to toasters and electric stoves."[508]

In 1940 Park launched his first personally-owned periodical, *Cooperative Digest*, a journal that served farm cooperative executives and agricultural leaders. It eventually developed a paid circulation of 15,000. Twenty-five years later it was still the only publication of its kind.[509] In 1942 Park began publishing a second magazine of which he was sole owner, *Rural Electrification Digest*[510]. "With the thought that hundreds of local electric co-ops would soon burgeon across the country, collectively spending hundreds of millions of dollars for supplies and equipment," Park, "conceived the idea of a trade magazine," that would have a local focus and would "meet the needs of these co-ops." *Rural Electrification Digest* was later published as *Co-Op Power*;[511] later it became *Farm Power*.[512]

One day in 1940 he met Howard E. Babcock, who was not only the founder and general manager of the co-operative known as the Grange League Federation Exchange (GLF), "which operated in

New York, Pennsylvania, New Jersey and bordering states," he was also at the time Chairman of the Board of Trustees at Cornell University. Babcock was also a charter member of *Cooperative Digest*, who at one point attempted to buy into the magazine for the purpose of extending the publication's coverage. Park resisted selling "him any stock in the journal, but told Babcock he could buy all the subscriptions he wanted." And he did. Almost overnight circulation of *Cooperative Digest* jumped from 200 to nearly 4,000. Babcock admired Park's business abilities. He made an unsuccessful bid to persuade him to move his family to Ithaca, New York, so that Cornell University could take advantage of his knowledge, business skills and organizational abilities. Park resisted but he left the door open a crack when he told Babcock that if he ever left North Carolina for Ithaca, it would be to run his own business. With this in mind, one day in March 1942 Babcock informed Park of an opportunity that forever changed the direction of his young friend's life. He told Park of a small, twenty-year-old, four-man advertising agency in Ithaca, New York, that was for sale, of which the Grange League Federation was its principal account.[513] He advised Park to buy it and move his family to Ithaca. When Park wavered, Babcock offered to lend him the necessary cash to buy the agency. Babcock's hunch proved correct; Park could not resist. On 1 April 1942,[514] Park journeyed to Ithaca, carefully investigated the advertising agency's business potential, discovered it had billings guaranteed for a year, and quickly moved to Ithaca. He never looked back.[515]

The business into which Park invested his money had the accurate but unimpressive name of Agricultural Advertising & Research. The agency did marketing research for its clients, primarily farmers. "With accounts billing about $2,000,000" annually, within four or five years he built his agency from an organization employing five people into one employing over 125. By 1944 his clients included "purchasing or retail cooperatives in Indiana, Ohio, Pennsylvania, Virginia, and North Carolina, and organizations like the Dairy League." The company was involved with marketing "various products ranging from ice cream, milk, grape

juice, tomato juice and canned and frozen vegetables."[516] Park had
no trouble repaying Babcock his money.[517]

Throughout the 1940s Park's agency grew rapidly. Branch
offices were established in New York City, Albany, Washington, D.
C., Richmond, Virginia and Raleigh, North Carolina. "Farm
cooperatives made up the bulk of his accounts. The company also
did work for blue chip national advertisers." For six years the
business continued to grow. Then, according to Park, he made a
mistake. He became involved in politics. In 1946 his firm handled
the advertising as well as the public relations campaign for New
York Republican Governor Thomas Dewey's 1946 gubernatorial
race. Two years later Dewey's political machine hired him to get
out the New York small-town and rural vote in his 1948 bid for the
White House. After Dewey was defeated by Truman that
November, Park vowed never again to get involved in politics. It
was not Dewey's loss that governed Park's remark so much as it
was that he almost lost all his agricultural clients.

Many of his clients were upset with his political activities and
after the 1948 election Park offered his GLF farm cooperative
clients the opportunity to change agencies—and several did. Those
who remained, however, did so because they had a vested interest
in a long-range project Park had spent a lot of time developing for
them. While trying to elect Dewey had slowed its evolution, the day
after the election loss Park plunged into this project with renewed
vigor. The origin of what he and the GLF members were
contemplating dated to the days shortly after the war ended.[518]

As far as agricultural prices were concerned, by 1945 farmers
increasingly believed they were getting the short end of the stick.
They bitterly complained about the countless regulations the
Federal government had imposed on them. Although they
acknowledged that Depression-era and wartime regulations had
been necessary, they contended that an intrusive post-war government was now unnecessary because both ordeals were over, but no
elected official seemed seriously interested in abolishing them.
They complained to Park that before the war, "you could sell
anything put in a can." And make money on it. Now things were

different. The Federal government was not only paying people NOT to plant crops, it was also engaged in a morass of other bewildering agricultural activities. His clients did not like the resulting mess. Their main bone of contention was that because of countless, confusing policies emanating from Washington, no market now existed for their perishable goods. The Grange League Federation (GLF) asked him if it was possible to set up a central selling organization that would enable them to successfully compete in the marketplace. Park listened carefully to his clients. After studying the problem, he told them that setting up a central selling organization would cost them $20,000,000. Not having that much money, and not willing to part with it even if they did, the GLF members sent him back to the proverbial drawing board to come up with another answer.[519]

Over the next several months Park contemplated several potential solutions to their difficulty. If the problem was that the government was preventing his clients from receiving higher food prices, there was little he could do without a massive shift in public opinion in favor of them. He therefore shifted his inquiry to another question. What would make people want to pay higher food prices? What he learned disturbed him, but it provided him with his first building block toward resolving the conundrum. With the help of research laboratories at Cornell University and other facilities, he discovered that although most Americans found plenty to eat each day, their stomachs were "usually stuffed with the wrong kind of food," so much so that it often made them ill. This finding ignited his curiosity and led him to focus on a phenomenon he saw daily: Americans never stopped complaining of their stomach ailments. He became convinced that this ever-recurring complaint, while obviously related to a poor diet, created among the public a general disrespect for food; average Americans did not particularly enjoy consuming their provisions. As a result, when a plate of food was set before them, instead of seeing something that caused their mouths to water, they saw an assortment of edible objects designed to fill an intestinal void; beyond that sentiment, food was neither appealing nor important;

as far as they were concerned, food was just something to eat to enable them to get through the day.

This observation led to another. In the past Park had frequently watched the behavior of housewives as they shopped at the grocery store. They purchased their groceries "in a grudging manner," he observed; they made their purchases with "the kind of reluctance and price watching" they did *not* exercise when buying perfume or beauty products. This attitude toward food was why they routinely attempted to purchase their foodstuffs at the lowest possible price; the thought of paying a high price for good quality food never seemed to penetrate their minds. He was determined to discover a way to overcome this attitude. Transforming it would be an arduous challenge, he believed, but it was a challenge well worth the time if, in the end, his GLF clients could obtain better prices in the marketplace.

The next building block toward a solution came some weeks later. At his own expense, Park "traveled to California and studied Sunkist's glamour treatment of the orange." Sunkist, he discovered, had overcome the suspicion barrier; no American housewife regarded a Sunkist orange as if it was just another scrap of food. Instead, housewives deemed a Sunkist orange as something fresh, something tasty, something well worth the price. In short, Sunkist had glamorized the orange. The food industry had done a good job in advertising its products but had done practically nothing to glamorize them. There was a critical difference. The answer to the GLF's problem, he concluded, was one of marketing. If Sunkist could persuade the public to buy its oranges, he could also persuade them to buy GLF products. Only one question remained: How?[520]

The use of national advertising to achieve this goal was out of the question. Advertising rates on a national scale were far too high to contemplate, especially since his clients were all small. There was no way they could afford to advertise nationally, even collectively. Park then gave some thought to moving his clients' products to distant states by rail. The problem here, he discovered, was that freight rates, like advertising rates, were also prohibitively high.

Devising a solution for his parsimonious clients remained a problematic headache, but he was sure he could come up with something. Then the third and final building block came into play.

Sometime in mid-1948 Park suggested to the GLF members that they collectively purchase the Green Giant company, which was at that time in financial trouble; it had, he pointed out, a widely recognized brand name, which was exactly what they needed. He also suggested they look into collectively purchasing the ailing S. S. Pierce company, which also had a widely recognized name. No one warmed to his suggestions. The GLF members told him they wanted nothing to do with Green Giant or S. S. Pierce. As their talks progressed, Park and the GLF members decided to look into the possibility of franchising their own brand label instead of using one already established.[521] The only way they could make such an enterprise succeed, Park told them, was to market their products with labels displaying a highly identifiable logo or trademark.[522]

Since the GLF members were unable or unwilling to bankroll the purchase of the Green Giant or S. S. Pierce companies, what was needed was the creation of an easily recognized symbol that grocery store consumers would immediately recognize for its superior quality, and one that would entice them to effortlessly pay a higher than normal price. Park's agricultural clients liked this idea and instructed him to find one. So long as the money involved in creating the logo did not threaten them financially, they were agreeable to whatever he might devise. Park now only had one problem. He needed a brand name, one that would move products, "something in which an overly cautious public could have trust and confidence." He assigned his head of research, Robert Flannery, to create an idea or a name—or something!—to crystallize his concept. Over the next few weeks, Flannery and the firm's employees considered several names, such as Irene Rich, Fanny Farmer and other popular appellations. They tested as many as 500 names.[523] Nothing, however, seemed to have what they were looking for: a name that was both high in recognition and one that would instantly be accepted and trusted by the public. Park ordered Flannery to do more testing. He even asked his employees for suggestions. A couple of weeks later, Flannery strolled into Park's office with the solution. He said: "Bring in Duncan Hines."[524]

When Flannery said those words, Park almost snapped his fingers. "Why didn't he think of it before?" he chastised himself. He instinctively knew Duncan Hines was the name he was looking for, the name that would solve all the GLF's problems.[525] While conducting his surveys, Flannery discovered the name housewives most frequently associated with good, quality food was that of Duncan Hines. His surveys also turned up another interesting fact: Duncan Hines's name was better known among all Americans than was President Truman's Vice-President, Alben Barkley, who was from Kentucky. In fact, more Kentuckians recognized Hines's name than they did Barkley's. This was all Park needed to know.[526]

Park now focused his goals. He now knew what he wanted. He wanted Duncan Hines's name and face on the labels of all the GLF's products. Hines's name was an authoritative one; it was widely respected and revered; it connoted strength and confidence. But most important of all, it was trusted. Park was sure a package featuring Hines would arrest the attention of housewives and induce them to buy the GLF's products. In his mind, Duncan Hines was a name well worth going after. Getting his cooperation, however, was another matter. Nevertheless, Park was determined to succeed where others had failed, and he soon put his master plan into action.

One of the things Park always insisted on before first meeting important clients was to be prepared. "Know everything you can about that person," was his motto before meeting anyone.[527] Therefore, before he scheduled an interview with Hines, he sent one of his employees to the various libraries in Ithaca to literally photograph every article they had on the man.[528] He quickly learned that Hines was not one to risk his reputation to make a dollar; wealth meant little to him. His philosophy, Park discovered, could be summed up in a sentence: One can easily earn another dollar, but if one loses his reputation, an opportunity may never again present itself to earn it back. This sentiment was not lost on him. Within days Park had absorbed so much information on Hines that he felt he knew him before he met him.[529] So confident was he that he could sell Hines on his future plans that he prepared "completely finished Duncan Hines labels, in full color, on dummy cans, cartons and jars so that" the food expert "could see what the concept would look like."[530]

When Park believed himself to be thoroughly prepared, he launched his plan. With help from a friend of his, Robert Wilson, Park called Hines at his Bowling Green home and requested a meeting. Hines, who expressed skepticism at Park's request, nevertheless accepted. A few weeks later in November 1948, Park approached the Waldorf-Astoria Towers in New York City, wearing a sartorial combination known to his later employees as "his Duncan Hines suit."[531] When Park was shown into a temporary meeting room the hotel had set up for the occasion, Hines was talking to someone from the Ford Motor Company who was trying to get him to endorse their latest automobile models. As he sat on the edge of his chair, Hines bluntly told the Ford executive that he did not endorse products, and that he used to drive a Ford but did not any longer because it "shook his liver." After he hung up, he turned to Park and said "I guess you want me to endorse something for you. Well, I am glad you heard that conversation and now know that I don't do that."[532] Hines, still agitated with the Ford executive, said rather acidly, "So, you're going to make me a millionaire." Park, knowing that Hines was more interested in keeping intact his reputation than in making money, quietly replied that, no, he had not asked for the meeting to make him a fortune. Rather, he was standing before him because he wanted to create food products in his *honor*. Park said, "By making your name more meaningful in the home, you can upgrade American eating habits."[533] Duncan Hines sat up at this statement. No one had ever said anything like *that* to him before. This young man was a little different from the rest of the dollar chasers he had been dickering with all morning. Park again reaffirmed to Hines that he had no interest in making any money from his famous name; rather, he was proposing a line of top-quality foods bearing

Hines's name that would complement what his eminent renown meant to millions of Americans. Park sweetened his offer; he told Hines that he could have complete control over anything bearing his name. Then he added the clincher. Since Park knew how Hines felt about Americans' eating habits and how disgusted he was with their regard for food, he told him he could help transform this attitude. He could encourage them to eat and respect foods which were healthy and disdain those which caused stomach problems. Park expanded on his initial remarks. He told Hines that if he allowed a company to use his name only on high-quality products bearing his personal endorsement, he would be doing his country a favor by directly influencing and upgrading American eating habits. This proposal had tremendous appeal to Hines; it affected his sense of honor. The concept of honor, Park realized, was the key in getting his attention.[534]

At the conclusion of their first meeting, Park left Hines with the necessary background material for his proposal. When they met for breakfast the next morning, Park showed him the product prototypes he had designed, each bearing Hines's name and face. "Hines picked up one and fingered it with some interest." The prototypes aroused his curiosity. As the conversation progressed, he turned one package over repeatedly, trying to decide if he wanted to go through with Park's proposal. After a few minutes, Park snatched up the others and eagerly showed them off. Forty-eight hours after their initial meeting, the two men agreed to a six-month trial partnership. One week later the two met again in Chicago, flanked by their lawyers, where they drew up and signed a contract, legalizing their temporary partnership. "Park gave Hines a certified check of a substantial amount to show he 'meant business.' In the contract,…there were escape clauses for Hines. He could pull out of the deal if his name and reputation were compromised in any way."[535]

As Hines saw it, if he was going to follow Roy Park's lead down this uncertain road, the younger man would first have to prove his competence and gain his trust. Park did not fail him, and over the next few months, Hines became immensely impressed with his honesty and forthrightness. In his mind Park was just like himself, only younger. The two grew to like each other very much. But many turns in the road had to transpire before that bridge was crossed.

Park did everything he could to win Hines's favor. The first task he embarked on was to "find out if housewives would pay a premium price for a premium brand." During December of 1948, with an investment of $50,000 of his own money, he "bought up quantities of canned goods from the supply sources of Boston's famed S. S. Pierce Company," replaced their labels with his own Duncan Hines labels and then placed them on grocery store shelves in upstate New York. "With radio and newspaper promotion to ballyhoo the event, the shelves were quickly emptied—at premium prices."[536] Park then began test-marketing several Duncan Hines packaged food products in New York, New England, Illinois and Chapel Hill, North Carolina.[537] He decided "to run a test of nine staple foods" featuring the Duncan Hines label. The "results of that test were all the encouragement" he needed. His research and instincts were right. The Duncan Hines name "moved" products. As he had hoped, Hines's name worked like magic. Interestingly, the most popular item removed from supermarket shelves was one of the prototypes Park had originally showed Hines: a box of cake mix.

A jubilant Park could not wait to tell GLF members of his successful tests. Unfortunately, Park was now faced with another problem. Although he had sold Hines on his concept, he had yet to prove to his GLF clients "that Duncan Hines could sell food as well as recommend it."[538] And that, increasingly, seemed unlikely. While Park was trying to lure Hines into a partnership, "enthusiasm among the farmers had dwindled and leading groups had disintegrated."[539] Said Park years later, "following the test marketing we went back to our farm cooperative clients with an encouraging report—only to find that there had been a shift in their management philosophy. They had decided to stick to their knitting by providing their farmer members with farm production supplies and leave the consumer marketing of processed foods to the pros in the consumer field."

Park now had a choice. He could dispose of the investment he had made in developing the Duncan Hines brand and turn his attention to other advertising and public relation activities, or he could plunge ahead with what he was sure was a winning formula. He decided the latter held the more promising road. But before acting, he sought the advice from someone whose judgment he always felt secure in seeking.[540] He turned to his friend, H. E. Babcock, who told him "to set up his own company and seek backing from bankers and investment brokers." Park took his advice. He "was almost too successful in selling the idea. His backers talked of millions. It seemed to Park that he would be squeezed out" if he was not careful. "He fought back and retained firm control over his infant company, though this meant considerably less money invested than his new partners had contemplated."[541] Toward the end of December 1948 Park changed the name of his Ithaca advertising firm to Hines-Park Foods, Inc.[542]

Park quickly made extensive preparations for his new company, which included plenty of advertising. Over the next three years he hired fifty advertising agencies to research, promote and advertise the line of products Hines-Park Foods unloaded onto supermarket shelves. He wanted to ensure that there would always be a vast pool of creative talent from which to draw.[543] Within weeks Hines-Park began accepting "applicants from other small companies for the Duncan Hines label." The only qualification Park insisted on was that their products maintain a consistent level of very high quality. Aware of the clauses in Hines's contract, Park did not dare insult the food expert with an inferior product that would sully his name. If he did, he knew the partnership and his potential fortune would evaporate without a trace. The member-companies of his food label would all have to offer the very best products in their respective fields. Park would settle for nothing less. With this in mind, Hines-Park was soon approving products from all over the nation: "chicken from Washington, tomato juice from Ohio and

New York, kidney beans from Ohio, coffee from Boston, pickles and relishes from North Carolina, crab apples from Michigan."

Originally, Park's arrangement with his food suppliers was to have them ship their products to a Hines-Park plant for repackaging under the Duncan Hines label, but freight rates were expensive. Then he had a brainstorm: "Instead of having the products brought to the label," why not bring "the label to the products...[?]" That operational short-cut solved the problem "of additional freight costs and the time loss in getting" his food suppliers' goods "into the grocery stores."[544] "Under the Hines-Park system relatively small food producers" were "enabled to compete on somewhat even terms with the goliaths of the food industry."[545]

The example of the St. Mary's Company, a packer of tomato and bean products from Sidney, Ohio demonstrates how the Hines-Park operation functioned. First, St. Mary's applied to be a supplier for Hines-Park Foods. After extensive testing in Hines-Park's laboratory and final approval given by Duncan Hines himself, it was licensed to carry the Duncan Hines label on selected products.[546] The company paid Hines-Park a one-time "flat fee and a fixed percentage of gross sales thereafter."[547] It paid a modest royalty for the use of the Duncan Hines name, and it also agreed "to devote 2% of its gross sales to Duncan Hines advertising"; 25% of that sum was allocated to Hines-Park's account for national advertising. St. Mary's then packaged and marketed Duncan Hines Tomato Juice to the public. Under the Duncan Hines label, the company could only market the recipe that was prepared and refined by the Hines-Park laboratory. Failure to abide by the recipe's exacting specifications would result in termination of the company's contract. The company was, however, free to market its Duncan Hines product as extensively as it wished.[548]

Within weeks of its opening, Hines-Park Foods was inundated with products; producers from all over the nation wanted them to sample, test and, they hoped, sponsor their wares. Space limitations prevented the company from testing all of them in Ithaca, and Park soon made arrangements for all testing to be done in Indianapolis,

Indiana.[549] Suppliers for Hines-Park knew better than to tamper with a Duncan Hines-approved product. They would have been foolish if they did. All franchise holders reported increased sales for products bearing the Duncan Hines label. Why tamper with success?

Despite Park's best efforts, the initial results were good but not good enough. In a March 1949 meeting with Hines, Park asked his famous partner to extend their six-month agreement for another six months. Hines, who had up to that time been keeping tabs on Park's activities but not actively involving himself in them, asked him point blank if he was making any money on his venture. Park said no, he was not. Hines asked him why he had not asked for his help. "Because," Park confessed, "I did not think I could afford you." Hines had to sit down for this. All his suspicions about Park vanished. The young man really was sincere. Hines then told Park he would help him all he could if he would pay his expenses. All he had to do was ask.[550] By September 1949 Hines-Park had licensed sixteen food packagers which were ready to distribute sixty brands of food featuring the Duncan Hines label[551] with products ranging from "bread and jam to fancy peaches and pears."[552] Sales for the second six-month period went better, primarily because Duncan Hines rolled up his sleeves and went to work. Park impressed Hines with his business acumen and organizational abilities, and their friendship grew into a tight bond. Therefore, it was no surprise when on 14 October 1949, Roy Park, with Duncan Hines as his full partner, formally established Hines-Park Foods, Inc.[553] Under an arrangement insisted on by Hines, the 2% royalty he received from the company's sales went to the Duncan Hines Foundation, in which he owned no stock.[554]

By the middle of 1950 Hines-Park "had thirty companies signed for 150 products, and some eighty dairies had qualified to carry" a soon-to-be-available ice cream product.[555] Since the initial licensing of their company's first products, their laboratories had tested more than 500 varieties of food; only one-fifth of them measured up to Hines's demanding expectations. Although the company would later be known for its cake mixes, the first star in its product lineup was ice cream. In June 1950 production began on Duncan Hines Ice Cream.[556] The ice cream was developed by the Lehigh Valley Cooperative Farmers dairy at Allentown, Pennsylvania, the assets of which, before production began, totaled $3,000,000. The introduction of the ice cream line forced the cooperative to spend $1,250,000 in new plant equipment just to keep up with the demand. Two weeks after Lehigh Valley announced it was ready to manufacture and distribute the instantaneously famous dessert, it produced one million pint containers bearing Hines's name. The initial sales of vanilla, chocolate and butter pecan ice cream were, according to a company spokesman, "terrific." At forty-three cents a pint, the dairy cooperative was, financially, in seventh heaven. The ice cream's secret, like many of the products bearing its famous logo, was its extreme richness; it was 25% heavier than other ice creams[557] and contained 33% more butterfat than similar products on the market.[558]

As promised, Hines kept his word to Roy Park. He rolled up his sleeves and went to work for his partner. He was, first and foremost, a salesman, and he once again demonstrated his abilities in persuasion. For most of the latter part of 1950 he and Clara went everywhere promoting Duncan Hines Ice Cream. They crisscrossed the country, making appearances in person, in newspapers, on radio, even on the new medium of television. In short, they went wherever Park asked them to show up. No town was too insignificant to promote their products. As 1950 gave way to 1951, he continued to spend the majority his time promoting the ice cream bearing his name. His travels would make many men his age dizzy and exhausted, but, surprisingly, he showed no sign of slowing down his hectic pace—or wanting to. The breadth of his travels was especially surprising since he almost never traveled by plane or train; instead, he preferred to drive.

National advertising for the ice cream began with the July 1951 edition of *Look* magazine, among other publications.[559] Later that month, Park announced that his company was ready to enter the cake mix market. He said his company was not going to enter the field in a test-marketing mode, as it had in the past; instead, it was going to mount a full-scale campaign to introduce what he believed was the finest cake mix on the market. He said the company would soon begin production with devil's food, white, yellow, and spice flavors.[560]

16

THE WORLD OF DUNCAN HINES

In September 1949 Hines and Clara took another extensive dining tour of New York City. With his guidebook's sales office in New York becoming increasingly busy, the two made a convenient excuse to visit it and indulge themselves in that city's extensive restaurant cuisine. As usual, they lodged in the Waldorf-Astoria hotel. After visiting the sales office and its manager Frank Watts, they were off to the restaurants. When reporters learned of Hines's arrival in their city, they cornered him for an impromptu press conference that evening. Hines, never one to turn down publicity, told the press about his day on the town:

> I went to Lindy's, he began. "First, we had borscht. No, I don't mean beet soup. It was pure beet juice, perfectly clear, and we put sour cream in it. Then [we ate] sturgeon. Then we had rye bread that was like a spring; when you squeezed it, it bounced back. Then a new kind of drink, not alcoholic, celery juice. Delicious! Then those things, what do you call 'em, blintzes. I had one with sour cream and one with cherry

preserves. With coffee I had a French cruller. Oh, I forgot the cheesecake. It was this thick.

Hines spread his thumb and forefinger about six inches apart. One reporter remarked that it sounded as if he did not have a balanced meal. Hines laughed, saying, "I don't eat it. I just taste. If I ate all that, I wouldn't be able to sleep at night."

Hines was still excited about the previous day, which he was only too happy to relate. "Yesterday Mrs. Hines and I went up in Connecticut and ate at four different places. I just tasted. You know how to taste? For sweet and sour, you use the tip of your tongue. To tell what herbs are in a dish, you put it in the back of your mouth and roll it around for a while. Don't swallow it right down like an old hound dog back there in Kentucky."

Hines then related that he had just been interviewed on a heavily prepared radio show. He said of the experience, with decisive finality, that he did not enjoy it. "I don't like a script," he said. "I tell 'em, 'When you're going to ask me a question, beckon like this, and I'll be ready to answer. If you want me to stop talking, hold up your hand.' That's all the script I need."

Another reporter, changing the subject, asked him what was New York's best restaurant. Hines's opinion on this was always changing. This time he said that it was the Newport at 18 East 60th Street, but then Hines shook his head and fretted that it was much too expensive for most Americans. When he discovered among his inquisitors a New York-based female reporter for the Louisville *Courier-Journal,* he quickly befriended her. "Now write this down for the people in Kentucky," he asked her. "Say I'm happy to see that the good restaurants south of the Ohio [River] are cleaning up. And say I'll be happy to get home and eat two-year-old ham, cornbread, beaten biscuits, pound cake, yellow-leg fried chicken, and corn pudding. And you can say what I think is the best eating-place in Kentucky: The Beaumont Inn in Harrodsburg."[561]

On 15 March 1950 almost a week before his 70th birthday, Hines and Clara left Bowling Green for another lengthy trip. Their plans were to travel "to Chicago for three days, San Francisco for a week, to Los Angeles for ten days and to Phoenix for two weeks and back home the first of May." He hoped they would get to New England on their next trip in "the later part of June" because, said Hines, "I am hungry for some of that super-duper New England food.... "562

When Hines and Clara arrived at the Green Gables Restaurant in Phoenix, Arizona on 14 April, members of the "Duncan Hines Family" gave him a belated gift for his birthday, a new Cadillac convertible automobile. This had been their practice since the end of the war. Hines accepted neither fees nor gifts from others and the only way his "family" members could make him accept the vehicle was if they all contributed equal donations toward its purchase. The restaurant where the festivities for the nearly month-late birthday celebration took place was as colorful as Hines himself. Guests were met at the door of the Green Gables by a mounted knight-in-armor; then they were heralded by trumpeters dressed in Errol Flynn-styled Robin Hood costumes. At the apex of the evening's jubilant repast—the presentation of the car—a small boy in a medieval costume presented Hines with a satin pillow upon which lay a certificate of ownership and a set of golden keys to the Cadillac. This was followed by a silver-plated armored knight who rolled a cart into the dining room; upon the cart rested an enormous birthday cake. When it was placed in front of the guest of honor, Hines heartily blew out the candles. The knight then presented Hines with a sword and asked him to stand so he could cut the first slice of cake. As soon as Hines placed the first carved piece upon a glass plate, a stringed ensemble commenced playing sweet melodies and continued their acoustical merriment through-out dinner while a soloist sang a plentitude of Kentucky ballads. As the orchestra played throughout the evening, the guests heartily consumed the wealth of food before them, which included "hors d'oeuvres, canapes a la russe, Miami green mock turtle soup aux quenelles, lobster cocktail supreme a la Parisienne, hearts of palms salad (flown in from Rio di Janeiro), Green Gables dressing-garlic toast, Golden Wisconsin pheasant (flown in from Wisconsin), sauce bigarde, potato souffle, cauliflower a la Aubrel, Vesuvian dream, demitasse cognac" and many other exquisite delicacies. On each dinner menu were the words, "Happy Birthday and Hats Off to You, Duncan Hines. Sincere best wishes to one, who, more than any other, has placed greater opportunity for gracious living before the nation's motoring, dining and vacationing public. We, your family and your thousands of followers throughout America who have benefited by your untiring efforts, extend our appreciation."[563]

For most of the latter part of 1950 Hines and Clara went everywhere promoting Duncan Hines Ice Cream. They criss-crossed the country for their company, making personal appearances wherever they were needed. They didn't mind. Their travels gave them an excuse to visit some new restaurants throughout the country, as well as call on old favorites. To cite just a few of the places they visited that year, on 10 September 1950 Hines and Clara ate a tasty meal at the Doll House at 1518 South Main Street in Salt Lake City, Utah. Eleven days later (21 September), they dined at the Airport Restaurant in Wichita, Kansas. Also on that same hot September day they visited an establishment known as "The Farm" where they posed for photographers in front of an enormous display of Duncan Hines Ice Cream. Upon arising in Wichita the next morning (22 September), Hines and Clara continued their promotional duties. Hines gave the local newspaper an interview. Later, just before heading off for another engagement, the couple posed once again for Wichita photographers while eating from cartons of Duncan Hines ice cream.

Early the next month (3 October), while on a publicity tour for Duncan Hines Ice Cream in Flint, Michigan, they found themselves at the doorstep of Cromer's Restaurant at 500 North Saginaw, where they sampled the sour cream cabbage slaw, hot cloverleaf rolls and other popular favorites for which the restaurant was known. Eleven days later (14 October), after a New England promotional tour, the couple were in Whitman, Massachusetts, visiting yet again the Toll House and his good friends, Ruth and Kenneth Wakefield. Less than two weeks later (26 October), they were seated at a table in the Swiss Chalet restaurant at Chicago's

Bismarck Hotel, where they dined on onion cake, among other things, with his other special friends, the proprietors of the Lowell Inn, Arthur and Nelle Palmer.[564] They did not always travel to see others; sometimes others traveled to see them. A few months later (29 January 1951), they were honored with a visit to Bowling Green by movie and radio personalities Gene Autry and Smiley Burnett.[565]

At the 10th annual Duncan Hines Family Dinner held at the Morrison Hotel in Chicago on 8 May 1951, Hines told those gathered at the event that he and Clara had traveled through 39 states since they had last gathered a year earlier. While on these travels, said Hines, he been given both the time and the opportunity to reflect upon the many notable and significant changes in the restaurant industry that had transpired during the previous fifteen years, including advances in sanitation and better preparation of food. With this change, he noted, had come a wider acceptance among the American public in attitudes toward eating out. He cited as evidence the more than 40 million people who now ate out every day. He congratulated the restaurateurs for their efforts in upgrading their kitchens and making American restaurant cuisine respectable. He told them that the ranks of the Duncan Hines Family would continue to swell because he was getting fifty restaurant recommendations in the mail every day. Everyone, it seemed, had a new adventure in good eating for him to explore; something, he told them, should come from his imminent investigations. In the meantime, he urged them to join the American Restaurant Association if they had not already done so; the association was full of ideas to help them improve their trade. Likewise, he urged all hotel and motel managers in attendance to subscribe to *Hotel Monthly* and *American Motel* for new ideas on how to make their businesses even better. Hines insisted that they should never stop improving their establishments, whether for dining or lodging or a combination of the two. He told them that "there is no question but that cooking in public eating places in America is improving faster perhaps than many of you realize. A gratifying percentage of the public are becoming more food conscious and they will not patronize places where the food is not consistently good.... All over America thousands and thousands of people are giving serious thought about choosing the right place to eat."[566] Hines was very proud of his "family" members and the part they had played in changing how Americans viewed the restaurant industry—and just as proud of the considerable part he had played in bringing about that transformation.

At this same gathering Hines told several anecdotes from his many years on the road. Most of the stories he told that evening were ones he had recounted many times before. He did tell a new story, however, one that came about during his recent trip to Mexico. He had arrived in Tamazunchale at the home of a friend, whom Hines would only identify as Col. Zelinsky. "It was rather late for dinner," said Hines, but the hour of the day was immaterial as far as the Colonel was concerned. Soon after he and Clara had arrived at their host's home, Col. Zelinsky announced that he had arranged to serve them an exceedingly fine dinner, one that would make their mouths water for more. The Colonel told the couple that his cook would be serving wiener schnitzel that evening; it was, he boasted, the best wiener schnitzel ever served in Mexico. Hines, his interest peaked by the Colonel's braggadocio, agreed to try it. But when dinner was finally served, Hines quickly changed his mind. "When the wiener schnitzel was brought," he said, "I thought it looked very queer."[567] It was then that he felt a sinking feeling in his stomach. "Experience should have taught me," he confessed, "that I was asking for trouble [when I agreed to eat] a European specialty prepared...in a dusty little Mexican town. I should have asked for frijoles refritos and tortillas and let it go at that." As Hines was about to stab his fork into his meal, he examined it more carefully. "What I saw appalled me," he said. "The Colonel's pride and joy was unlike any wiener schnitzel I'd ever seen, and I've never seen anything like it since, either. It was an odd color that I couldn't quite make out in the dimly lighted room, and it curled up at the edges like an old shoe that has laid out in the sun and the rain for a long time. The odor that arose from it was, to say the least, unpleasant. I certainly wasn't going to eat that!"[568]

Thinking fast, he remembered that one should not drink any water in Mexico unless he was crazy or desperate, so he asked Col. Zelinsky to get him a bottle of beer. "While he was gone," said Hines, "I cut off one corner, wiped it off with my napkin and stuck it in my pocket. When Col. Zelinsky came back, I told him that I was awfully sorry, but I had forgotten that I was under doctor's orders and was not allowed to eat any meat. But that it looked so good that I hadn't been able to resist trying one bite. This seemed to satisfy him, but when I looked at it the next morning, I concluded that it was a piece of stewed burro's ear, for it was [as] blue as anything. I still don't know what would have happened to me if I had tried to eat it."[569] When Hines left Tamazunchale, he did so with few regrets, but he couldn't help wondering if someone had missed a burro lately.[570]

While Duncan Hines had no doubt left his mark on America's social landscape, as the decade of the 1950s began his thoughts repeatedly turned to a question that increasingly vexed him. How was he going to dispose of the hobby that had become a publishing success? More pointedly, could he relinquish control of what he had started? And did he really want to?

17

THE OFFICE LIFE

By 1951 Duncan Hines had, as the cliché goes, "too many irons in the fire." When he turned seventy-one in March, he knew he was not immortal. He no doubt wondered what Clara's future would hold should he suddenly pass away. With this thought hanging about the periphery of his consciousness, he began to probe into the possibility of finding someone to take over his book publishing business. He wanted someone in whom he could have complete trust, someone who would make the decisions he made, someone who would continue to promote his business as he did. Although he greatly trusted Roy Park, he chose not to ask him for help in this matter. Park had his hands full promoting his name via canned and boxed grocery products; asking him to assume control over his book publishing operation seemed inappropriate. So he looked within the ranks of his family for help. One of the first people he turned to was his sister's son, also named Duncan Hines. For a short time the younger Hines worked for his famous uncle, but he quit after about three weeks because his uncle was partial to "blowing up" at him over usually inconsequential matters. The sad truth is that while reason told Hines he needed to transfer his business over to another, his emotions would not allow him to relinquish control. Adventures in Good Eating was his child. Like a parent, he had nourished it, developed it and witnessed its spectacular growth. The mere fact that someone, particularly a relative, might come along and suggest some (probably efficient) modifications was more than he could bear; the situation could be likened to a famed portraitist watching a mischievous seven-year-old draw a mustache on a work of art upon which he had labored for many years. Nevertheless, between 1950 and 1952 Hines tried to find someone to adopt his creation wholesale with the unmentioned proviso that it not be changed in any way. As he was to learn, painfully, it was a qualification no one could accept.

One of the people whom Hines had in mind as a replacement was an army air corp officer. A few years earlier, in 1946 and early 1947, Hines had spoken with his relative by marriage, Clarence Herbert Welch of Los Angeles, California, about taking over Adventures in Good Eating, Inc. In 1945 he learned Welch was considering leaving the armed services and asked him if he would be interested in administering the business affairs of Adventures in Good Eating. Hines admitted the financial aspects of his business was not his strongest suit. Although his background was in sales, public relations was where he really shined. Someone else, he thought, should handle the clerical responsibilities. Welch agreed to accept the position if he could conclusively determine there was enough money in it to support himself and his family.

In early January 1946 Welch visited Bowling Green and gave the business a thorough top-to-bottom investigation. Everything Hines had in his office was turned over to his discerning eye. He went through the company's financial records. He read every scrap of paper in the file cabinets. But after he had completed his probing study, he was still puzzled as to how the man made any money. It all seemed so chaotic. To Welch's organized mind, Hines's methods of accounting and office organization were enough to drive anyone crazy. It was a patchwork operation, not an efficient, businesslike venture. He finally concluded that Adventures in Good Eating was nothing more than a glamorous hobby, and certainly not a business. After several frustrating months of trying to get some straight answers from Hines and his accountant/

bookkeeper, Cecil "Hoot" Holland, Welch decided not to run Hines's business, not only because he believed it could not generate enough money for him and his family, but also because he believed Hines was not serious about letting him manage it. There was also another reason. Between the time the subject was first broached and his decision not to accept, Hines had married Clara. In Welch's eyes, she swiftly took control of his business affairs and quickly rendered moot any service he could have provided.

Welch concluded later that even if Hines had never married Clara, it was unlikely he would have accepted the job. It was his contention that Hines, the printer, overruled Hines, the businessman. As he saw it, Hines was more interested in producing a high-quality book than he was in running an efficient business or making much money beyond his material needs. His reasoning in this regard came about one day after carefully examining Hines's books and business practices. He sat down with the older man and had a frank talk with him. Welch quickly came to the point. "Duncan," he said, "you've got a major problem with the book." Hines asked what was the matter. Speaking specifically of *Adventures in Good Eating* but also including in his remarks *Lodging for a Night* and the *Vacation Guide*, Welch said, "The problem is that it's too good, so far as the printing is concerned. It never wears out." He pointed out, for example, his practice of putting glue between the book's cover and its fly leafs. One could not pull back the book covers and easily pull them off the way one could with a standard paperback book. "That's a great book," Welch said to him. "That's a quality book. But Duncan, what you're selling is a directory. It's got to wear out every year." A fine, well-produced book, he added, had not only wrecked his balance sheet, it had also inadvertently slightly harmed his reputation. Recalling some letters he had reviewed in the files, he said, "You're getting complaints from people about restaurants that you've not recommended in four years, or you're getting complaints from people about restaurants that are no longer in business. Or you're getting complaints about a restaurant that has been deleted in your new book but is still in last year's edition. The problem is that your customers' old book hasn't worn out, and as a result they haven't bought a new one. What you're doing is making people keep obsolete directories. These directories you're selling should self-destruct every year because you've got to sell books. That's the nature of the business. And you're hurting your reputation, Duncan. When people try one of these old guidebooks, they're eating at places that are no longer recommended by you. And when the food is no good, they're saying to themselves that they don't understand how you got your reputation to begin with." Despite Welch's best efforts, Hines just could not understand Welch's reasoning; the thought of producing a cheap product horrified him. No matter how many times Welch explained that a cheaper quality directory would net him more money, he simply could not bring himself to lessen the quality of anything associated with his name.

Welch's other problem with his business practices was Hines's refusal to endorse products; this was, of course, two years before Hines met Roy Park. Welch told him, "You've got a fine name. You've got a great reputation. And if Duncan Hines endorses something and approves of it, then people will conclude that it must be good." Hines pooh-poohed this idea, branding it as "commercial." Welch countered that since the books produced by Adventures in Good Eating, Inc. were not making enormous sums of money, he should look at endorsements as "bread on the table." "You've got to increase your income," he said. Hines still contended that endorsing products was too commercial for his taste, and that the answer to any financial problem his company faced was to sell more books. Welch countered this assertion by contending that, based on his examination of the company's financial records, such as they were, selling more books was not going to help his profit margin. His books ignored inflation and were still sold at $1.50. The production costs were rising in spite of this fixed price and increased sales of the books would only exacerbate the company's financial problems. When it became apparent Hines would not see his logic, Welch gave up. He told others later, "I just can't change Duncan. He's a gentleman of the old school. His word is his bond, and he just doesn't think people would appreciate it if he incorporated my recommended changes."[571]

In 1951 Clara persuaded her husband to hire her half-brother, Bob Wright. The younger man worked for his famous brother-in-law for a few months. Wright's first job was billing those who rented the "Recommended by Duncan Hines" signs. Although his employment was brief, he developed some firm opinions about his famous in-law and his business. Hines, he believed, made most of his money from his sign rental business; he charged enough to cover his gas, lodgings and meals. Although over 9,000 establishments were eventually included in all three guidebooks, only 1200 to 1500 of them took advantage of the famous signs bearing Hines's approval. His sign rental business translated into an annual profit of almost $38,000 a year—a hefty sum when one considers that the average income in the United States in 1951 was a little over $3,000.[572]

Before the Second World War Hines had a profitable country ham business, but by 1951 it scarcely existed. The only ham orders he filled now were those for special friends—and only if they asked. When he received a request for a country ham, it was now his practice to go downtown and obtain one from Sam Nahm, a relation of Clara's first husband, who ran a Bowling Green feed store.[573] Sometimes he got his country hams from Jimmy Siddens in Bowling Green; other times he ordered one from a favorite outlet in Cadiz, Kentucky, a town well-known for producing marvelous slabs of Kentucky's favorite delicacy.[574] However, for some unexplained reason, in the summer of 1951, Hines briefly flirted with the idea of getting back into the country ham business—and he believed his young brother-in-law was just the person to carry out his plans. Hines had it all worked out. He had the young man's future all planned. He told his brother-in-law that he was going to be the manager of this new enterprise. All he had to do was travel deep into the western Kentucky countryside and arrange with ham producers to supply him with choice two-year-old country hams. Wright made one trip into the country with him to line up a couple of potential ham suppliers, but for some reason, after a burst of energy into this potential lucrative direction, nothing further came of his grandiose plans. It never got off the ground because Hines, as usual, had too many other projects going at once, and there was no time left for this one. After working for Hines for three months, Wright saw more rewarding employment opportunities and left Bowling Green for a job in San Francisco.[575]

Because of his age, and because of Clara's prodding, Hines slowed down his busy schedule. She insisted he not venture out on the highway as often. This was easier said than done; there were times when Hines could not avoid having a jam-packed agenda on his calendar. But most of his days throughout the 1950s were characterized by a relative peacefulness. Duncan Hines had just enough to keep himself busy. No more. No less. He could remain in Bowling Green for longer periods because his books continued to sell. Year after year, sales for all four publications increased. Keeping himself before the public to generate sales no longer seemed urgent. With the exception of the *Vacation Guide*, his books always sold out. Paul Moore, who oversaw book production from about 1947 through 1953, stated that a typical printing run for *Adventures in Good Eating* in the early 1950s was approximately 25,000 copies. A comparable printing for an edition of *Adventures in Good Cooking* approximated 17,000 copies, while a print run for an edition of *Lodging for a Night* usually came to about 10,000 copies. All three books far out-paced sales of the *Vacation Guide*, which rarely sold out of its annual 5,000 unit print run.[576]

Hines and Clara were not on the road these days nearly as much as they had been. For as much as three months of the year, they stayed home. A typical automobile trip at this time might take them north to Omaha, Nebraska, west to Seattle, Washington, south to San Francisco, California, and west to Dallas, Texas. They would spend three or four days in each city before eventually returning to Bowling Green. During these trips Hines seldom popped into restaurant kitchens unannounced, checking on the quality of the establishment's cuisine. By and large, that was a thing of the past. Besides, he did not have to since the public was now doing it for him. By 1950 his very active dinner detectives were still with him, but they had dwindled to about a dozen individuals. Although the general public was helpful to Hines's cause, his "detectives" were still the ones he trusted most.[577]

Many people worked for Duncan Hines, but the ones who made his operation an efficient one were his secretaries. By 1950 much of the post-war chaos Clarence Welch had witnessed four years earlier had vanished. To be fair, Welch inspected his operation at a time when book orders were coming in so fast that his office staff could barely keep up with the demand. But now the operation functioned like clockwork. Without his secretaries, Hines could not have put out any of his guidebooks, and he knew it. It is unlikely all their names will ever be known. Many of them, like Edith Wilson, Emelie Tolman and Olga Lindquist are long dead, but some employees have left behind their recorded impressions.

One such person was Mary Jo Agee, who worked for Hines during the early 1950s. Agee was a woman in her late twenties or early thirties with two children. She was several years older than her fellow office colleagues. "She was a short person who wore four-inch high-heels all the time, even while doing her housework," said one of her co-workers.[578] Her job was to fill book orders. She typed the shipping labels and sent customers their bills. When she finished these tasks, she gave the labels and bills to John Henry Foster, Hines's handyman and groundskeeper, who hand-wrapped all orders before taking them to the post office. Sometimes Foster's efforts did not suit the fastidiously neat specifications Hines laid down for him. Once Foster put the wrong label on a box of books, and the mistake sent Hines into a state of prolonged vocal exasperation. As always, however, he quickly cooled off within a few minutes. Sometimes, though, Hines hired employees who did not suit him at all. One woman he hired simply could do nothing right in his estimation and he soon dismissed her. She was not the only one. If an employee ever made a mistake, such as sending a customer a cookbook instead of a guidebook, it was usually only a matter of time before that person found employment elsewhere. As was the case in Chicago years earlier, his lack of a discernible criteria for selecting those he hired, caused him to have unnecessary fits. He knew what qualities in a person he did not like but apparently could not detect them during the initial interview. As a result, those he employed was a hit-or-miss affair.[579]

Mary Herndon remained in his employ from the summer of 1951 until the first couple of weeks in 1954. When she applied for the job, she had just completed two years of study at Highland Park Junior College in Highland Park, Michigan. Shortly after her graduation in May and her return to Auburn, a small town located 20 miles west of Bowling Green, she learned of an employment opportunity with Hines by way of a family friend, Hines's niece, Louise Hines. When she applied for the job, she expected to be interviewed by one of his secretaries. To her surprise, her interviewer was none other than Duncan Hines himself. With little fanfare she was hired on the spot and told to return the next day. She was given no tests or applications to fill out. She was hired on a trial basis to see how she would work out. Hines would quickly discover for himself if he wanted her to remain. On her first day on the job, he took her into his living room, offered her a seat at a card table, sat down across from her and began dictating letters. She found his style of dictation surprisingly eccentric. Unlike the straightforward, curt manner most businessmen used, his manner of dictation was much like his speech and train of thought: jerky, frequently unorganized, and filled with a profusion of jokes and ad-libs. The whole purpose of each letter was to amuse the reader. Entertainment was the most important consideration. She never anticipated a boss like this in secretarial school. As did his other secretaries, Herndon adjusted. When she typed her first letters, she asked the other secretaries if Hines was really serious about signing his correspondence "the head rooster." It was explained to her that he used that *nom de plume* only in letters to his friends. Nevertheless, for the first few days, his unusual method of dictation nearly drove her crazy, and she was more than thankful that another secretary took most of it.[580]

When his secretaries were not taking dictation for his thousands of friends, they often composed many of his letters. While personal letters required an individual response, they learned quickly the language to use when responding to a particular type of letter, such as someone asking if Hines would endorse a product or if he would check out a restaurant. "We pretty much knew what we had to write," said Herndon. Their replies were, more or less, form letters. "A lot of times," she said, "we would just write our own letters and he would read them and sign them."[581]

Her duties were numerous. Herndon sent out questionnaires to members of the Duncan Hines Family; made corrections in the guidebooks when the questionnaires were returned; transferred that information to new, upcoming editions; and prepared the prototype for each guidebook page before it was sent to Paul Moore in Nashville. Specifically, she sent correction cards to all establishments listed in the guidebooks to ascertain if there were any changes that differed from their last listing. When the information was returned, she had to make the necessary changes in the next edition's working prototype. All new changes in the listings, even if they were nothing more than little, insignificant details, were retyped. Paul Moore then transformed Herndon's cut-and-paste pages into a tentative text and returned it for final proofreading before she handed it over to Hines for his final inspection and approval.

In the early 1950s Clara and his secretaries saw the gradual ravages of age creeping into Hines's personality. Some days he was his usual self, but other days he was a little difficult to work with. Said Herndon, "He got to the age [where] sometimes he would do things and wouldn't tell us. Or he would try to tell us to do something in a way that we knew wasn't the right way. And sometimes we would have to go to Mrs. Hines and explain [the situation] to her and let her talk to him." He may have been called "the head rooster" but they knew who ruled the roost; he always listened to Clara and never questioned her judgment. She was his protector and friend. And she kept her husband's secretaries happy, when she could.

Herndon saw many things come in the mail while she worked for Hines. People sent him all manner of food to taste. But the item the office most received, it seemed, was fruitcake. They received so many fruitcakes at Christmas that Hines unceremoniously gave them to his secretaries to enjoy. In fact, there was no telling what might turn up in the mail. Once in July 1953, said Herndon, "somebody from Arkansas sent him a 600-pound watermelon." There is no record of how much postage was used to send it, or how long it took to dispose of it, but Herndon and her fellow employees all got a chance to sink their teeth into it.[582]

The woman who was employed by Hines longer than any other was Sara Meeks, a Bowling Green native who worked for him from 1951 to 1959. After leaving high school, she went to Bowling Green Business University[583] because Western Kentucky Teachers College at that time did not offer business courses.[584] She enrolled in 1950 and took the usual secretarial courses, which included typing, shorthand, bookkeeping, and penmanship. After graduation in May 1951, the college's employment department learned that Hines needed an employee and directed her to his doorstep.

Meeks soon found herself taking most of Hines's dictation, much of which was directed to Roy Park. She was also assigned other chores, such as proofreading the guidebooks. "I didn't know much about the marks that you were suppose to make when you were proofreading," said Meeks, but she did "know that if there was a place that [Hines] no longer wanted to be listed, we would write *T/O* through the listing," which was a shorthand signal for "take out."

The task Meeks felt most honored to undertake was billing the sign rental clients. Her duties were simple enough. She kept track of two sets of signs; one set was 16" wide by 20" inches high, while the other set was somewhat smaller. She also kept track of what she charged each customer who used them; Adventures in Good Eating, Inc. charged its customers $20 for the sign and $10 each year for the tags that were attached to little hooks in the sign's design. The tags indicated the year of the latest recommendation; if the year was 1950 but the sign's tag read 1949, it meant the establishment's recommendation had not been renewed. All information pertaining to the sign rentals was kept in an office safe in twelve heavy, metal books, one for each month. Each book told whose rent was due. For instance, there was a metal book for all January rentals, another for all February rentals, etc. For Meeks the busiest month—and the heaviest book—was September. Once each month, she opened the safe and retrieved the metal book for that segment of the calendar. Meeks never tired of this assignment and found it "an honor" that Hines let her do it, because she knew how important it was to him.

Many owners of the establishments Hines recommended would buy more than one sign. Some of the extra "Recommended by Duncan Hines" signs they bought were nailed to roadside billboards, so passing motorists would see them. Some proprietors bought as many as ten signs and nailed them to fence posts. Needless to say, it pleased Hines when they did this. The income he derived from his sign business was also used to pay his employees, who received a weekly salary (in 1951) of slightly over $40 or, more precisely, a monthly salary of about $165, which was considered good pay at the time. Hines offered no benefits, such as retirement or health coverage but, in that day and age, few employers did. Employees were encouraged to save their money, not spend it.[585]

On her first day on the job, Sara Meeks was introduced to Edith Wilson, the office manager, who had been efficiently running the office since 1946. In Hines's office the red-headed Wilson displayed a stern self-discipline and an exacting attention to detail. Hines valued this quality, and he owed her (and Clara) a debt of gratitude; thanks to them his business and financial affairs were not a total mess.

At about the time Meeks came there for employment, Hines had been having problems with Mrs. Wilson. Earlier in the year, she informed him that she was going to leave to pursue a career as a legal stenographer and court reporter. It is unclear as to precisely why Wilson left him, but it could be that the pleasure of working for Duncan Hines had worn off. The two were temperamental opposites. Hines was usually a relaxed, easygoing individual, taking his time in whatever he did. Wilson, by contrast, was just the opposite. As his office manager, she did not exactly treat her fellow employees like marionettes, but by all accounts she ran a tight ship. But Hines and Wilson were, however, alike in one respect; there were times when both could become rather volatile if their tempers were stretched beyond a certain point. The two were both of Scottish descent, and the human chemistry between them, over the years, may have added more than a few gray hairs.[586] Wilson probably left Hines when she had endured his lackadaisical business practices long enough. She probably also surmised that Hines's inefficient office conditions, as she saw them, would only get worse with time. He would never change his passive manner of running his business. She may have concurred with Clarence Welch's assessment that Hines's business was only a highly successful hobby.[587] Although Sara Meeks did not get to know Mrs. Wilson very well, she remembered the older woman as "maybe a little pushy. She felt her importance. At least that was the way the young girls who were working there felt toward her." Although Mrs. Wilson was very kind to them, Meeks added that, "I felt like there was friction at one point between she and Mr. Hines and Mrs. Hines. I felt like her days were numbered, and evidently they were."[588] That may very well have been the sentiment in the office at the time, but it is contradicted by those who knew Edith Wilson in her later years. Until the day she died (30 September 1993)[589] she had nothing but complimentary things to say about Hines—and especially about Clara; she was always very proud that she had once been employed by Duncan Hines.[590]

Although Hines was suddenly without an office manager, he assumed he could find a replacement without any trouble. But in this case he was wrong. Over the next few months looking for an office manager to replace Mrs. Wilson proved to be a frustrating experience, and it ultimately led to his handing over his entire business operation to Roy Park. At first, everything looked rosy. In February 1952, eight months after Edith Wilson left for greener pastures, Hines replaced her with another office manager, a young man named Donald H. Molesworth, who had been recommended to him by acquaintances who thought very highly of his organizational and business skills. Molesworth, he was told, was the one who would increase sales and transform his office staff into a crackerjack operation.

Not long after Molesworth had been hired, he began earning his keep by firing several of Hines's employees, who, in his estimation, were not worthy of a paycheck. In March 1952 Molesworth fired a woman who had been serving as the office stenographer. In her place, he hired nineteen-year-old Wanda Richey, a young woman who had graduated from high school a year earlier. On her first day on the job, Richey was surprised that her office companions were approximately her own age; she had expected the staff to be much older. Her new friends and co-workers were Sara Meeks and Mary Jo Agee, among others. Over the next month or so, Molesworth continued hiring and firing other secretaries until he settled on an office crew he believed to be reliable. When he fired the office's billing clerk, he gave the job to Richey. A few days later, he asked Mary Jo Agee to take Richey's place as stenographer.

As billing clerk, Richey's job was "to bill the people we shipped the books to." The only other job Richey was required to do was take dictation when Meeks was out of the office. At first she felt intimidated at the prospect of taking dictation from a famous man like Duncan Hines, but the first time he asked her to come into his office for a dictation session, he went out of his way to make her feel comfortable. As Mary Herndon had discovered, so now did Richey: taking dictation from Hines was quite an experience; no one in secretarial school had ever prepared her for such colorful expressions. Overall, though, she enjoyed the five months she worked for him, offering that he "was not hard to work for" at all. Richey left Hines for another job in August 1952. When the day came to tell him the news of her imminent departure, she dreaded the experience. She thought he might chew her out. But when she went into his office to tell him of her decision to leave, he surprised her with his thoughtful understanding, and as she walked out the door that afternoon, his blessing "left a very good impression."[591]

Donald Molesworth, on the other hand, did not even attempt to make a good impression. His co-workers hated him. Molesworth, who was in his late twenties or early thirties, was by all accounts, an attractive young man who let it be known that from now on he ruled the roost.[592] And he crassly reminded everyone that he had Hines's blessing to run Adventures in Good Eating, Inc. as he saw fit. "I don't think he went over with any of us very well," said Mary Herndon. "I was not impressed."[593] None of those under his thumb could stand his arrogant, overbearing manner. Meeks said that one day "he came in," and announced that "he was our boss" and let them know it in no uncertain terms. Molesworth's personality notwithstanding, for a time he had the run of the place and forcefully took charge of the company's day-to-day operations. So confident was Hines in the young man's abilities that he even gave him a company car, which, said Meeks, "was really something in those days. You didn't hear of a company car that often." For a while Hines was very happy with Molesworth. The young man was bringing in plenty of new business. But one day in June, after only four months on the job, Hines abruptly fired him and angrily told him never to set foot in his office again. The cause of the rift was probably ignited when Hines inspected the company car that Molesworth was driving and discovered candy wrappers and "other things" in the floorboard that made him wonder if his company car was being used for recreational rather than business purposes.[594]

J. T. "Top" Orendorf, who usually served as Hines's Bowling Green attorney, was in his office the following day when Molesworth came to see him. Orendorf had been expecting this meeting. Upon his arrival in Bowling Green, Molesworth had consulted with him, and asked Orendorf for advice on the pros and cons of working for Hines. The lawyer told the young man that while it was not generally well known outside Bowling Green, Duncan Hines's temperament could on occasion "flare up from time to time," particularly as he got older. Orendorf advised Molesworth that he had better protect himself, just in case his employment became an incompatible affair. Molesworth followed the lawyer's advice and got a written three-year contract outlining the terms of his employment. Hines thoroughly trusted the judgment of the party who had recommended Molesworth, so he eagerly signed the document the young man shoved under his nose. Now Molesworth sat before Orendorf, astonished, suddenly without a job, wondering what to do about it.

Orendorf wrote Hines with regard to Molesworth's predicament. He also talked to Hines's certified public accountant, Cecil "Hoot" Holland, who kept possession of all his bookkeeping records. Orendorf said, "Hoot, I've got this lawsuit, and I have to know in this lawsuit what happened to the business after this young man went there." After examining the books, Orendorf concluded that Hines could not defend Molesworth's firing on the grounds that he caused Hines to lose business; nor could Hines use the argument that Molesworth was inefficient; on the contrary, every indication showed that he had increased sales perceptively; in fact, in the short time he had worked for Hines, sales had doubled. After looking at the figures, Orendorf could only conclude that Molesworth "was a fine salesman" and that Hines had no grounds for firing him. Orendorf attempted to discuss the matter, but Hines "just blew up" saying Molesworth was "no count" and refused to talk about it. His mind was made up. Molesworth was not going to work for him—contract or no contract. "As a last resort," on 23 June 1952, Orendorf filed a lawsuit against Hines in federal court. Since Hines's usual attorney was on the other side of the argument this time, he hired Bowling Green's G. D. Milliken, Jr. to defend him.[595] On 13 November 1952, a jury trial was held. The case could not be tried in a Kentucky court, because Hines's business had originally been incorporated in Illinois, so the trial was held in Federal court in Bowling Green. All current and former employees who had worked for Hines during Molesworth's tenure were summoned to testify at the jury trial, which began at 9:00 A.M. that morning and was resolved the same day.[596]

During the course of the trial Milliken, acting on Hines's behalf, repeatedly tried to demonstrate the things that Molesworth had not done well.[597] Milliken contended that Molesworth had methodically changed the structure of Hines's office to the point that it was unrecognizable to his employer. All Hines wanted in an office manager was someone to maintain the structure he had created—and make it run smoothly; he did not need to employ someone who was anxious to tear it apart, even if it was at times inefficient.[598] Sara Meeks, like the other employees who had worked under Molesworth, had to testify against him. "I was supposed to testify that this man did not do a good job…and I remember that when I came off the stand, Mr. Hines looked at me," nodded his head approvingly, and said softly 'good job.' "He was happy with what I had said."[599] The definitive moment during the day-long trial came when Hines's own accountant, Cecil "Hoot" Holland, took the witness stand and testified that, based on the company's bookkeeping, Hines's business had prospered during Molesworth's tenure.[600] Toward the end of the day the jury returned their verdict in favor of Molesworth. To put the contentious proceedings to rest, an order of satisfaction was filed in court six days later by both parties on 19 November 1952. In the end, Hines was ordered to pay Molesworth (who, by the time of the trial, had moved to Westminster, Maryland)[601] a sum of $8,850,[602] a considerable figure by 1952 standards. Despite his financial loss, Hines was glad the trial was over. Said Meeks, "He was so happy to get rid of [Molesworth] that he didn't care what he had to pay him."[603]

Thanks to Edith Wilson's inauguration of a sensible work arrangement for Hines's operation in the mid-1940s, by 1950 there were four employees working for Hines at all times, although sometimes their duties would overlap. Their desks were arranged in a circle in the middle of the office. Since the area where they worked was not large enough for Hines to have his own office, he spent much of his time in the building's adjacent living quarters. There he worked through the morning, ate his noonday meal in the kitchen, took his ritual afternoon nap, which lasted until about 2:00 P.M., and worked some more until 5:00 P.M., when everyone went home.[604]

Although his employees worked hard for Hines and were not disloyal to him, they did draw the line in one respect. Hines revered the cooking skills of his black maid, Myrtle Potter, and so gave her free rein in their kitchen. Each day Mrs. Potter ensconced herself in their kitchen, preparing new concoctions for the noonday meal. More often than not his employees were the beneficiaries of these sumptuous, sometimes spectacular meals, usually compliments of Clara. Unfortunately, their palates were used to plain, home-cooked country food. The culinary gifts Clara proffered were sometimes so rich they could not finish them—and sometimes could not swallow them. As a result, they stealthily flushed many a meal down the toilet. They did not want to hurt the Hines's feelings, so they always said they immensely enjoyed the food. "They liked different foods than we did," said Sara Meeks. "They were used to these gourmet foods, and we were used to country cooking, like peach cobbler and chocolate cake, but when it came to all these tortes and things like that, we didn't know what to think of it."[605] Mary Herndon, who also did her share of flushing, added that "they used a lot of liquor in some of the recipes...and neither Sara Jane nor I were not very fond of that taste. So I guess we told a few white lies from time to time. If we didn't have time to flush it down the toilet, [the food] got shoved into our desk drawers real quickly, and we hoped that Mr. Hines wouldn't have us get something out while he was standing over our shoulder." Sometimes, "as soon as we'd taste it in front of him, we'd race each other to the toilet as soon as he went out the door. We'd enjoy some of it, too," but some of their samples, particularly the desserts, were so laden with alcohol they dared not strike a match in the bathroom for fear the toilet bowl would burst into flames.[606]

18

PASSING THE TORCH

One of the many companies licensed to sell Duncan Hines products was Nebraska Consolidated Mills, Inc. The company was primarily a flour milling operation with little experience in consumer marketing. That quickly changed. Under the able leadership of Allan Mactier, the company's ambitious 32-year-old president,[607] Nebraska Consolidated worked out a satisfactory franchise agreement with Roy Park to sell flour-based products. A few months after the contract was signed, the small milling company began producing sixteen different kinds of cake and specialty mixes.[608] Headquartered in Omaha, the company operated mills in four Nebraska cities, and one in Decatur, Alabama. After more than a year of laboratory and consumer testing, they introduced the Duncan Hines Cake Mixes in Nebraska and Iowa on 26 June 1951. In the winter of 1952 Nebraska Consolidated launched Duncan Hines Buttermilk Pancake Mix; in April 1953 it was followed with Duncan Hines Blueberry Muffin Mix. "All mix recipes were developed in Nebraska Consolidated's kitchens, with the help and supervision of Duncan Hines and his staff."[609] While other mixes had been marketed as "just add water or milk" convenience items, the new company altered the formula: they left in the dried milk and disposed with the dehydrated eggs.[610] Using

Hines's name proved a boon to the new enterprise: three weeks after the Duncan Hines cake mixes were introduced in supermarkets in Omaha, Nebraska, the product captured 48 percent of the cake mix market.[611] If Roy Park ever worried about his company's future, his thoughts of failure vanished after this success. From that point forward, Hines-Park Foods, to use Park's apt word, "snowballed."[612]

Products from Hines-Park were not at first widely available; initially, they were found only in supermarkets in selected cities. But once the company managed to firmly ensconce its products on supermarket shelves in targeted markets, it expanded to other geographical sections. For a variety of reasons, Park believed it the wiser strategy to infiltrate the nation's supermarkets methodically rather than blanket the country with its products. His strategy proved sound, for in time most of them, particularly the cake mixes, began to catch on with the public through the best advertisement of all: word-of-mouth.

The best test of the public's approval of the cake mixes was at the cash register. In mid-1952 Nebraska Consolidated Mills reported on its sales in Iowa and Nebraska: "All the Hinky-Dinky Stores ran out.... Safeway ran out during the afternoon, too, so we set out with two five-ton trucks and delivered 389 cases directly to the seventeen Safeway Stores in Omaha and Council Bluffs." Within the next few months the plant delivered to supermarkets in these two states over 10,000 cases of Duncan Hines cake mix. That spring Hines-Park arranged to make their products available in the South. As in other states, housewives rushed to the supermarket to buy them. The cake mixes out-performed all other products. For example, on the first day that they were available in Bowling Green, Kentucky, one store's entire supply of 1,400 packages was exhausted in just a few hours. The same phenomenon was replicated in grocery stores across the country. Everyone, it seemed, had to sample the latest Duncan Hines product.

Meanwhile, sales for Duncan Hines Ice Cream were going through the roof. By December 1951 ninety-five plants in locations from Los Angeles to Boston churned out nearly 3 million cartons

of the expensive dessert each month, and there seemed to be no
end to the public's appetite for it.[613] By early 1952 the rich,
flavorful dairy product was available in 39 states.[614] The company's
fortunes were further sweetened in July 1952 when the Duncan
Hines ice cream bar was made available.[615]

By the end of 1951 Hines-Park had approved 165 different products from 120 food producers. The array of food Hines endorsed
included twenty jams and jellies, eighteen jars of pickles, three
types of mushrooms, and eleven ice cream toppings.[616] The company's product line-up also included fruit sherbet, salad dressing,
ketchup, steak sauce, Worcester sauce, chili sauce, and sea food
sauce. There was also a Duncan Hines Bread, which first appeared
on supermarket shelves on 6 May 1952. Each loaf sold for about 25
cents, and it soon became one of the company's better sellers;
much credit to its success was due in part to its recipe of un-
bleached flour, honey (instead of sugar), and plenty of milk.[617]
Hines said that if a list could be compiled of his three-year-old
company's products it would become dated before the print was
dry. In a short time the firm's strategic and organizational efforts in
placing and marketing its merchandise were successful enough to
make the rest of the food industry take notice.[618]

When a grocery store customer bought a box or can from
Hines-Park's product line-up, his decision was often influenced by
Ag Research, Hines-Park's advertising arm. In 1949 Ag Research's
advertising budget was only $10,000; by 1952 that figure had
climbed to over $1,000,000.[619] But advertising alone could not
account for the firms's spectacular sales. This was proved when L.
W. Hitchcock of the James H. Black Co. reported to Hines-Park
executives of an experiment he conducted in Chicago. With the cooperation of a Chicago food distributor and several grocery stores
it supplied, Hitchcock put Duncan Hines salad dressing on
supermarket shelves to see if anyone would buy it based on the
strength of Hines's name. For five weeks there was "no advertising,
store signs, no promotion of any kind." The results were
phenomenal. No matter where the salad dressing was displayed,
supermarkets quickly sold all available stock. When it was later

advertised in Chicago, Milwaukee and Minneapolis, supermarkets sold almost 9,000 cases in a few days.[620]

To promote the introduction of the company's cake mixes, Roy Park put his best salesperson to work. Duncan Hines, with Clara at his side, journeyed across America on a public relations campaign to let the American public know what was waiting for them on supermarket shelves. As a pure public relations ploy, Park arranged for several cities and small towns to celebrate "Duncan Hines Day" or "Duncan Hines Week," each of which was highlighted by an appearance by his famous partner.[621] These promotional appearances were punctuated by scores of color newspaper advertisements as well as Hines's appearances on radio and television. Throughout the promotional tour, when he was not entertaining a bevy of reporters, Duncan Hines was being hailed as a ceremonial guest of honor in dozens of cities across the country. During these public tributes to his integrity and character, Hines was often given the key to the city or an equivalent honor as he stood in front of a supermarket where his company's cake mixes were on sale.[622] He was on the road nearly every day, or so it seemed. His schedule would have exhausted most men his age, but Hines never complained; he was the center of attention and reveled in it.

By 1953 three flavors from the Duncan Hines line-up—white, yellow and devil's food—had captured ten percent of the national cake mix market. Earlier that year Hines-Park Foods had "brought out other Duncan Hines mixes—for pancakes and waffles, gingerbread and muffins." All sold very well. One year later, in the summer of 1954, according to a survey taken in the Southern states for *Progressive Farmer* magazine, "the Duncan Hines cake mixes ranked fourth behind Aunt Jemima, Pillsbury and Swansdown, and the pancake mix was fourth behind Aunt Jemima, Pillsbury and Ballard's. In the Spokane market, Duncan Hines cake mixes were now "third behind Betty Crocker and Pillsbury, while the muffin mix" was first. A Fort Wayne, Indiana, market survey, released in October 1954, revealed the Duncan Hines cake mixes to be "ahead of all other brands." When the cake mixes were introduced in Des

Moines, Iowa in 1951, within months they had garnered 26% of the market; by 1954 they had snared 41% of it.

The Duncan Hines brand changed the way housewives perceived cake mix preparation, and its introduction stirred up the industry. "When they originally appeared on the market," reported *Advertising Age* in an article reviewing the brand name's spreading popularity, cake "mixes were promoted mainly as a convenience product." Housewives who bought a box were expected to follow the printed instructions: "Just add water and pop in the oven.... The Duncan Hines mix turned the tables on the established brands by telling the housewife to add two fresh eggs as well as water." Adding authority to the product, the cake mix package carried a picture of Duncan Hines next to his statement: "I have found that strictly fresh eggs mean a bigger, better cake...in appearance, flavor and freshness." This approach to manufacturing cake mixes attracted an increasing number of consumers and was soon copied by other food production firms.

By the mid-1950s the objective that Roy Park had originally set out to accomplish—to create a product people would respect and enthusiastically purchase regardless of its price—had largely been met. When asked about his success, Park explained that marketing "quality" was a sound selling approach, "because it recognizes the desire and ambition of every American to move up toward a higher standard of living. It's not enough...to stress nutritional values. Food has tremendous possibilities for glamorizing, and we should sell all the joys that go with good eating."[623]

As Hines-Park Foods was expanding, Duncan Hines's life was taking all sorts of interesting turns. In October 1952 he began appearing regularly on network radio with Roy Park. According to one newspaper account, Hines inaugurated "a five-day-a-week radio show over the Mutual Network," the purpose of which was "to feature chats about good food, where to find it, and where to spend the night after you have eaten it."[624] Meanwhile, Hines was honored on Broadway, when his persona was acknowledged in *Guys and Dolls* in the song "If I Were a Bell." He even had a horse race named after him: Omaha's "Duncan Hines purse." None of this publicity hurt his syndicated newspaper column which by November 1951 could be read in 100 newspapers around the country with a combined circulation of 20,000,000.[625]

In the summer of 1953 Adventures in Good Eating, Inc., was overhauled. The change came when Hines finally concluded he was no longer physically able to maintain his hectic pace of life. While he had been looking for a capable person to manage his business, in the end he turned to Roy Park, who had no qualms about operating it. Running it was the least he could do for the person who had helped make him a wealthy man. Of course, because Hines-Park was located in Ithaca, Park could not operate it from Bowling Green. Therefore, on 29 July 1953,[626] Adventures in Good Eating, Inc. was relocated to Ithaca, New York, and reconstituted as the Duncan Hines Institute with Roy Park as its president.[627] The institute's activities included not only publishing the guidebooks and cookbook but also leasing the famous "Recommended by Duncan Hines" signs.[628] In early 1954, six months after Park had staffed his Ithaca organization and assigned them specific duties, Hines relinquished his daily responsibilities. In his hands, Hines was sure, Adventures in Good Eating, Inc. would continue serving the public responsibly. The new books still retained Hines as its "editor-in-chief," but the older man had almost nothing to do with the final product.[629] Park hired his own "dinner detectives" to uncover America's best dining experiences. Each "detective" was given a territory to cover, and as a team they inspected the growing number of listings that kept filling the guidebooks' pages. Their number eventually totaled thirty-seven individuals armed with notebooks that read "Duncan Hines Sent Me." They did efficient, excellent work, but they were not cut from the same cloth as those that worked with Hines. They were more or less products of man-in-the-gray-flannel-suit-America who did not become giddy, as had their predecessors, over finding a restaurant that served "real" mashed potatoes.[630]

Nevertheless, with characteristic thoroughness and profession-alism, Park spared nothing on his new endeavor. His "conception of what the guidebooks should encompass outstripped anything

Duncan Hines alone had been able to accomplish."[631] Regular purchasers of *Adventures in Good Eating* could detect a difference as soon as they laid eyes upon the new edition. Unlike the plain, bright red books Hines produced, the new version was a multi-colored, modern-looking affair that featured a happy family of four dining within the atmospheric confines of luxury and splendor.[632] As editor-in-chief, Park wrote the introductions to each guidebook. Toward the end of his remarks, he added that the Duncan Hines Institute's three guidebooks now listed a combined total of over 10,000 eating and sleeping establishments. Park closed with a subject dear to Hines's heart: restaurant cleanliness. "Nothing is more important than cleanliness," wrote Park. "The sanitary conditions under which food is prepared, cooked and served are important in promoting and safeguarding your health." In a bow to Hines's influential crusade over the past two decades, he wrote that in recent years, "many laws have been passed in states all over the nation to safeguard the public's health." As Hines did before him, Park warned readers that "people eating out should give sufficient thought to the kitchen of a public eating place...rather than be guided solely by chromium fronts and attractive interior decorations."[633]

Another aspect regular purchasers of *Adventures in Good Eating* noticed about the new book was that it was made of cheaper material. Gone was the sturdy, high quality publication Hines had created. It was now a paperback book, one that could easily fall apart after a year's use. Gone also were the spacious margins large enough to write notes alongside the restaurants in question; now the listings were tightly packed. Also, while guidebook buyers certainly had more entries than ever from which to choose, they were also hard to read. The biggest void in the new editions, however, was the pleasure in reading it. Park replaced Hines's folksy writing style with one that was sparse, business-like, and to the point, mainly because, at a still static price of $1.50 and an ever expanding number of listings, it had to be. While the new guidebooks lacked Hines's special sparkle, blame for the compact look and their curt, terse style should not go to Roy Park; rather, it should go to Hines. Thanks to him, among other extenuating factors, by 1955 there were so many good restaurants and quality lodgings from which to choose that Park found it increasingly difficult to compress all his information in a single volume.[634]

While the abundance of fine restaurants and quality lodgings was now Park's headache, not Hines, the famed eater did not slow down too much. At age 74 he had a lot of life left in him, and he put it to good use as the roving ambassador for the Duncan Hines Institute. Radio and television appearances between restaurant meals began to occupy more of his busy schedule. And he was still entertaining to read about. One day in January 1954 Hines told his local newspaper about his problems with the department of agriculture. Possibly because he resided in the countryside, census takers had listed his occupation as that of "farmer." Because of this unwanted classification, for several years the department had been sending him, in his words, "enough literature on crop raising to satisfy half of Kansas." Exasperated by this waste of paper, he told the census takers that the only things that grew on his property were weeds.[635]

Throughout 1954 the reading public saw plenty of Duncan Hines, perhaps more than they had in the previous five years combined. He seemed to be featured either on the cover or within the pages of every major publication in the country. As the year began, he and Clara were the subjects of the 12 January edition of *Look*, the popular, pictorial weekly newsmagazine. In this extensive piece, Hines revealed his choices for what he believed were the ten best motels in America. The genesis for the piece came in the early fall of 1953, when *Look* asked him for help on a piece about motels designed for the traveling public. With the prospect of 40 million vacationing Americans traveling across their nation that summer by car instead of the traditional way—which before the Second World War was by train—*Look* magazine felt that readers needed guidance from a pre-eminent authority. The magazine pointed out that in the coming year a dwindling number of Americans would frequent hotels; they would instead be traversing the far reaches of the countryside in their new automobiles and would be miles away from large cities—and most hotels. Due to this development, consequently, more Americans than ever would be sleeping in the next best form of accommodation: motels. Times were changing, and that included types of accommo-dations. What better way to inform the public on where to stay, what to look for in a good motel, and which ones to avoid than to get such information from America's best known traveler, Duncan Hines, whose book, *Lodging for a Night,* listed over 3,000 potential places? Besides, if it was recommended by Duncan Hines, how could American travelers go wrong?

After thinking it over, Hines agreed to let one of the magazine's photographers follow him and his wife around on one of their cross-country tours of America, one that was to take them through 44 states. Hines picked a wide variety of motels for his *Look* article, "ranging from huge highway hotels to cozy overnight bungalows." His list was based on several factors, including cost, convenience, and hospitality. His ten best motels included: 1) *The El Rancho Grande* in Brownsville, Texas, which had such "luxuries as a swimming pool and room service." Hines also liked the fact that "warm food and cool beverages [were] delivered by bicycle." 2) *The Fort Humboldt Motel* in Eureka, California featured "home-like cottages and a folksy hospitality that includes furnishing the guests with radios." 3) *The Guest Ranch* in Cheyenne, Wyoming was an attractive, Western-styled motel that offered "private sitting porches where its guests" could "chat and relax." 4) Then there was *The Key* in Fort Wayne, Indiana. Hines liked this "million-dollar motor hotel" because it represented "the combined merits of a downtown city hotel and the economical conveniences and atmosphere of a country motel." 5) *The Yankee Traveler* in Plymouth, Massachusetts was a "contemporary Cape Cod-style motel" giving motorists in New England an opportunity to experience a chance to relax "in the true traditional hospitality of the early New England inns." 6) *Bacon's-by-the-Sea* in Fort Walton Beach, Florida was a "rustic motor inn" located on the sandy beaches of the Gulf of Mexico; one of its luxuries was a motorboat. 7) *Tourinns* in Wilmington, Delaware was an "ultramodern motel" that provided "living-room-type bedrooms" and even offered a special quarters for pets. 8) *Desert Caravan Inn* in Spokane, Washington was a "modern motor hotel...built in the midst of picturesque pines." 9) *The El Rancho* motel in Myrtle Beach, South Carolina was an "extensively landscaped motel" which faced 7 miles of beach and provided "women guests with gardenias in season." 10) *The Franciscan Motor Hotel* on North Highland Avenue in Hollywood, California had "a Hollywood swimming pool, with service and atmosphere to match."

Hines reminded his readers of how far the motel industry had come in two short decades. "In less than 20 years, a few scattered roadside cabins have multiplied to more than 40,000 motor courts.... Each year, about 2,000 new ones happily hang out their gleaming 'no vacancy' signs." The reason for their growth and the source of their popularity with tourists, said Hines, was not difficult to understand. "Motels, built on main highways, are easily accessible without the nuisance of city traffic. Cars parked conveniently near lodgings save bothersome trips for extra baggage and forgotten items. With no plush lobbies to dress up for, they stress informality." Another reason they were popular, particularly with adults traveling with children, was that they were affordable. Hines wrote, "As a rule, motels are less expensive than hotels because there is little or no tipping involved. However, as motel prices edge upward, more and more of them are relying on such sure-fire tourist attractions as swimming pools, air-conditioning, free television, children's playgrounds and running ice water to lure and lull the weary traveler."

Hines provided *Look*'s readers with updated instructions on how to pick a good motel. One tip was that "a neat and tidy outside appearance...[was] the best indication of clean rooms inside." He asked readers to note if the lawn and shrubbery had been cut, if the driveway was neat, and if the paint was fresh. Before checking in, he advised travelers to look "around to see if it is in a quiet location—far enough from the highway, railroads and noisy night spots—to enable" one to have a quiet rest. If the motel passed this test, there next came another barrier, the motel receptionist. A good indicator of whether a motel was worth staying in could be found in the behavior of the person at the reception desk. First impressions in any situation always the most important, and Hines pointed out how receptionists make or break a motel's business. "A courteous, pleasant receptionist," he wrote, "is an important indication that your stay will be a pleasant one. Don't hesitate to ask to see the room before signing the register. One glance at the room and its furnishings will tell more than the lengthiest assurances from the desk clerk."

If the receptionist hesitated, Hines's advice was to drive on. But if the receptionist showed a potential guest the room, Hines advised his readers to put it to the final—and ultimate—test: the inspection. Hines advised readers to check the furniture for dust, to inspect the bed sheets for cleanliness, to see if the bedsprings were adequate, and to make sure there were "plenty of good-sized towels" in the bathroom. He also suggested that one should not walk out of the room before being perfectly satisfied that plenty of hot and cold water was instantly available. He advised readers to check the "heating, ventilation and lighting facilities." Even windows had to be checked. "A screened window that can be raised and lowered easily," he wrote, "is always desirable—sometimes even with air conditioning." Rooms, he said, should also have "good-sized closets, extra hooks in the bathroom, [and] sufficient drawers." All, he insisted, were "assets of a better room." Lastly, there was the subject of safety. "Safety measures," he wrote, "such as inside locks on room doors, night watchmen and lights [that are] kept on all night are important for adequate protection." Nothing, it seemed, escaped his attention. These were his standards and, he implied, they should be his readers' as well.

Finally, Hines could not pass up a chance to comment on those motels which had dining facilities. If the food looked and smelled good, he said, proceed further. He informed his readers to "use your eyes for such small details as clean catsup bottles and covered sugar bowls. They often reveal kitchen conditions." Hines concluded the Look article by instructing his readers in the ways of becoming "a good motel guest." To do that, Hines wrote, "follow the four rules of the road—courtesy, caution, compliance and common sense." He had traveled in excess of 2 million miles, he said, and so far those rules had worked for him magnificently.[636]

Hines accumulated much credibility within the motel industry. Some years earlier, around 1946-1948, he had been approached by a group of highly reputable stockholders who had the idea of opening a chain of Duncan Hines Motels. Hines thought it over for a while but "regretfully declined to join the venture." He felt that in doing so he would be getting away from his "original purpose of guiding people to the best places that were then already in existence."[637]

About this time the public began to learn of his most recent hobby. A few years earlier, in 1948, Hines began developing a new bit of business to entertain the press—and, later, television audiences. He would empty his pockets and show off his large collection of unusual wristwatches. Whenever he and Clara would go anywhere, he would arm himself with at least a dozen timepieces, almost all of which made some sort of noise, and entertain himself and anyone else for long stretches of time. His wrists were usually adorned with his prized timepieces such as his handsome gold watch, which was a duplicate of President Eisenhower's, or his "regulation pocket watch with a fob made from a $50 gold piece."[638] It was not uncommon for him to carry fourteen wristwatches on his person wherever he went. While most of these devices were of modern design, one was 150 years old and was still in excellent operational condition.[639]

On his trips throughout the country Hines was constantly purchasing a new toy to play with, always a gadget of some kind, one which he was sure would also delight a friend or relative. He was enchanted by gadgets and acquired plenty of them. Their usual defining characteristic was their usefulness. Roy Park knew of his partner's watch hobby and made it a practice to give him a new one every year. One year Park sent Hines a watch with an alarm in it. As he tried it on, Hines made everyone laugh when he said that he was going to set its alarm off in church so the preacher would cut the sermon short.[640] A few months later, when a reporter from the

Louisville *Courier-Journal* interviewed him, Hines pulled from his pocket the watch with the $50 Mexican gold piece fob and thrust it into the reporter's face, saying with characteristic humor, "This one is handy in case my wife takes all my money, so I'd still have the price of a hamburger for two." Showing off his wrist watches, the alarms of which could sound off not only every hour but every fifteen minutes, he said as he pulled them from his left coat pocket, "These alarm watches sometimes come in handy. I can always set one or the other of them to go off and remind me of an important appointment any time an encyclopedia salesperson gets about ready to pin me down."[641]

Still a child at heart, Hines sometimes played practical jokes. He was known to bring home from his travels little gifts for his employees. On one occasion, however, one of these jokes did not particularly amuse them. A few days earlier while he was in Chicago's Marshall Field department store, he spotted a can of "French-fried Mexican agave worms." They were expensive, at two dollars per can. He ordered a couple of units and sent them to Bowling Green. Later, when he returned home, he opened the worm-filled containers, nicely arranged the edibles on a silver tray, and offered them to his employees. "They looked like big matches that cowboys use," he said. "I told the girls in the office that it was a delicacy from France—and they ate them like candy—they loved them. Two days later I showed them the can—and they wanted to kill me. It was just the name. As long as they didn't know what it was, they liked it."[642]

19

DUNCAN HINES GOES TO EUROPE

In the spring of 1954 Hines and Clara went to Europe for the first time, accompanied by their close friend, Nelle Palmer, the operator of the Lowell Inn in Stillwater, Minnesota.[643] It was a "just for fun" trip, Hines told reporters as he prepared for his excursion,[644] adding that he was not going to spend his time hanging around "crumbling castles or stuffy museums." Instead, he said, "I want to see everything that is new and modern, including a few watch factories in Switzerland!"[645] He and Clara took a train from Bowling Green to New York City, where they were met by Roy Park upon their arrival. Before heading off to Europe, however, Hines, Clara, Park, and a couple of reporters drove 30 miles into the New York countryside to dine in nearby Banksville. Their destination? La Cremaillere a la Campagne, a French restaurant owned and operated by Antoine Gilly in a 100-year-old home. As they headed toward their destination, Hines said with a wistful grin, "I can taste those cheese cigarettes of Antoine's right now. Heavy cream, egg yolks, grated Parmesan—"

"Duncan!" Clara blurted out, laughing, "Remember, you're supposed to be saving some space for Europe."

When the party arrived at La Cremaillere a la Campagne, Hines asked M. Gilly what restaurants in Paris he should investigate, remarking "that he was willing to try anything but snails." Later, in the middle of their feast, one reporter asked Clara if her husband was a fussy eater. "Not at all!" exclaimed Hines, answering the question for his wife as he reached out to help himself to another cheese cigarette. "Take breakfast," he said playfully but with a straight face, "One of my favorite breakfasts is ice cream and corn flakes. What could be simpler than that?"[646]

The Hines and Nelle Palmer set sail upon the French luxury liner *Liberte* for Paris on 8 April 1954. While on board they were treated to "floor shows, dancing, [an] orchestra, horse races, and bingo games." While playing bingo, Clara won 72,000 francs, or a little over $200. Later, the chef on the liner "gave the Hines a special dinner in their honor." The multi-course dinner was served over several hours in a very leisurely manner. The Hines dined on such delicacies as fresh Russian caviar; clear vegetable soup; lobster with an elegant, rich sauce; green asparagus with another rich sauce; broiled Porterhouse steak with the chef's own version of Hollandaise sauce; potatoes, which, in Hines's words, were "fixed up real fancy"; green vegetable salad topped with what Hines judged as "a super-duper dressing"; a souffle; assorted fruits; and a wine of a very good year. Hines was most impressed with the size of the asparagus; he recalled later that they were "served as whole spears and these spears were about eight inches around the base. They were either white, green, or green and white, tender from top to bottom and were served with delicious sauces. To eat them you dip an asparagus spear in the sauce and bite off a chunk and repeat until all is eaten, and it's quite a feat to eat them and not dribble the sauce on your face."

At Captain Jacques Leveque's orders, the crew gave their honored guests a grand tour of the ship. They let Hines linger at great length in the ship's kitchen, or galley, where the master food critic found waiting for his inspection thirty-six "varieties of cheeses, eight kinds of fresh fruits and all kinds of fresh vegetables." Hines especially appreciated the fact that "when chicken was on the menu, the first-class passengers were served French chickens, which are smaller but plumper than the American variety"; they also had, he said, "a more delicate flavor." Another observation that pleased Hines was that the ship's cooks prepared their meals "entirely with butter—no lard or grease."

The manner in which his meals were served fascinated and delighted Hines. At the traditional ten-course "Captain's dinner," he noted that one course of the meal, fois gras or goose liver, was served with truffles from a huge platter, the center of which featured "a unique barnyard scene. The figures of the various animals," particularly the geese and the barn, "were made from a mixture of bread and lard, chilled and then painted.... The caviar was served from a boat carved from ice, and when time came for dessert, the cakes were served in lighted, colored, spun-sugar baskets."[647]

When the Hines and Mrs. Palmer disembarked in France at LeHavre, they almost hated to leave, but there was the whole European continent ahead of them, so they boarded a boat train for Paris. Once inside the city limits of the French capital, the threesome began exploring the French restaurants of the famed metropolis. As they had hoped, no matter where they ate, they found good food. "All of the French food," said Hines later, "was so wonderfully seasoned by the chefs that I never once reached for the salt or pepper during my stay in France." However, to his discomfort, he noticed that the French liberally poured more sauce on their food than he cared to witness.[648] The most memorable restaurant the threesome discovered during the next few days was the tiny Chez La Mere Michel, which specialized primarily in seafood; Hines swooned over their scallops.[649] He later said of the owner, Maud Michel, "I had fun with that old lady that runs that place. She brought out some real old brandy. I kissed her on both cheeks and I got her around the waist and give her a slap and she said, 'Oh, you're a nice man.'"[650]

Next the Hines and Mrs. Palmer dined at the Plaza Athenee, an elegant restaurant where they were the luncheon guests of George Marin. At this meal they savored the culinary joys of "melon with Bayonne ham, (thin, sliced raw ham),[651] Turbot souffle, roast chicken with green beans and peas, fresh strawberries and pink champagne." At the small but intimate Relais de Porqueralles, "they feasted on the famous bouillabaisse, made of all sorts of fish lobster, crab, mussels and shrimp and served, from a huge platter, with a thin fish soup." Their greatest meal of the day came later at Laperrouse, where they dined on "duck and chicken, cooked with herb sauces."

A day or so later Hines was the guest of honor at a nearly five hour luncheon in which he was made a member of the Parisian society of Cercle des Tourists Gastronomes. At this dinner, he and Clara were served large portions of "fresh truffles in pastry shells, broiled sole, roast duck with browned new potatoes and green peas, fresh strawberries on ice cream with spun sugar cookies," or what the French prefer to call sweet biscuits.[652] Hines enthusiastically approved of the manner in which the French consumed their meals. "Eating, to your Frenchman," said Hines, "is not just a way of appeasing his hunger, but a gustatory experience. Each course—indeed, each mouthful—is savored and thoroughly enjoyed before he passes on to the next." There was no bolting and beating it here. Hines was also greatly impressed by the attention that French restaurateurs paid to keeping their restaurants clean. "For example," he observed, "as soon as there is a speck of ash in an ash tray, the tray is whisked away and replaced by a clean one."

However, if the indoor restaurants of Paris gladdened Hines's heart, the ones on the city's sidewalks did not. "The famous sidewalk cafes were a disappointment to us," said Hines later.

We'd looked forward eagerly to dining under the gay umbrellas and watching the *boulevardiers* and *demimondes* of Paris walking up and down, but alas for romance. A horde of flies, gnats, and other bugs that I couldn't identify swarmed over us and our table, and our sparkling bon mots were lost in the cacophony of sound the like of which I'd never heard. Every automobile in Paris seemed to have two horns and no muffler. Nell[e] and Clara shouted at me, I shouted at Nell[e] and Clara, and we all shouted at the waiter. We ate inside for the rest of the trip.[653]

Once outside of Paris, they quickly forgot the city's congested turmoil. In fact, they grew quite fond of everything they encountered. While the Hines and Mrs. Palmer spent a little time between meals visiting the usual tourist attractions that Americans frequent, they primarily concentrated their energies on eating the rich food for which French cooks are so famous. For the most part, they avoided eating establishments that were well known to American tourists in favor of the small, native restaurants "where unusual food was to be found."[654]

After exploring the French countryside for several days, they crossed the French border into Belgium, where they made their way to Brussels and to L'epaule de Mouton, a restaurant well off the beaten tourist path. The restaurant, founded in 1660, still seated only twenty-eight persons, but it was, they discovered, well worth the trip. The restaurant's staff of four prepared and brought to their table "smoked ham from [the] Ardennes forest, consomme of black cherries, lobster bisque, filet cooked with white wine and tarragon sauce, chicken 'flamed' at the table, [and] veal with cream sauce." While in Brussels "they were met...by Paul Hebert, their driver from the travel agency in London, and a Humber Pullman limousine, by whom and in which they were driven during their remaining tour of the continent." When they arrived in Amsterdam a day or so later, they dined on rijistafel, a rice-based Indonesian meal, in a Balinese restaurant. They also seated themselves at the table of one of Europe's famous restaurants, an establishment that had been in continuous operation since 1300 and had been located in the present building since 1627; amazingly, it had become a mecca for foreign tourists, even though it sported the unappetizing name of "The Five Flies."[655] The trio also dined at the Lido, which served 300 patrons on four floors and employed 140 persons, leaving a customer-employee ratio that guaranteed the finest in personal service. Though the food was marvelous and service spectacular, what most impressed Hines during his stay in the country was the dress of Belgium's waiters. He observed that, no matter where he went, all the Dutch waiters, wore "long, dark Prince Albert coats."[656]

From Belgium the threesome next crossed the border into Germany and soon descended upon Frankfurt, where they enjoyed "wonderful German sausages, both pork and beef," at Zum Gemalte Haus, a wine stube. There they also downed sizable portions of "German potato salad, pickled pork and sauerkraut."[657] This meal remained one of Hines's most memorable during the entire course of his vacation. He particularly liked "the pickled pork, the bratwurst, and the kartoffel-salad."[658] The stube served no bread, so Hines bought some from a peddler who entered the premises from the street "with loaves tucked under his arms."[659] Hines later said they were the best loaves of bread he had ever eaten anywhere.[660]

The next day the three journeyed to Heidelberg, where they lunched at the famous Zum Seppel or "student's inn." While they enjoyed the food, they were more entranced by the "rows upon rows of steins on the wall, bearing the coats-of-arms of the famous students who had eaten there—including Bismarck." They next traversed into the folds of the Black Forest, where "they lunched at a small inn on a mountain top and were introduced to the inn's specialty, *trout bleu*, (i.e., blue trout)." Said Hines later, "The trout are caught, slit open and cleaned and dropped into boiling water flavored with herbs. The fish is served, in a half-moon shape, complete with head, tail and fins and is a lovely shade of blue. If the fish doesn't turn blue, then it isn't fresh. The flavor is delicate and most delicious."[661] While their only culinary disappointment while visiting Germany was that they were unable to find a restaurant that served German pancakes, they had better luck in their next European country.[662]

The next day they crossed the border into Switzerland and thrilled to the country's "mountains and storybook houses." At the Stadt-und-Rathskeller in Lucerne, they encountered a new dining experience, the house specialty, cheese fondue. As he waited to be served this meal, Hines was told that this regional specialty was made from two different types of cheese. When it was set before him he noticed that the Swiss cheese treat was served along with a chafing dish filled with white wine; in his eyes this was truly a culinary adventure. Later he related how it was consumed: "They gave us long forks with which we speared squares of rye bread, which we swished around in the fondue, popped it into our mouths," and ate them. Later Hines learned of the traditional protocol that accompanied the eating of this dish: the person who let the bread fall from his fork had to pay for the dinners of the others in his party. "He probably pays the cleaning bill, too!" Hines cracked. After being alerted to this tradition, Hines later said he "didn't know he was so dexterous."[663]

The Hines and Mrs. Palmer next visited Lausanne's Ecole Hotelier, the world's oldest hotel school, which was first opened by the Swiss government and the Swiss Hotel Association in 1893; by 1954 it had graduated over 5,000 students.[664] Later, when they dined and lodged in Switzerland's Grand Hotel Victoria-Jungfrau, the Hines and Mrs. Palmer experienced new dining pleasures. They sunk their teeth into many wonderful treats during their stay, including "rice pudding (pureed) with candied fruits and sauce, apple fritters with vanilla sauce, strawberry fritters (whole fresh strawberries dipped in batter and then French fried)," and the "three filets"; the latter consisted of "beef with mushroom, pork with a slice of truffle, and veal with a slice of fois gras." Also delectable but unusual, in Hines's view, was the orange juice; it was made from "blood" oranges from Spain, which, he said, "was as red as tomato juice but very good."[665]

After having satiated themselves on the luxurious taste sensations of Switzerland's rich cuisine, they eventually set off for Italy. Before they arrived at the Italian border, however, they crossed into France again, stopping for a meal near Avignon, a city in the southeastern section of the country, near the confluence of the Rhone and Durance Rivers. Their driver took them 6 miles outside the city to the best restaurant they dined in during their entire European excursion: Le Petite Auberge at Sauneterreonly, which had been operated by a retired insurance agent for the last five years.[666] Their meal began with hors d'oeuvres "which were out of this world," said Hines. Each hors d'oeuvre was served with its own sauce and swallowed, as Hines aptly put it, in "two bites." These scrumptious delicacies included "artichoke bottoms, tiny cooked onions, rice with Smyrna raisins and cumin, cooked fennel root, celery root with anchovy sauce, tiny beets, cooked mushrooms, chopped parsley and chervil, tiny tomato slices and tiny asparagus with shredded carrot." Finding the hors d'oeuvres to their liking, Hines and his party forged ahead to the next course, which consisted of "mussels fried in butter (almost a fritter), cockerel roasted over charcoal, veal kidneys, parfait with strawberry ice, coffee and mousse with ground nuts on top." As they headed for the next country on their agenda, the meal they consumed that day was one that would stay embedded in their treasure book of culinary memories for years to come.[667]

When they finally crossed over into Italy, the first city they pointed their limousine toward was Venice. Upon their arrival, Hines and Clara and Mrs. Palmer decided to first pay a visit to the American Consulate. But to their surprise, finding a comfortable route was a bit difficult. Since no motor launch was available to make the trip, Hines and his party had no choice but to ride in a gondola across Canal Street. At this, Hines objected. He firmly let it be known that he was not going to ride across town in a gondola, and that was that. However, after much coaxing by Clara, Hines relented, snorting all the while as he stood up in the craft, Venetian style. It had been raining just before they boarded their craft to make the "treacherous" crossing, the seats were wet, and Hines "was determined not to ruin a good suit of clothes. As a result he almost fell into the water."[668] Said Clara later, "He didn't fall out, but it was a touch-and-go proposition."[669]

While they tasted many types of Italian cookery during their tour of the country, Hines was dismayed with some of the fare they consumed. "I was mightily disappointed in the Italian spaghetti," Hines said later, because "it didn't have any oomph to it, no authority at all." While he did enjoy the ice cream and cookies he found in Italy, the country's coffee, he decided, he could do without. The Italian coffee, he said, "was strong, black, bitter, and almost thick enough to float a spoon. Half a cup at a meal was my limit." Hines later attributed his disappointment in some of the Italian cuisine to French chefs; the French food they had so recently consumed had "dulled" their appetites.[670]

The only bad meal Hines and his party encountered during their culinary adventure occurred in Venice, the day after their visit to the American consulate. While dining at what was reputed to be one of Venice's finest restaurants, they were served an assortment of appetizers. These consisted of "shrimp, crab and—baby octopus." Hines later told reporters that the baby octopus was "the snag" in his trip. The creatures, he observed, "had been cooked and [were] served cold with an oil dressing.... They resembled little rubber balls about an inch in diameter. I'm a great believer in eating regional delicacies and I've always advocated that course of action, but I never expected to be confronted by an octopus."[671] Hines said that inasmuch "as it was served intact with all its little feelers, head and big eyes, it was quite a task...to nibble on it."[672] Then, turning pale at the thought of the experience, Hines said the truth was that, when he put the octopus in his mouth, he just "couldn't choke the damn thing down."[673] Eventually he managed to "down one, and Clara ate two."[674] Rolling his eyes heavenward, he said, "I can't see why people would eat those crazy little octopus things unless they were intoxicated."[675]

From Italy, the threesome made their way back to London, England, where they stayed at the Savoy Hotel. Upon their arrival, "the 'red carpet' was rolled out for them by the institution's 1500 employees." Hines thought it marvelous that the hotel employed 92 chefs just to prepare for 300 guests. Perhaps one of the most pleasant meals of their trip came when the Savoy's chefs served them plate-loads of "English steak-and-kidney pie and excellent roast chicken." They also enjoyed the hotel's strawberries, and felt obligated "to sample the traditional British favorite, roast beef, and for that" they dined at "the world-famous Simpson's-on-the-Strand, where [a] white-coated chef carved it at [their] table."[676]

During their stay in London, the Hines and Mrs. Palmer also attended the Derby at Epsom Downs as guests of the Savoy management and were afforded the chance to see the Royal Family arrive in state. To return the favor of the wonderful reception the Savoy management had given them, Hines hosted what he termed a "Kentucky breakfast." Hines made arrangements to have a country ham flown over from the U. S., which, when served, was accompanied with red-eyed gravy, fried eggs and hot biscuits. The night before the breakfast was given, Clara "had to show the Savoy's French chef how to make the gravy and the biscuits,"[677] using the same recipe served at the John Marshall Hotel in Richmond, Virginia.[678] Despite her best efforts, Clara later remarked that while the biscuits were good, they "wouldn't have recognized their Kentucky cousins."[679] The only criticism they made of their stay in England was a trivial matter. Their room at the Savoy Hotel was a bit cool, said Hines, because "the British don't believe in sleeping in heated rooms."[680]

Soon afterward, the three sailed for America from Southhampton on the Queen Mary.[681] Hines was astonished at how much food the ocean liner carried to feed what amounted to a small city. He discovered that during the course of a single round trip voyage, the Queen Mary carried "thirty-five tons of meat, twelve and a half tons of poultry, six tons of potatoes, fifteen tons of poultry, six tons of fish, thirty tons of vegetables, 300 barrels of flour, six tons of sugar, a thousand crates of fresh fruit, 5000 quarts of milk, two tons of butter, and over four thousand quarts of ice cream. The china, glassware, and table silver total[ed] more than a half-million pieces". The three enjoyed their pleasant voyage across the Atlantic and were the featured guests of a cocktail party given by the staff captain on the Verandah Grill, a small dining room on the top deck, where they were served "consomme flavored with tarragon, filet of sole, excellent pressed duck, salad, and dessert."[682]

Hines and his party finally arrived in New York on 8 June 1954; they had been away from American shores for exactly two months. Upon his return to America, Hines was swamped by reporters. While most celebrities who return from Europe are asked about the sights, scenery and places they saw, the press corps neglected to do this; instead, all their questions to Hines were, in one form or another, "What did you eat in Europe and where did you eat it?"[683] After he checked into a hotel, Hines was more than happy to tell the press the details of his culinary adventures in Europe. While he enjoyed a double bourbon on the rocks in his suite at the Ambassador Hotel, Hines told reporters, "We had more fun than a case of monkeys, but I'll be durned glad when that train gets in tomorrow night and I get me some hot biscuits."[684]

When asked about his impressions of his first trip to Europe, Hines confessed to being a bit confused by the many customs he encountered. He recalled asking a waiter in Italy, "How the devil can you make coffee so lousy? If I drink this, I won't have to shave for four days. It'll stop all growth." He also recalled another cultural novelty—for him: eating cheese for breakfast in Holland. Then there was all that alcohol. Keeping in mind that he regarded alcohol primarily as a beverage to soothe the nerves on late afternoons or evenings, or as a beverage to be lightly consumed with certain dishes, Hines confessed to being "aghast" at the sight of German citizens openly quaffing beer. He also did not relish the prospect of seeing the natives of France starting their day with a glass of white wine.

As he related his experiences, he tended to dwell on the food he did not enjoy, especially the unappetizing fare he consumed in Italy. Hines then recounted his experience with highway robbery on the train ride he took from Florence to Venice. While enroute "he ordered three ham sandwiches, some oranges, and mineral water." He gave the vendor "1,500 of those Italian bucks," or about $2.40. Said Hines of this meal, "Why, [the size of] the ham in those sandwiches you could put in front of your glasses and still read the morning paper." He also did not like the butter he found in Europe; everywhere he dined, except for France, the butter tasted sweet. "I like a little oomph in my butter," he said, "so when the waiter wasn't looking, I just put some salt on it." The dinner hours were not to his liking, either. "People don't eat over there until ten o'clock in the night. Hell, I'm scared when it's dark. I want to go home."

Despite Hines's complaints, he had many positive things to say about his European trip. He liked the omelets in France, the desserts in Belgium, the rye bread in Baden-Baden, and the honey in the Black Forest. As stated earlier, Hines was surprised to find that there were no German pancakes in Germany and, while in Lucerne, he took note of the absence of pies, poundcake, and smoked sausages. Despite his disenchantment with Italian food, he confessed that he swooned over that country's noodles. Prodded a little further, he said that the ravioli was the best he had eaten in his life. Prodded still more, he said he had a special fondness for the rice and shrimp he ate in Venice, particularly because it was "the only garlic-seasoned dish" he was served while in Europe. Despite his dislike of the way the French and Germans so freely consumed their alcoholic beverages, he did approve of the way they approached food in general. "They don't beat it and bolt it over there," he said. He also approved of the way they kept their table knives sharp. "The knife is always as sharp as a razor, hence you never see anyone eating food off" the blade.[685] Overall, he said,

> My reaction to Europe is I should have tried it twenty years ago. Clara and I met some fine people over there. Their eating habits may be different from ours, but that doesn't necessarily mean they're worse. The same goes for their food.... People in Europe eat a lot of bread, and the bread is tasty. Beef, lamb, and chicken are good. Butter is good and unsalted. Asparagus is served in stalks about eight inches long and about three inches around the base. Generally, there's no drinking water on the table unless you order it by the bottle and pay extra for it. There's no bourbon in Europe, either, so I drank Scotch. Mrs. Hines tried what they call aperitifs.

Hines said that the most "delectable" dish he encountered on his tour of the European continent was something not served there at all but on the ocean liner Liberte: "tiny French peas. It was the seasoning that made them something to remember throughout my life in this and the next world." Later, commenting on the food he found in France, Hines said,

I found that the French were apt to use too much sauce on things. They'd douse it over meat in a way that would contaminate everything else on the plate. One lunch I went to in Paris started at one and ended at four-thirty. The squares of butter had flower decorations in red in the center. Jelly, but pretty. In Nice, the butter came in fluted ribbons, and we had five waiters serving our table. The coffee cups at breakfast held half as much again as our American cups. Wherever we went, I avoided ground up meats. Also, I was careful to see that the meat we did eat was thoroughly cooked. I wasn't going to take a chance on the raw flesh of some varmint I didn't even know the name of.[686]

He confessed that he did not appraise the European restaurants as severely as he did those in America, stating, coyly, that he restrained himself when he had an urge to visit a restaurant's back door "to see if they throw their garbage to the neighborhood dogs." His European restaurant tour was primarily charted, he said, by the advice given him from well-traveled friends, ones thoroughly trustworthy in matters of European gastronomy. When asked if he could read French, he said he could not, but that, when in doubt, he always asked the headwaiter what it was—a practice he had entreated Americans to exercise for the past two decades. It did not matter if Americans could not read the menu, he said. It "might have twenty-two letters and turn out to be gull. Matter of fact there were gull eggs on the menu of the Queen Elizabeth. If you're not sure of the cookin', order ham and eggs. And if the yoke don't stand up above the white like the morning sun, those eggs are no good, see?"

After displaying for the press the number of wristwatches he had strapped to his arms, he pulled out of his trouser pocket a new timepiece, a wristwatch he had bought in Switzerland that was made of glass on both sides and displayed a dozen wheels silently clicking away but bringing him the time. "Took two men three months to make this," he said. "Cost a bit, but it saves me money. I'm so dad-blamed busy winding these watches up I don't have time to buy drinks for some blamed redhead."

The conversation returned to food. Comparing the cuisine on the French and English ocean liners, Hines said that the "French spend so much time making it look pretty. On the English boats the food is very good, but they don't doll it up so." He parted with one last critique of France's food. "Over there the vegetables are swimming in sauce and you can't taste the flavor of the vegetables. Next time I go, I'm going to take me a little boat to put the sauce in."[687]

When all but one reporter had left, the moment Hines had been waiting for had finally arrived: his first meal in America after having been away from its cuisine for eight solid weeks. And Duncan Hines knew exactly what he wanted. He went to a nearby restaurant, sat down at a table, and consumed a hearty, robust meal of ham and eggs. It was the perfect way to end his trip.[688] Said Hines, with a wink, "I'd almost forgotten how good they can be!"[689]

20

WE DEDICATE THIS BOX...

In 1955 the Duncan Hines Institute published two volumes. The first was Duncan Hines' Dessert Book, a collection of Hines's favorite after-dinner recipes; it was followed later in the year by the ever-so-slightly autobiographical Duncan Hines' Food Odyssey.[690] The Dessert Book was a standard paperback book. As was Adventures in Good Cooking, the Dessert Book was compiled from recipes submitted by restaurants and Hines's many friends and family members. As was the case with the older book, blank areas were filled with household hints, suggestions, admonitions, and an assortment of Duncan Hines homilies. The book contained a total of 555 recipes, which made it a comprehensive range of sugary confections guaranteed to satisfy anyone with a craving for something sweet to eat.[691] The book was distributed through Pocket Books, a mass-market paperback publisher, and an initial print-run of 250,000 copies was ordered, thus enabling it to reach "a much broader cross section of the country" than Adventures in Good Cooking ever had. The volume is still a treasured volume in the libraries of hundreds of cooks.[692]

Later that year Duncan Hines' Food Odyssey hit bookstore shelves. Originally titled There's No Accounting For Tastes, it was touted as an autobiography; but with the exception of the first two chapters, there was little autobiography in it. A more appropriate title should have been *Duncan Hines' Travelogue*; the book, an entertaining read, was essentially a tour of the many restaurants Hines had visited over the years, accompanied by a short discussion of his recent activities with the Duncan Hines Institute.[693]

On 9 May 1955, at the 14th Annual Duncan Hines Family Dinner in Chicago, attended by approximately 300 members of his restaurant and lodging listings,[694] Hines predicted, presciently, that "by 1975 the average homemaker will spend an average of only 15 minutes a day [preparing food] in the home compared to the 90 minutes she spends today." [695] But he spent most of his time speaking at great length of his recent travels. He told the crowd that, earlier in the year, he and Clara had covered 10,000 miles in their automobile in three months. As they were driving through Texas, he said, they stopped in Beaumont. As was the case more often than not, it was not long before a newspaper reporter showed up. When Hines mentioned that he was on his way to Mexico, he was asked if he was carrying a pistol.

"NO!" Hines said, adding that he "would not know how to use one." Within twenty-four hours Beaumont's citizens presented him with a Stetson hat instead of a gun so he would not seem out of place upon his arrival. Hines liked the hat so much that he wore it during the entire time he was in the country and said that because of it, he had no trouble with the Mexican natives or anyone else.

While they were traveling through Mexico, he said that he and Clara had to watch what they put in their mouths. "In Mexico," he said, "we ate no unpeeled fruit and no uncooked vegetables, thus no illness." They encountered few unsatisfactory edibles during the course of his trip. On two occasions, however, they slipped up. At one forgotten spot on the map, they attempted to eat some frijoles—or Mexican beans. Said Hines, "I like beans, but what I was served had been pulverized and apparently mixed with axle grease, so I ate none. One taste was enough." Another time, in Metamoras, Mexico, just across the Rio Grande from Brownsville, Texas, he and Clara were invited by a friend to try Mexican quail at the Cucaracha Cafe, the name meaning Cockroach. When he saw it, Hines roared with laughter. "What a name for a restaurant!" Of the meal itself, he said that "the quail turned out to be our common black-bird. The breast was black as pitch." After their meal, he and Clara made no plans to return to the Cucaracha Cafe; being served blackbird had quenched their curiosity. Later, when they saw a billboard advertising the delights to be consumed at the Striped Skunk Restaurant, they did not even bother to stop—or slow down; they figured that, after consuming "Mexican quail," there was no telling what "regional favorite" that questionable restaurant would dump onto their dinner plates.[696]

Hines was a creature of habit. Although he enjoyed traveling, he did not like to upset his daily routines, and he could become quite annoyed if he could not fit his quotidian rituals into his schedule. One ritual he insisted on was going to bed at nine o'clock. When attending a dinner party while in the company of others and nearing the hour when his body demanded rest, he had several stratagems for getting to bed when he wished. One of these was to wear two or three different wristwatches on his arm, the alarm for each set a few seconds apart. Therefore, when he was seated at the dinner table and the hour was growing late, it was not unusual for one of his wristwatches to suddenly blast into action, making loud, disruptive, easily heard noises. When, moments later, another of his timepieces shattered the evening's congenial atmosphere, those in his party knew that he had something better to do.

On one occasion, while he was a guest on a radio program, Hines decided he did not care for the line of questioning. Therefore, as he spoke, he surreptitiously reached into his coat pocket full of watches. Suddenly, one of the wristwatch alarms began emitting an annoying, irritating sound. While the radio technicians turned numerous dials and flipped an army of switches in an effort to keep the cacophony off the air, Hines furiously turned the timepiece over and over in his hands and shook it as he pretended not to know how to turn it off. Within a few seconds his spot on the show was cut short and, as he had hoped, he was quickly dismissed by the show's host.[697]

Sales of Duncan Hines products continued to soar. Not only was Hines-Park, Inc. involved in marketing quality foodstuffs, it was also carving out a niche for itself in the food appliance arena; by the end of 1955 it had licensed over fifty kitchen items brandishing the Duncan Hines name, "from cooking ranges to a Duncan Hines coffee-maker."[698] In September 1955, speaking before the southern district of the Advertising Federation of America in Alabama, Roy Park reported that gross "sales of Duncan Hines foods at the retail level amount[ed] to about $50,000,000 a year," and proudly stated there were now over ninety licensed food manufacturers in the program "with advertising appropriations totaling approximately $3,000,000 annually."[699] He also told them about a year-old enterprise his company had inaugurated, the Duncan Hines Signet Club. Park described this as "a travel and credit service,...with some 50,000 members whose credit cards [were] honored by 2,300 Duncan Hines-recommended eating, lodging and vacation places in Canada, Mexico and points of interest in the Caribbean," as well as in the United States. Members could essentially "eat at the best restaurants" in America and "pay for their meals at the end of the month."[700] Hines liked the idea and wished something like it had been available fifty years earlier.[701]

As the end of 1955 rolled around, Duncan Hines had quite a bit to be proud of. Twenty years had passed since he had mailed that unique 1935 Christmas card to keep others from pestering him. As he dropped his cards in the mailbox, he had no idea what he was setting into motion. He had never wanted to be famous, let alone a public icon—although he certainly did not mind the adulation and attention he had since received. Initially, he had only wanted to give the public a publication they could use so they would stop irritating him with questions. Twenty years later his name was revered, respected and better known than most Americans. Over 100 million products bearing his name were now sold throughout the world. Sometimes, being irritated paid off.[702]

On 7 May 1956, at the annual Duncan Hines Family Dinner in the Grand Ball Room of Chicago's Sheraton Hotel, Hines remarked on his role in raising restaurant and lodging standards when he said, "You know, I have been called a crusader by some of my good friends in the press, radio and television. They are referring to my crusade for good food, good service and good accommodations. If what I have been doing is called a crusade, then I will continue to be a crusader." He would continue his crusade, he said. But just around the corner was an accolade that proved to be the ultimate honor, one that vaulted his fame far beyond that which he had already achieved and continues to this day.[703]

Three months later, on 17 August 1956 the Duncan Hines Institute and Hines-Park Foods announced their merger with the Procter & Gamble Company, a large corporation based in Cincinnati, Ohio, whose main product lines at the time were "soaps, detergents, drug products and shortenings."[704] Some months earlier, P&G had decided to expand its line of grocery products, specifically flour-based mixes, and chose to purchase Nebraska Consolidated Mills, which manufactured the Duncan Hines cake mix products. J. Allan Mactier, president of Nebraska Consolidated, announced that the corporate giant's direct purchase of his company included all research and production facilities, and that capital funds created by the sale would be used to continue the company's bakery flour and mixed-feed divisions.[705] Simultaneously, Procter and Gamble also announced it had acquired not only exclusive rights to use Duncan Hines's name but also, through an exchange of stock for an undisclosed price, both the Duncan Hines Institute and Hines-Park Foods, which Roy Park would continue operating from Ithaca as its president.[706] As part of the deal, Park became one of Procter & Gamble's vice-presidents, no doubt to protect his interests. The acquisition also included an agreement that P&G would not harm or hamper the smaller company's guidebook and credit card business.[707] Explaining his company's friendly acquisition, Procter and Gamble executive vice-president, Howard J. Morgens, said that "since housewives are showing an increasing interest in buying shortening already mixed with flour, sugar, and other ingredients, it seems quite logical for Procter and Gamble to extend its interest to prepared mix products."[708] Morgens added that the company was gratified by "Hines' confidence in the ability of Procter & Gamble to protect and extend the reputation of high quality foods which is associated with his name."[709] And P&G had big plans for that name; by the end of 1956 the corporate giant had introduced twelve mixes in their new line of Duncan Hines baking products: flapjack, buttermilk pancake, blueberry muffin, hot roll, yellow cake, spice and coffee cake, sponge cake, marble cake, white cake, angel food cake, burnt sugar cake, and fudge brownie.[710]

Although his organization was now a subsidiary of another company, Park continued working in Ithaca at the Duncan Hines Institute as if nothing had happened, overseeing, protecting and sanctioning all food products associated with the Duncan Hines name.[711] Publication of the guidebooks and the cookbook continued; at the end of 1956 *Adventures in Good Eating* was in its 49th printing; *Lodging for a Night* was in its 39th; *Adventures in Good Cooking* was about to be published for the 26th time; and *Duncan Hines Vacation Guide* was about to see its 11th revision.[712]

After Roy Park took control of his partner's book business, there was little left for Hines's employees to do; by the middle of 1954 they had found employment elsewhere. Only Sara Meeks was retained for her services, which mainly consisted of watching the office. Now that the sign business was being administered in Ithaca, she did not even have that to occupy her hours. Once Park took over, said Meeks, "there was nothing to do there except Mr. Hines' personal correspondence. And that's why I got to stay on, because he liked the way I did his letters, I guess." Hines and Clara, she said, still "traveled a lot.... Sometimes for two or three weeks. But he wanted someone to be in that office in case a visitor would stop by, and to take care of the mail, and answer the phone. And that was my job. It was very boring for a while, because I was there by myself all day." Although there was little to do, she dutifully came to work each day about eight in the morning and stayed until five that afternoon because, she said, "I was afraid he would call and check on me." Hines subscribed to various newspapers and a host of magazines. Taking advantage of her paid indolence, she sat at her desk and read.

When she took Hines's dictation and typed his correspondence, most of it consisted of personal matters he conducted with his many friends, including restaurant owners whose establishments he had recommended, as well as some of his former dinner detectives.[713] By the mid-1950s Hines's daily mail had declined a bit, down to 140 letters a day.[714] Perhaps the biggest daily chore she performed was sorting and collecting all letters pertaining to business now transacted in Ithaca. When Hines was home, he opened his own mail. If he could not answer a letter, said Meeks, and "didn't know what to do with it, or if it was anything that needed a reply, he'd say 'send this to Roy Park,' and we would have big envelopes going out to Roy Park" daily. Another of her duties was to plan his trips. This was fairly easy to plot out, because if the couple had nothing important scheduled, they seldom traveled more than 150 miles a day. If she needed anything while they were gone, John Henry Foster, the black custodian and groundskeeper, who lived in the little house on the property, was there to help. Foster also cut the grass, kept the property looking neat, and did all the odd jobs that required regular attention. If Meeks needed Foster to run an errand for her, which was a rare occasion, she would ring a farm bell to signal him to come into the office. Every now and then travelers would see the huge Duncan Hines sign in the front yard and stop by for a visit. "Oh, they would get so excited," she remembered. "They would come in and look around the office. He had a lot of pictures of himself and a lot of awards, and they just thought it was wonderful." After several months of genuine boredom, Meeks informed the Hines that she wanted to quit. They persuaded her to stay a while longer. A while longer turned out to be a few more years.[715]

Little evidence remains of Hines's daily activities after the Procter and Gamble purchase. When he was not traveling, he spent his leisure time at home with his nieces and nephews. They would drop by to see if he would entertain them, because they knew his real love was entertaining others, and he was never short of ideas, particularly when he wanted to play cards.[716] He was also full of mischievous stories. Hines liked to tell everyone that each morning he would wake up and eat two breakfasts. The first breakfast consisted of a cup of coffee, a task he was better off preparing for himself anyway, considering how finicky he was about how it should taste. When he had finished consuming a cup or two, it was his habit, he said, to shuffle the chairs, dishes, pans and any other objects at his disposal until Clara woke up and fixed him his second breakfast, which usually consisted of another cup of coffee, orange juice, and corn flakes topped with a large dollop of vanilla ice cream.[717]

The full array of Duncan Hines cake mixes did not appear on grocery shelves until very late in 1957. Procter and Gamble spent the last few months of 1956 and practically all of 1957 giving their new products little improvements—a result of the most intensive consumer testing program in the company's 120-year-old history.[718] More than 40,500 blind taste tests were conducted nationwide. This massive testing led the company to expand the size of its baking mix laboratories and test kitchens. The company examined and analyzed every aspect of its mixes. Nothing was left to chance. As for packaging the final product, P&G engaged the services of one of the best-known experts in the area of industrial food package design. Before the new packages were put on grocery shelves, P&G executives knew—because of their exhaustive research—exactly what psychological buttons to press to make housewives ignore their competitors and purchase their new products. The biggest factor executives were counting on, though, was the famous signature logo. Because Duncan Hines's famous smiling face and logo were emblazoned across the top of each package, automatically conveying to many a guarantee of quality, no one was too worried about its success.[719]

In July 1957 a columnist for the Louisville *Courier-Journal* caught up with Hines as he was about to embark on a trip to Alaska. Hines looked forward to his excursion. Alaska, he joked, would be a spot on the earth where he would not be recognized and where people would not be asking him out to eat, forcing him to put on his Sunday clothes for the occasion. While his books had collectively sold around two million copies in 21 years, Hines said, "I've never made a cent off the books.... The money I make comes from other sources." One of those sources now came in the form of hefty royalties from Procter and Gamble for using his name. Although his cut only came to a fraction of one cent for 24 packages, there was something that those who thought he got a raw deal failed to consider. As he pointed out, his critics did not take into account that every "20 minutes some 20,000 packages" of those cake mixes were being purchased. After a while, he said, that added up. The income he received from that venture alone was more than ample to make his semi-retirement a comfortable one.[720]

In the fall and winter of 1957, Hines appeared on several radio and television programs. On 6 November 1957, he appeared as a guest on CBS Radio's "Sez Who Show" and made an appearance as a guest on CBS television's "To Tell The Truth." His media appearances were not sporadic; listeners in the middle Atlantic states could still hear him each weekday on a Mutual Radio Network program called "Let's Travel,"[721] which was broadcast over more than 300 stations.[722] As 1957 faded into 1958, Hines began to slow down. While he may have tried to continue his hectic schedule, he took things a little easier. As the end of his eighth decade approached, he began letting Clara do more of the driving. They would start out each day taking turns at the wheel once an hour, but, after lunch, Clara more often than not took the wheel for the rest of the day.[723]

In December 1957 *Adventures in Good Eating* celebrated its 50th printing, which now included nearly 3,000 restaurants. *Lodging for a Night*, meanwhile, had recently gone through its 40th printing,[724] and Hines's cookbook, *Adventures in Good Cooking*, had expanded its scope to include 700 recipes.[725] Five months later, on 5 May 1958, this accomplishment was brought up at the Duncan Hines Family Dinner, which was held once again in Chicago. Roy Park announced at this meeting that there was a new development in the sale of the guidebooks; Park said that he had begun selling them to the nation's libraries—something Hines had never considered; over 3,000 public libraries stocked their reference shelves with each annual edition.[726]

By August 1958 Procter and Gamble was having a hard time keeping the grocery shelves full of their new Duncan Hines cake mixes. Their smoother batter, which created a moister cake, was proving to be very popular. As expected, because the Duncan Hines name was affixed to their packages, they moved at a dizzying rate. At Ralph's Market in Los Angeles, California, 800 dozen packages of Duncan Hines cake mix, measuring 34 feet long by four feet deep, disappeared in a few days. At the Oakwood Super Market in Kingsport, Tennessee, store manager Dale Simpson reported that his 517-case display of Duncan Hines cake mixes sold out in three weeks. The Duncan Hines display of 350 cases at the Gold Star Market in Levant, New York, sold out in two weeks. In West Patterson, New Jersey, a 250-case display was set up on a Tuesday afternoon and was sold out by Friday. The store ordered fifty more emergency cases of the cake mix just to get through the weekend.[727]

No one remembers exactly how Hines's diagnosis for cancer came about, but the best recollection is that he was in Florida visiting family and friends in January 1958, when he felt ill enough to visit a local doctor who gave him his suspicions. Hines arranged through his Bowling Green physician, Dr. A. D. Donnelly, to be examined in Nashville, Tennessee, and it was there that he was officially diagnosed as having lung cancer. Although he remained active for a few more months, from that point on until his death, he was in and out of the Bowling Green hospital, suffering greatly, waiting for the inevitable.[728]

In September 1958 Sara Meeks' daughter was born and by that time Hines had become seriously ill. Meeks kept telling Clara, "I can't come back to work. I don't have anyone to keep this baby." Clara responded by saying, "Sara, I can't believe you would do this.

WE DEDICATE THIS BOX...   259

[Mr. Hines] has been so good to you over the years, and he needs you now to help with his correspondence, and you've just got to come." Meeks reluctantly agreed after it was explained to her that she did not have to come to work every day, but only on days when she was needed to write some letters. Therefore, when she was needed, Meeks took her baby to work with her. Hines paid her by the hour rather than put her on a regular salary. The overall experience, however, "was a pain in the neck," Meeks recalled. Nevertheless, she was sympathetic; she could plainly see that Hines needed some one to help him. "He was not well at all. He didn't care" about anything, she said. While she was trying to write his letters, her baby cried all day long, and while it did not bother Hines, it certainly bothered her. Sometimes Myrtle Potter, their black cook, would carry the child into the living quarters while Meeks typed. After a while, Meeks could plainly see that bringing her child to work did not sit very well with Clara, so occasionally she found a baby-sitter.

By January 1959, Hines had lost much weight. Even though he was gravely ill, he never complained.[729] He spent much of his time in bed, sometimes seeing guests and assorted friends. In retrospect, that he should meet his end as a result of lung cancer was not surprising. In the days before Americans knew for certain that cigarettes were harmful to one's health, Hines smoked them to his heart's content. "I almost never saw him without a cigarette in his hand," said Mary Herndon.[730] He always had a package of cigarettes and matches lying on a nearby table, ready to grab for his use. He would never carry them around in his shirt pocket; instead, when he was about the house, it was his habit to sit on the sofa in front of the coffee table, tear off not just a corner of the cigarette package but the entire top and chain smoke them one after another until they were gone.[731] In the end, his pastime proved to be his undoing. At 7:30 AM on Sunday, 15 March, 1959, eleven days before his 79th birthday, Duncan Hines died in bed in his Bowling Green home.[732]

21

AFTERMATH

Duncan Hines's body remained at his home until about an hour before his funeral. The funeral services commenced at 2:00 P.M. on 17 March 1959, at the Christ Episcopal Church in Bowling Green.[733] After the service had been performed, he was laid to rest next to his siblings in Bowling Green's Fairview Cemetery.[734] One month later, Hines's estate was probated in Warren County court. According to the terms of his will, Clara was named executrix of his estate and was notified that he left her an estate worth $25,000.[735]

On the occasion of his death, Hines was remembered for his gentle Southern sense of humor and how this quality emerged from the pages of his publications. Also remembered was "his criteria for evaluating eating places" which insisted on "cleanliness, courtesy, and ample portions served unobtrusively."[736] Said the Louisville *Courier-Journal*, "Hines was a perfectionist, as a real gourmet must be. He demanded not only excellent fare at the table, but decent service and a clean kitchen.... His influence on American cooking was considerable.... His accolade was enough to keep many small, out-of-the-way eating places in business."[737]

H. B. Meek, dean of the School of Hotel Administration at Cornell University, summed up Hines's importance to American culture when he said that "while Duncan Hines' appraisal of public restaurants could not be expected to be infallible, his listings constituted a real service to the traveling public. To the operating restaurateur, Mr. Hines was equally helpful in that he recognized quality and publicized it."[738]

A few days after his death, he was eulogized in Congress by Rep. William Natcher, a native of Bowling Green, who stated that "All America has benefited from Duncan Hines' 'hobby,' and every time a diner feels the satisfaction and glow that results from an excellent repast he can be grateful to Mr. Hines for recommending the restaurant that prepared the meal."[739]

Clara Hines's life changed little after her husband's death, with one exception. She felt uncomfortable living 2 miles from Bowling Green's city limits and wanted to live in town. The home she had shared with her husband was rather small for her tastes so she decided to sell it. She had enough money from Procter and Gamble royalties to build a sizable home, so she built one three times as large. Early in 1960 she purchased a tract of land in Bowling Green's upscale suburbs and built a three-bedroom home.[740] On 1 June 1960 it was announced that her once-famous home had been purchased for $32,500 by W.B. Hardy, a funeral director from the nearby community of Smith's Grove. Hardy took possession of the property on 1 July 1960 and immediately announced plans to turn the property into a second site for his funeral home business, adding that he would construct an adjoining $10,000 chapel to the existing structure.[741] Today, when one drives by the building, he can easily distinguish where the structure Hines constructed ends and the newer addition begins.[742]

In the fall of 1962 American travelers assumed that the 1963 Duncan Hines guidebooks would soon be issued for the coming year. But they and the proprietors who profited from them were to be disappointed. In late November each member of the Duncan Hines Family received in the mail a letter from Roy Park which stated some devastating news, which said that "publication of the Duncan Hines Travel Books will be discontinued for 1963. Sales of the books and the display of official Duncan Hines signs will continue until 31 December 1962. Unsold books...after that date may be returned for refund. If you are leasing official signs, you will receive special instructions concerning lease termination, refunds and returns....This is, of course, a major decision. It means the suspension of a publishing activity which has provided a valuable service to American travelers for 27 consecutive years. It means that all of us...will be ending a long and friendly business association with you."

He explained his decision to terminate the business. He had concluded that

> the American traveling public no longer need[ed] the services provided by the Duncan Hines Travel books. The great need of 27 years ago has been erased by the remarkable upgrading of eating and lodging facilities all over the country. Today's traveler is no longer a hardy pioneer challenging an uncharted sea with a stomach of iron and a back of steel. No matter his personal tastes, his financial well-being, or the direction of his wandering, the traveler today has a near infinite choice of high quality eating and lodging places. For example, Duncan Hines could find less than 200 places he thought worthy of mention at the time he published his first list of superior eating places. But today it is next to impossible to list all the worthy eating places in a practical-size[d] book. The same is true of places to lodge. The tremendous growth in the lodging field...has also greatly lessened the need for travel guide books.

In his farewell letter Park pointed out

> the reliance of motorists on guide books has been reduced further by the rapid growth in turnpike and tollway traffic. Almost every toll or limited access highway has many convenient eating and lodging places which adequately serve the hurrying traveler. In view of all these changes, I believe you will agree that the traveling American has moved past an era of concern and moved into an era of confidence about traveling. That America now really loves to travel (but no longer views a

guide book as a glove compartment "must") is a great tribute to the pioneering efforts of Duncan Hines. Mr. Hines' uncompromising crusade for improved hospitality along America's highways...played a vital role in the constant upgrading which has brought about the present happy state of affairs across the country.

He thanked everyone and wished them well. And the service which began with an unusual Christmas card became another relic of America's cultural history.[743]

Some quarters were saddened by Park's announcement. "The American roadside will not look the same again," the New York *Herald-Tribune* editorialized. "Within the next few months every one of those thousands of 'Recommended by Duncan Hines' signs, which hang in front of restaurants, hotels and motels and have become almost as familiar to motorists as Burma-Shave advertisements will be removed from the highways and by-ways of the U. S." By June 1963 the last of the familiar signs with the distinctive logo had been eliminated from America's roadside culture. While they lasted, the public snapped up the remaining Duncan Hines travel books; by the time the last one had been purchased, more than five million books had been sold. After 31 December 1962, they became collector's items.[744]

Some months after Roy Park made his stunning announcement, he moved his company from Ithaca, New York to Procter and Gamble's company headquarters in Cincinnati, Ohio. He remained with them as a consultant[745] and left the organization in 1969,[746] using his accumulated wealth to enter the multimedia field that would, in time, make him one of America's wealthiest men.[747] He was an astute businessman, and his company's profits increased at an annual rate of 22 percent each year between 1963 and 1988. For Park the communications business was more of a congenial avocation than a ruthless, cutthroat enterprise. Chester Middlesworth, who looked after Park's communication properties in Kentucky and North Carolina, said of his employer, "Even though he has a great deal of money, he does not strive or plan hour after hour for money." Through Park's eyes, what he did for a living was just easy.[748]

The years slipped by, a couple of decades passed, and then Clara Hines died at her home at 7:45 A.M. after "a lengthy illness" on 8 August 1983, surviving Duncan Hines by twenty-four years. She was taken to the Gerard-Bradley Funeral Home and later buried near her husband.[749] By then the Duncan Hines books were nothing more than a memory. And to most Americans, the name Duncan Hines was just a name on a cake mix box. After his death Hines's face was removed from the cake mix packages, leaving only the familiar Duncan Hines logo, which remains to this day. In time, the man for whom the cake mix was named was largely forgotten.

Roy Park died of cardiac arrest on 25 October 1993, at Columbia-Presbyterian Medical Center in New York City. At the time of his death he was eighty-three and still living in Ithaca. Shortly before his death, Park was listed in *Forbes* as the 175th richest man in America; he owned twenty-two radio stations, eight television stations and 144 publications, mainly periodicals located in the North Atlantic and Southern states. His estimated net worth was $550 million. Park once admitted that although he made plenty of money over the years, the most fun he had while making it was through his association with Duncan Hines.[750]

In December 1997 Aurora Foods of Columbus, Ohio bought the Duncan Hines brand from Procter & Gamble for $250 million. Matt Smith was appointed to run the Duncan Hines division in 1998. He was followed in that position two years later by Michael Hojnacki.

Several factors contributed to the termination of the Duncan Hines guidebooks. As Roy Park stated when he ceased publishing them, by 1962 there were far too many good restaurants and lodgings to be listed in a single volume. The day had passed when one book could contain them all. Perhaps his best reason, though, was an unspoken one: Duncan Hines was no longer around to actually recommend anything. After his death, somehow the phrase "Recommended by Duncan Hines" didn't mean as much.

When Americans travel today, it is mostly by Interstate, and the choices offered on restaurant menus from one end of this highway system to the other are increasingly limited and familiar. Writes David Schwartz,

> Whether in Massachusetts or Montana, run-of-the-road family restaurants seem to interpret American cuisine as breaded pork chops, Salisbury steak and fried fillet of (unnamed) fish accompanied by green beans out of a can.... Bogus theme restaurants with their decor ordered from a design catalog may serve regional specialties, but all too often the meals come as prepackaged, portion-controlled servings that were cooked up in a factory kitchen, flash-frozen and shipped halfway across the state to be microwaved back to some semblance of life—not a state of affairs that would have cut much mustard with the man from Bowling Green.[751]

The interstate highway system has inadvertently created an American public who not only has forgotten how to enjoy the experience of traveling but the art of roadside eating. Many, if not all, have never practiced the pleasure of discovering little wayside restaurants that offer a smorgasbord of regional delights especially prepared in subtle and distinctive ways that can be found nowhere else. To any cultured palate a country ham cured in Hawaii is vastly inferior to one cured in Kentucky. Likewise, the pineapple dish prepared in a Hawaiian restaurant is stupendously better than one prepared in a rural Kentucky tavern. In his "autobiography" Duncan Hines saw the day of widespread regional differences ending, but he was optimistic that they would somehow always be with us. "Some regional preferences go on and on, pretty much unchanged from one year to the next," he said.[752] And he was right. Regional specialties still exist, the desire to cook recipes native to one's geographical location will probably never die, and the food to prepare it will probably always be in abundance. Millions of families have recorded the recipes of countless regional dishes and many of these have found their way into American restaurants. All one needs is the will to seek them out, taste them, and savor the joy they afford.

In his 1938 *Saturday Evening Post* article, Milton MacKaye said of Duncan Hines after meeting him that there was "through his conversation a tender and touching attachment to such items as unsweetened corn bread, white, first-run maple syrup, and properly cured hams, which at once stamps him as a sentimentalist and poet."[753] MacKaye was correct, but Hines was more than that. He was a true American original who changed our expectations toward restaurants and what one should find when entering them. He created within the public mind an attitude that restaurant kitchens should be immaculately clean and above suspicion. In time, thanks to him, restaurant patrons came to demand that criteria, no matter where they dined. They believed their dining experiences should be ones to remember, not regret.

So the next time the reader dines in a restaurant that affords him a memorable meal, the savory pleasure of which causes his tongue to sparkle and brings a smile to his face, he should remember Duncan Hines for a moment and lift a glass to toast his memory. Somewhere, you can be sure, Duncan Hines will wink and reciprocate the gesture.

[1] Cartoon, *Moonbeams* (December 1958): 6. *Moonbeams* is Procter and Gamble's company magazine.

[2] Cora Jane Spiller, Interview with Louis Hatchett (Bowling Green KY): 10 May 1994.

[3] n.a., *Descendants of Henry Hines, Sr. 1732-1810* (Louisville KY: John P. Morton & Company, 1925) 10. CSA is an abbreviation for Confederate States of America.

[4] Spiller, 10 May 1994.

[5] *Park City Daily News* (Bowling Green KY), 16 February 1920.

[6] Spiller, 16 August 1993.

[7] *Descendants of Henry Hines, Sr.*, 10.

[8] Spiller, 10 May 1994.

[9] Edward Ludlow Hines, autobiographical paper, no. 1 and no. 2, n.d., n.p.

[10] Spiller, 16 August 1993.

[11] *Times-Journal* (Bowling Green KY), 16 February 1920.

[12] *Park City Daily News*, 16 February 1920. The master commissioner and circuit court clerk are now two separate positions.

[13] Spiller, 16 August 1993.

[14] Ibid.

[15] Milton MacKaye, "Where Shall We Stop For Dinner?," *The Saturday Evening Post* (3 December 1938): 211:17.

[16] Robert Spiller, 16 August 1993. Although his father was a Democratic Party stalwart, Duncan Hines was a lifelong member of the Republican Party. He never referred to President Harry S. Truman as "the President," but preferred instead to jocularly anoint him as "that son of a bitch."

[17] Cora Jane Spiller, 16 August 1993.

[18] Ibid., 16 August 1993 and 10 May 1994.

[19] Ibid., 16 August 1993.

[20] Kentucky Registrar of Vital Statistics, file no. 29188.

[21] Spiller, 16 August 1993.

[22] Kentucky Registrar of Vital Statistics, file no. 29188. Kentucky's Department of Vital Statistics gives Markham Hines death date as 12 October 1917, but that may have been when it was filed. The family Bible states his death as 10 October 1917.

[23] Spiller, 16 August 1993.

[24] *Park City Daily News*, 4 December 1951.

[25] Spiller, 16 August 1993.

[26] *Park City Daily News*, 6 December 1935.

[27] Spiller, 16 August 1993.

[28] *Park City Daily News*, 18 August 1948.

[29] *The Times-Journal*, 7 October 1905.

[30] *Park City Daily News*, 18 August 1948.

[31] William Warner Hines fact sheet, Kentucky Library, Bowling Green, Kentucky.

[32] Spiller, 16 August 1993; Warner Hines lived at No. 4 Proctor Court which is now across the street from Western Kentucky University's South Hall.

[33] *Park City Daily News*, 18 August 1948.

[34] Spiller, 16 August 1993.

[35] Jane Morningstar, typescript, Kentucky Library, n.d.

[36] John Porter Hines, "Reminiscences of Green River," 1.

[37] *College Heights Herald*, 13 January 1956.

[38] *Park City Daily News*, 19 June 1961.

[39] Interview with Caroline Hines Tyson, 27 July 1994.

[40] Spiller, 16 August 1993 and 25 March 1994. This last enumerated child was the only one not to have been born in Bowling Green. Shortly before the baby's birth, Cornelia had come down with consumption, and Edward had taken her out west because of her declining health.

[41] *Bowling Green Gazette*, 31 December 1884.

[42] Spiller, 16 August 1993.

[43] *Courier-Journal*, 29 August 1992.

[44] Although Hines says in his autobiography that his birthplace was torn down to make way for the Bowling Green High School, in this he is mistaken; that institution is several blocks from the place of his birth. Duncan Hines, *Duncan Hines' Food Odyssey* (New York: Thomas Y. Crowell, 1955) 6.

[45] John L. Andriot, ed., *Population Abstract of the United States* (McLean VA: Andriot Associates, 1983) 1: 304.

[46] *Park City Daily News*, 29 September 1943.

[47] Spiller, 16 August 1993.

[48] Interview with Robert Wright, 25 May 1994.

[49] Hines, *Food Odyssey*, 6-8.

[50] Ibid., 7.

[51] Ibid., 8.

[52] Spiller, 16 August 1993.

[53] David M. Schwartz, "Duncan Hines: He Made Gastronomes Out of Motorists," *Smithsonian* 15 (November 1984): 92.

[54] Anna Rothe, ed., *Current Biography 1946* (New York: H.W. Wilson Company, 1945) 259.

[55] Hines, *Food Odyssey*, 122.

[56] Spiller, 16 August 1993.

[57] John Porter Hines, "Reminiscences of Green River," 1.

[58] The Bowling Green Junior High School occupies the site of this now extinct institution. St. Columba closed in June 1911.

[59] Spiller, 16 August 1993 and 10 May 1994.

[60] Ibid., 16 August 1993. The Rochester house was located in a small hamlet nestled just outside Bowling Green's city limits known as Forest Park. The site of the home is now a block or two from the campus of Western Kentucky University, just across the L&N railroad tracks on the Morgantown pike.

[61] Hines, "Reminiscences of Green River," 1.

[62] Spiller, 16 August 1993.

[63] The Bowling Green Business College was located in downtown Bowling Green on College Street between 11th and 12th Streets.

[64] *Park City Daily News*, 8 January 1950. The building that Hines attended no longer exists. It was moved to another location a few blocks away in 1899 when the building was razed by fire. The castle-like edifice that replaced it was also razed by fire in the 1960s.

[65] Duncan Hines, *Duncan Hines' Food Odyssey* (New York: Thomas Y. Crowell, 1955) 13.

[66] Interview with Cora Jane Spiller, 16 August 1993.

[67] Ibid., 16 August 1993 and 28 June 1994.

[68] Milton MacKaye, "Where Shall We Stop For Dinner?," *The Saturday Evening Post* 211 (3 December 1938): 80.

[69] Spiller, 16 August 1993.

[70] Hines, *Food Odyssey*, 15.

[71] *Courier-Journal* (Louisville KY), 7 July 1957.

[72] MacKaye, "Where Shall We Stop for Dinner?," 80.

[73] Lesley Poling-Kempes, *The Harvey Girls: Women Who Opened the West* (New York: Paragon House, 1989) passim.

[74] Hines, *Food Odyssey*, 16-17.

[75] James A. Cox, "How Good Food and Harvey 'Skirts' Won the West," *Smithsonian* 18/6 (n. d.): 136.

[76] Hines, *Food Odyssey*, 16-17.

[77] *Courier-Journal*, 7 July 1957.

[78] Hines, *Food Odyssey*, 18.

[79] Spiller, 16 August 1993.

[80] Telephone interview with Jean Brainerd, Wyoming State Museum, Cheyenne WY, 2 September 1994.

[81] Hines, *Food Odyssey*, 1.

[82] Ibid., Peerless City Directory, comp., *1902-1903 Cheyenne Wyoming City Directory* Tribune Press (Greeley CO) 94. In the *1902-1903 Cheyenne Wyoming City Directory,*
Harry P. Hynd is listed as the proprietor of the Capitol Bar, not Harry Hynd's Restaurant. Hynd ran the dining facility with the help of his wife Nellie. The restaurant must have been the first one on the street that caught Hines's attention, because the same city directory shows there to be eighteen restaurants then serving Cheyenne denizens.

[83] Hines, *Food Odyssey*, 1-6.

[84] Spiller, 16 August 1993.

[85] MacKaye, "Where Shall We Stop for Dinner?," 82.

[86] Hines, *Food Odyssey*, 18.

[87] Joseph M. Carey, the owner of the ranch, was Wyoming's senator (1890-1895). After he was defeated in his re-election bid, he returned to his lucrative law practice. He entered politics again in 1911, becoming that state's governor in 1915. He died in 1923. Hines's friend, Robert D. Carey, became Wyoming's governor (1919-1923). He later served as a US Senator from Wyoming from 1930 until his death in 1937.

[88] Duncan Hines, *Duncan Hines' Food Odyssey* (New York: Thomas Y. Crowell, 1955) 18-19. The Careys are erroneously referred to in this book as the Gearys.

[89] Adventures in Good Eating, Inc. v. Best Places To Eat, Inc. and Carl A. Barrett, civil action no. 1844 (1940), Procter and Gamble, Duncan Hines collection, 30. Although Hines believed this incident to be in 1903 or 1904, chronology does not support this assertion. Also, from this same source, Hines states that he lived "eleven" years in the western states; he was there for, at best, almost seven. It is possible that this is the stenographer's error, mistaking the word "seven" for "eleven" while transcribing Hines's recollection.

[90] Interview with Maj. Gen. Richard Groves, 10 August 1994.

[91] *Wyoming Census, 1880,* (Cheyenne WY), 306. Mary Jennings Jeffres was born in 1844.

[92] Groves, 10 August 1994.

[93] Telephone interview with Jean Brainerd, Wyoming State Museum, Cheyenne, Wyoming, 2 September 1994.

[94] *Cheyenne Daily Leader,* 22 December 1903.

[95] *Wyoming Census, 1880* (Cheyenne WY) 306.

[96] Groves, 10 August 1994.

[97] Charles Apple, ed., *1884 Cheyenne, Wyoming City Directory* (Cheyenne WY: Leader Steam Printing Co., 1884) n.p.; Charles Apple, ed., *1895 Cheyenne, Wyoming City Directory,* (Cheyenne, Wyoming: Leader Steam Printing Co.,

1895) n.p.; Peerless Directory Company, comp., *1902-1903 Cheyenne, Wyoming City Directory* (Greeley Co: Tribune Press, 1902) 55. Chaffin's greenhouse was first located in Cheyenne at 352 Ransom; after 1895 it was located at 1718-1722 Central Avenue.

[98] Groves, 10 August 1994.

[99] Phil Roberts, David L. Roberts and Steven L. Roberts, *Wyoming Almanac* (Laramie: Skyline West Press, 1994). It would be illuminating to know the exact date that Hines left his job as a Wells-Fargo relief man, but Robert Chandler, resident historian of the Wells-Fargo Company in San Francisco, California, says that the answer will never be known, because all the company's files from that time were destroyed in the fiery aftermath of the San Francisco earthquake of 18 April 1906.

[100] Duncan Hines, *Duncan Hines' Food Odyssey* (New York: Thomas Y. Crowell, 1955) 19.

[101] Hines, *Food Odyssey*, 20. In this source, Hines says his employer was the Wells-Fargo Company. This is either his mistake or the book's editors, because in every other account Hines states that his employer was the Green Copper Company. Wells Fargo's company historians concede that the Green Copper Company may possibly have been briefly involved in some small way with their company, but its ties with them were only tenuous. In fact, they had never heard of the Green Copper Company.

[102] *Cheyenne Daily Leader*, 28 March 1903.

[103] Ibid., 22 December 1903.

[104] Ibid., 28 March 1903. Maj. Richard H. Wilson was the commanding officer at Fort Slocum from 1904 to 1906.

[105] Groves, 10 August 1994. Eva, it seems, continued to live with Florence at one time or another for the rest of her life.

[106] New York Department of Health, Bureau of Vital Statistics.

[107] Interview with Maj. Gen. Richard H. Groves, 8 September 1994.

[108] Ibid., 10 August 1994.

[109] Chicago, Illinois, city directory, 1906. In the fall of 1905 they made their first home at 4628 Lake Avenue.

[110] Adventures In Good Eating, Inc. v. Best Places To Eat, Inc. and Carl A. Barrett, civil action no. 1844 (1940) 15. According to the 1905 and 1906 Chicago city directories, when Hines was first employed by the J. T. H. Mitchell Company, the firm operated out of room 1201. Shortly after he was hired, the firm moved downstairs four floors to room 816 where the office remained until Hines left the firm.

[111] Milton MacKaye, "Where Shall We Stop for Dinner?," *The Saturday Evening Post* 211 (3 December 1938): 80.

[112] Interview with Robert Wright, 25 May 1994.

[113] Interview with Cora Jane Spiller, 16 August 1993.

[114] Chicago, Illinois, city directories, 1908, 1909, 1911, 1912 and 1913. It must have been hard for his relatives to keep up with him. In the first few years of their marriage, Duncan and Florence Hines moved to a new address nearly every year. In 1907 they moved to 4123 Drexel Boulevard; that was followed by a move one year later to 4217 Berkeley Avenue. In 1910 they moved to 4335 Greenwood Avenue, which was followed by yet another move in 1911 to 1123 East 47th Street.

[115] This apartment is no longer in existence; it was torn down after World War II, probably a victim of a 1950s urban renewal project.

[116] Adventures in Good Eating, Inc. v. Best Places To Eat, Inc., 18-19.

[117] MacKaye, "Where Shall We Stop for Dinner?," 80.

[118] This restaurant is still in existence and remains quite popular.

[119] Adventures In Good Eating, Inc. v. Best Places To Eat, Inc., 14.

[120] Ibid., 15-16.

[121] Chicago, Illinois, city directories, January 1915; July 1915. In 1914, Hines and Joseph A. Coyer started the National Sample and Color Company; Hines was its president and Coyer its vice-president. Nothing is known of this foray into entrepreneurship, not even the nature of the company itself, but it must not have been very successful; the business was listed as a going concern in the January and July issues of the 1915 Chicago city directories, but by the time the January 1916 edition was published, the firm was no longer listed.

[122] Chicago, Illinois, city directory, 1917.

[123] Adventures In Good Eating, Inc. v. Best Places To Eat, Inc., 2; Chicago, Illinois, city directory, 1928. Both Rogers and Company and the Mead-Grede Printing Company were located at 2001 Calumet Avenue at the corner of Calumet and East 20th Street.

[124] Adventures In Good Eating, Inc. v. Best Places To Eat, Inc., 3-4. In a 14 June 1997 conversation with William Jenkins, a retired professor of government at Western Kentucky University and a man who had conducted considerable research into Hines's past, he related to the author the nature of the "advertising specialties" Hines sold as a traveling salesperson. Jenkins is convinced that these objects, also referred to as "printing ideas," were the little office knick-knacks on which companies advertise their names, such as pencils, key-chains, fans, erasers, calendars, etc. In fact, in the sales trade they are still called "advertising specialties."

[125] Duncan Hines, *Duncan Hines' Food Odyssey* (New York: Thomas Y. Crowell, 1955) 60.

[126] MacKaye, "Where Shall We Stop for Dinner?," 80.

[127] Spiller, 16 August 1993.

[128] Adventures In Good Eating, Inc. v. Best Places To Eat, Inc., 3. It was while Hines was learning the use of his new vehicle that he was given the news of his father's death. Duncan's father, Edward Hines, had retired to his peaceful bungalow on the Gasper River in Warren County, Kentucky, some years earlier. In either late 1918 or early 1919, not long after the death of his son, Markham, the elder Hines's health began to deteriorate. Because of his condition, his family brought him back to Bowling Green where they could better look after his needs. At first he stayed at his daughter Annie's home at 902 Elm Street, but he was later moved to his son Porter's residence at 1337 Park Street, where he died at age 77 on Sunday 15 February 1920, at 12:55 P.M.

[129] Ibid., 5.

[130] Spiller, 10 May 1994.

[131] *Illinois Census, 1920,* Chicago, Illinois.

[132] William Lawren, *The General and the Bomb: A Biography of General Leslie R. Groves, Director of the Manhattan Project* (New York: Dodd, Mead & Company, 1988) 54.

[133] In the 1940s Leslie Groves, who by then had risen to the rank of General, became the director of the Manhattan project during World War II; later he was immortalized in the 1989 Paul Newman film *Fat Man and Little Boy.*

[134] Groves, 8 September 1994.

[135] Maj. Gen. Richard H. Groves to author, 8 October 1994.

[136] Duncan Hines to Mrs. Leslie R. Groves, 11 March 1950.

[137] Duncan Hines, *Adventures in Good Eating* (Chicago: Adventures in Good Eating, Inc., 1936) 9. Hines was probably trying to render a well-turned romantic phrase. In fact, he avoided driving at night.

[138] Spiller, 10 May 1994.

[139] MacKaye, "Where Shall We Stop for Dinner?," 80.

[140] Spiller, 16 August 1993.

[141] MacKaye, "Where Shall We Stop for Dinner?," 80.

[142] Ibid.

[143] David M. Schwartz, "Duncan Hines: He Made Gastronomes Out of Motorists," *Smithsonian* 15 (November 1984): 88.

[144] MacKaye, "Where Shall We Stop for Dinner?,"16.

[145] *Courier-Journal* (Louisville KY), 4 April 1941.

[146] Schwartz, "Duncan Hines," 88.

[147] Press release, Duncan Hines Institute, Inc., Ithaca NY, February 1959, 3.

[148] "Duncan Hines 1880-1959," General files, Kentucky Library, Bowling Green KY, 1959.

[149] James A. Cox, "How Good Food and Harvey 'Skirts' Won the West," *Smithsonian* 18: 130.

[150] Schwartz, "Duncan Hines," 87.

[151] Ibid., 88, 90.

[152] Adventures In Good Eating, Inc. v. Best Places To Eat, Inc., 16. Hines's notebook was constantly being updated with additions and subtractions. Between 1905-1930 there were many more restaurants that had been listed, but in 1930 there were about 200.

[153] Schwartz, "Duncan Hines," 88, 90.

[154] Spiller, 16 August 1993 and 10 May 1994.

[155] Chicago, Illinois, city directory, 1928. This firm was located at 320 East 21st Street at the intersection of 21st Street and Calumet Avenue, just one block from the Mead-Grede company.

[156] Chicago, Illinois, city directory, 1930. It was located at 124 Polk Street in Chicago.

[157] Adventures In Good Eating, Inc. v. Best Places To Eat, Inc., 6.

[158] Chicago, Illinois, city directory, 1934. E. Raymond Wright, Inc. was located at 856 West Adams Street.

[159] Hines drove his own automobile, not a company-provided one; nor did the company pay his gas, oil, and repair expenses. He bore those costs himself.

[160] Adventures In Good Eating, Inc. v. Best Places To Eat, Inc., 7-12.

[161] Unfortunately, the author has been unable to determine in which Chicago newspaper the article appeared. There were more than a half-dozen operating in Chicago at the time.

[162] *Courier-Journal*, 16 April 1941.

[163] Schwartz, "Duncan Hines," 90.

[164] Exactly how many restaurants his memorandum notebook actually contained will never be known conclusively as it has not survived, possibly because it was treated as a fluid, disposable document.

[165] *Courier-Journal*, 7 July 1957.

[166] n. a., "Meet Duncan Hines," *Moonbeams* (November 1958): 5.

[167] Duncan Hines, *Duncan Hines' Food Odyssey* (New York: Thomas Y. Crowell, 1955) 28.

[168] Adventures In Good Eating, Inc. v. Best Places To Eat, Inc. and Carl A. Barrett, civil action no. 1844 (1940) 19-22.

[169] Adventures In Good Eating, Inc. v. Best Places To Eat, Inc., 21-22. Almost all the collected material Hines used to create his initial publication and any other paperwork from his days in Chicago is long gone. In the deposition cited above, Hines said (p. 22): "...in moving twice from Wright's [business] to my home and [then later to] Kentucky [,] I discarded many of those [files] because

they became too bulky and too cumbersome to handle. Many of the magazines and things of that like were too voluminous and I discarded lots of those…"

[170] Hines incorporated Adventures in Good Eating, Inc. in May 1936.

[171] Hueser was probably one of Wright's employees.

[172] Adventures In Good Eating, Inc. v. Best Places To Eat, Inc., 23-24.

[173] Interview with Edward Beebe, 7 March 1995. Months earlier, Harold Beebe had suggested to Hines that he put his restaurant knowledge in a book.

[174] Invoice # 5897.

[175] Milton MacKaye, "Where Shall We Stop for Dinner?," *The Saturday Evening Post* 211 (3 December 1938): 16.

[176] Duncan Hines, *Adventures in Good Eating* (Chicago: Adventures in Good Eating, Inc., 1936) 9-10.

[177] Ibid., 11.

[178] Ibid., 30. A typical dinner at the Beaumont Inn in 1936 cost about $1.25.

[179] David Schwartz, "Duncan Hines: He Made Gastronomes Out of Motorists," *Smithsonian* 15 (November 1984): 94.

[180] The restaurant was Kleeman's, located at 212 Sixth Avenue, North.

[181] Undated Chicago newspaper clipping.

[182] Another fact about himself that Hines revealed in this article was that he would drive "to Chicago Avenue to buy the household coffee" and then drive clear over "to No-Man's Land on the north shore for milk and cream."

[183] Hines, *Adventures in Good Eating*.

[184] Hines never referred to this group as "dinner detectives." That term was first used two years later by Milton MacKaye in his widely read 1938 *Saturday Evening Post* article on Hines.

[185] "Meet Duncan Hines," *Moonbeams* (November 1958): 5.

[186] Interview with Cora Jane Spiller, 10 May 1994.

[187] Milton MacKaye, "Where Shall We Stop for Dinner?," *The Saturday Evening Post* 211 (3 December 1938): 16.

[188] Adventures in Good Eating, Inc. v. Best Places To Eat, Inc. and Carl A. Barrett, civil action no. 1844 (1940) 26.

[189] Interview with Edward Beebe, 7 March 1995.

[190] "Meet Duncan Hines," 5.

[191] Interview with Robert Wright, 25 May 1994.

[192] MacKaye, "Where Shall We Stop for Dinner?," 16.

[193] Invoice #9080.

[194] Invoice #9226. This particular order was processed more quickly than others. It was placed by Hines on 11 August 1937 and was ready for delivery on 27 September 1937. In addition, surviving invoices reveal that it took the Wright Company—from the date of order to the date of delivery—approximately 45 to

60 days to produce one of Hines's books. Hines once stated that he made seven cents on each book. If this was the case, however, his business was definitely dropping into a bottomless pit of debt, because at that rate he was only earning $350.63 for 5,009 units—not enough to even pay his printing bill. Moreover, it is unlikely that taxes and operating costs subtracted $1.43 from each manufactured unit. Hines usually sold all his books, and 5,009 copies at $1.50 per copy gave him, theoretically, $7,513.50. With 40% of the profit on each book going to his distributors, a more realistic figure is that Hines was left with $4,508—still a substantial amount in 1937.

[195] Invoice #9558.

[196] Duncan Hines, *Adventures in Good Eating*, 2nd ed. (Chicago: Adventures in Good Eating, Inc., 1937) 198.

[197] Adventures In Good Eating, Inc. v. Best Places To Eat, Inc., 23.

[198] This was an interesting, indeed, amusing act for a man who just two years earlier was tired of being pestered with telephone calls.

[199] Hines, *Adventures in Good Eating*, 2.

[200] Ibid., 11.

[201] MacKaye, "Where Shall We Stop for Dinner?," 16-17.

[202] John Dunning, *On the Air: The Encyclopedia of Old-Time Radio* (New York: Oxford University Press, 1998) 440-41. McBride's radio show was heard on WOR, New York (1934-1940); CBS (1937-1941); NBC (1941-1950); and ABC (1950-1954).

[203] Joseph Gustaitis, "Prototypical Talk Show Host," *American History* 28/6 (Jan/Feb. 1994): 48-49.

[204] Spiller, 10 May 1994.

[205] Hines, *Adventures in Good Eating*, 12.

[206] MacKaye, "Where Shall We Stop for Dinner?," 17.

[207] Hines, *Adventures in Good Eating* (Bowling Green KY: Adventures in Good Eating, Inc., 1941) xv.

[208] Ibid., xiii-xv.

[209] MacKaye, "Where Shall We Stop for Dinner?," 17.

[210] Interview with Maj. Gen. Richard Groves, 10 August 1994.

[211] What follows is a seven-month record of the Hines's vehicular peregrinations across the North American continent. The purpose of what follows is to give the reader an idea of what the Hines's recreational life was like during this time. It is also as complete a record as is available of their final year together. This information comes from a 1937 expense sheet and travel log, among other sources.

[212] Duncan Hines, *Adventures in Good Eating*, 17th ed. (Bowling Green KY: Adventures in Good Eating, Inc., 1941) 295.

[213] Duncan Hines, *Duncan Hines' Food Odyssey* (New York: Thomas Y. Crowell, 1955) 136. Mader's is still the same Old World Bavarian restaurant it was when Charles Mader first opened for business in 1902. It was located at 1041 North 3rd Street; the address is now 1037 North 3rd Street.

[214] Hines, *Adventures in Good Eating*, 109.

[215] Ibid., 97.

[216] Ibid., 234.

[217] Ibid., 172.

[218] Ibid., 107. This establishment was located at 1132 Auburn Street.

[219] This restaurant was located at 619 North Michigan Avenue.

[220] Hines, *Adventures in Good Eating*, 105.

[221] Ibid., 104.

[222] The Lowell Inn is still in existence and is operated by the Palmers' son, Arthur.

[223] Hines, *Food Odyssey*, 138.

[224] Hines, *Adventures in Good Eating*, 168.

[225] Hines, *Food Odyssey*, 139.

[226] Hines, *Adventures in Good Eating*, 168.

[227] Milton MacKaye, "Where Shall We Stop for Dinner?," *The Saturday Evening Post* 211 (3 December 1938): 82.

[228] This was most probably Gordon McCormick.

[229] Hines, *Food Odyssey*, 248.

[230] Hines, *Adventures in Good Eating*, 106.

[231] This restaurant was located at 128 East Main Street.

[232] This restaurant was located at 137 East Broad Street.

[233] Hines, *Adventures in Good Eating*, 229.

[234] Groves, 10 August 1994.

[235] Donnelley's offices were in Chicago at 350 East 22nd Street; the books were manufactured in their printing plant in Crawfordsville, Indiana, at 1301 East Wabash Avenue.

[236] Contract with Duncan Hines and R. R. Donnelley and Sons Company, March 1938.

[237] Hotel receipt, St. Charles Hotel, New Orleans, 18 March 1938.

[238] Hines, *Adventures in Good Eating*, 175.

[239] Documents, R. R. Donnelley & Sons Company with Duncan Hines and Adventures in Good Eating, Inc., 14 February 1938-2 May 1938.

[240] Hotel receipt, Walnut Park Plaza, Philadelphia, 21 May 1938.

[241] Hines, *Food Odyssey*, 32. The hotel is located at 2 East 55th Street.

[242] Hines, *Adventures in Good Eating*, 209.

[243] Hines, *Food Odyssey*, 32-34.

[244] Receipt from R. R. Donnelley to Duncan Hines, 1 July 1938.
[245] MacKaye, "Where Shall We Stop for Dinner?," 17.
[246] "From Hobby to Publishing," *Publisher's Weekly* 134 (6 August 1938): 354-55.
[247] Hotel receipts, Deshler-Wallick Hotel, Columbus OH, 11 August 1938.
[248] Hines, *Food Odyssey*, 150.
[249] Hotel receipts, Commodore Perry Hotel, Toledo OH, 22-23 August 1938.
[250] This restaurant was located at 436 Huron Street.
[251] This restaurant was located at the intersection of Madison and Erie Street.
[252] *Park City Daily News*, 7 September 1938.
[253] *Chicago Daily Tribune*, 7 September 1938. The funeral was held in the chapel at 4227 Cottage Grove Avenue. The author has not yet located the grave site.
[254] I. A. Bench (secretary to Duncan Hines) to Franklin M. Watts, 9 September 1938.
[255] Ernie Pyle, Scripps-Howard news service, 10 September 1938.
[256] Trade-Mark certificate, United States Patent Office, 28 February 1939. On 19 September 1938, Hines filed an application with the United States Patent Office to have Adventures in Good Eating, Inc. registered as an official trademark under the protection of the laws of the United States. On 28 February 1939, Hines was awarded Trade-Mark No. 365,202, and it remained in force for twenty years.
[257] Horace Sutton, "Wayfarer's Guardian Angel," *Saturday Review of Literature* 31 (27 November 1948): 38.
[258] Duncan Hines to I. A. Bench, 27 November 1938.
[259] Interview with Cora Jane Spiller, 16 August 1993.
[260] M. Lincoln Schuster to Duncan Hines, 30 November 1938.
[261] Duncan Hines to Frank M. Watts, 9 June 1939.
[262] Adventures in Good Eating, Inc. v. Best Places To Eat, Inc. and Carl A. Barrett, civil action no. 1844 (1940), 31.
[263] Milton MacKaye, "Where Shall We Stop for Dinner?," *The Saturday Evening Post* 211 (3 December 1938): 17.
[264] Phyllis Larsh, "Duncan Hines," *Life* 21/2 (8 July 1946): 16.
[265] MacKaye, "Where Shall We Stop for Dinner?," 80.
[266] Anna Rothe, ed., *Current Biography* (New York: H. W. Wilson, 1946) 261.
[267] Interview with Mary Herndon Cohron, 29 August 1994.
[268] Clementine Paddleford, "60,000 Miles of Eating," *This Week Magazine* (12 January 1947): 12.
[269] David M. Schwartz, "Duncan Hines: He Made Gastronomes Out of Motorists," *Smithsonian* 15 (November 1984): 92.

[270] MacKaye, "Where Shall We Stop for Dinner?," 80.

[271] Ibid.

[272] Schwartz, "Duncan Hines," 92.

[273] Milton MacKaye, "Where Shall We Stop for Dinner?," *The Saturday Evening Post* 211 (3 December 1938): 82.

[274] Ibid., 80.

[275] Duncan Hines, *Adventures in Good Eating*, (Bowling Green KY: Adventures in Good Eating, Inc., 1941) 26.

[276] MacKaye, "Where Shall We Stop for Dinner?," 80.

[277] Their guest told the Wakefields, as she made her exit, that she would send them a check.

[278] Duncan Hines, *Duncan Hines' Food Odyssey* (New York: Thomas Y. Crowell, 1955) 72.

[279] MacKaye, "Where Shall We Stop for Dinner?," 81-82.

[280] Hines, *Food Odyssey*, 72-73.

[281] Clementine Paddleford, "60,000 Miles of Eating," *This Week Magazine* (12 January 1947): 12.

[282] Hines, *Adventures in Good Eating*, 148.

[283] Hines, *Food Odyssey*, 73. After 37 years of feeding the public, the Wakefields retired from the Toll House in 1967. It folded as an institution about 1970. Frank Saccone purchased the building in September of 1972 and reopened it in June 1973. Ruth Wakefield died at age 73 in 1977. At 11:30 P.M. on 31 December 1984, fire swept through the historic structure, demolishing it completely. Kenneth Wakefield, then 87 years old, said he would miss it. *Brockton* [Mass.] *Enterprise*, 2 January 1985.

[284] Paddleford, "60,000 Miles of Eating," 12.

[285] Hines, *Adventures in Good Eating*, 117.

[286] Hines, *Food Odyssey*, 169-71.

[287] MacKaye, "Where Shall We Stop for Dinner?," 81.

[288] Hines, *Food Odyssey*, 115-17.

[289] Ibid., 123.

[290] Hines, *Adventures in Good Eating*, 81.

[291] Hines, *Food Odyssey*, 123-24.

[292] Ibid., 124.

[293] MacKaye, "Where Shall We Stop for Dinner?," 82.

[294] *Fort Lauderdale* [Florida] *News and Sun-Sentinel*, n.d.

[295] MacKaye, "Where Shall We Stop for Dinner?," 82.

[296] Hines, *Food Odyssey*, 125.

[297] MacKaye, "Where Shall We Stop for Dinner?," 82.

[298] Hines, *Adventures in Good Eating*, 225.

[299] Phyllis Larsh, "Duncan Hines," *Life* 21/2 (8 July 1946): 17.

[300] Hines, *Adventures in Good Eating*, 135.

[301] MacKaye, "Where Shall We Stop for Dinner?," 82.

[302] Hines, *Adventures in Good Eating*, 215.

[303] Duncan Hines to I. A. Bench, 11 December 1938.

[304] Interview with Cora Jane Spiller, 16 August 1993.

[305] Proposal for Directories, R.R. Donnelley & Sons Company to Adventures in Good Eating, Inc., 1 February 1939.

[306] Milton MacKaye, "Where Shall We Stop for Dinner?" *The Saturday Evening Post* 211(3 December 1938): 82.

[307] Proposal for Directories.

[308] Adventures in Good Eating, Inc. v. Best Places To Eat, Inc. and Carl A. Barrett, civil action no. 1844 (1940) 36.

[309] *Boston Herald*, 23 June 1939.

[310] Spiller, 16 August 1993.

[311] The Morrison Hotel was located in Chicago at the corner of Madison and Clark Streets and was popular with businessmen because of its central location.

[312] Interview with Elizabeth Duncan Hines, 30 August 1993. She should have been scared, as this was one of the few known instances where Duncan Hines drove at night.

[313] Duncan Hines, *Adventures in Good Cooking* (Bowling Green KY: Adventures in Good Eating, Inc., 1939) ii.

[314] Interview with Caroline Hines Tyson, 27 July 1994.

[315] Elizabeth Duncan Hines, 30 August 1993.

[316] Spiller, 16 August 1993.

[317] Interview with Sara Jane Meeks, 7 June 1994.

[318] Spiller, 16 August 1993.

[319] The Bowling Green bank that held his office was on State Street between Main and 10th Streets.

[320] Spiller, 16 August 1993 and 10 May 1994.

[321] Ibid.

[322] Ibid., 10 May 1994.

[323] Meeks, 7 June 1994.

[324] Spiller, 10 May 1994.

[325] Meeks, 7 June 1994. In the 1950s, long after Hines had moved his office and home outside of town, when a secretary took dictation from him, it was usually done in his living quarters. The office was one large room and giving dictation was not only distracting to the other employees, it was also annoying to Hines; listening to his secretaries bang away on their typewriters without losing his train of thought was no environment in which to give dictation. Therefore,

Hines had a small office in his living quarters for this purpose, which he called "the library." When Meeks first saw it, she wondered if Hines belonged to a book club. The sight of so much reading material led her to believe him to be a voracious reader. She said that "when he would come back from a trip not only would there be a pile of letters on his desk waiting for him to answer, but there would also be on the floor an enormous pile of magazines, newspapers and especially books that had accumulated in his absence.... He had a lot of books." The library was "right by the window, and I would sit there and take dictation, and then, when I would finish, I would go back to the office to type the letter, and then he would come out there and sign it." Hines needed the library so he could concentrate as he composed material for both magazine articles and the material in his books, activities he could not accomplish if he had the constant clatter of the office about him. But in mid-1939 the "library" was just a thought and months away from realization. In the meantime Hines had to contend with the cramped office space and its physical limitations.

[326] Spiller, 16 August 1993.

[327] Interview with Thomas C. Dedman, 19 May 1994.

[328] Duncan Hines, *Lodging for a Night*, (Bowling Green KY: Adventures in Good Eating, Inc. 1939) vi-vii.

[329] Ibid., viii-ix.

[330] Ibid., 250.

[331] Jack Bruce to Duncan Hines, 25 April 1939.

[332] Duncan Hines Cave City Rotary Club speech, 18 August 1943.

[333] Duncan Hines to F. H. Marquis, 1 June 1939.

[334] R. R. Donnelley & Sons Company to Duncan Hines, 1 September 1939.

[335] Interview with Cora Jane Spiller, 10 May 1994.

[336] Interview with Cora Jane Spiller, 16 August 1993.

[337] Interview with Duncan Welch, 7 March 1995.

[338] Emelie E. Hines death certificate.

[339] Marriage certificate for Duncan Hines and Emelie E. Tolman, Aransas County, Rockport TX, issued 9 December 1939; returned and filed by W. R. Ellis, Justice of the Peace, 11 December 1939, no. 224.

[340] Spiller, 16 August 1993.

[341] In 1994 the author visited this still standing structure at 1032 College Street, between 10th and 11th Streets. Most of its interior was exactly as Hines and Emelie left it. All the bathroom arrangements were still intact—the floor tiles, the sink, the toilet, even the old-fashioned bathtub; none had been replaced.

[342] Spiller, 10 May 1994.

[343] Ibid., 16 August 1993 and 10 May 1994.

[344] Warren County Deed Book, # 186, 11 October 1939.

[345] *Oklahoma City Times*, 4 December 1939.

[346] E. Eastman Irvine, ed. *The World Almanac and Book of Facts for 1939* (New York NY: World-Telegram, 1939). Some of that year's top ten non-fiction best sellers included *Mein Kampf* by Adolph Hitler; *Listen to the Wind* by Anne Morrow Lindbergh, which had sold 200,000 copies by 1 March; *A Peculiar Treasure* by Edna Ferber; *Alone* by Richard E. Byrd; and *Benjamin Franklin* by Carl Van Doren, which had sold 187,000 copies by 1 June.

[347] Duncan Hines to Frank M. Watts, 28 December 1939. One should note that *Adventures in Good Cooking* had sold reasonably well in three months, considering that it was given almost no publicity.

[348] Interview with Larry Williams, 31 March 1995.

[349] Interview with Paul W. Moore, 31 August 1994; interview with Larry Williams, 31 March 1995. The original name of the Williams Printing Company was the Folk-Keeling Company, which was purchased by brothers Roy and Fletcher Williams on 8 August 1911 and thus acquired its new name. The business did relatively well for a number of years; when the Depression began, the Williams brothers saved their company from bankruptcy by making their relatives and a friend co-owners. The owners of the firm were Roy and Fletcher Williams, their brother, Tom Williams, their brother-in-law E. A. Burgstrom, and James Overall; each invested $1,000. When they needed more cash, the Williams brothers' two sisters, Clara and Ruth, collectively put up another $1,000. The $6,000 they pooled together enabled the firm to keep the bank from closing its doors. During the Depression, when most Nashville printers were permanently closing their doors for lack of business, the Williams firm was kept alive mostly by their largest customer, the Life and Casualty Insurance Company. The Williams Printing Company's first address in Nashville was 161 4th Avenue North; the company moved in 1933 to 417 Commerce Street, next door to the Ryman Auditorium. In 1983 the firm moved to another Nashville address. The Commerce Street location was the only one of which Duncan Hines was familiar; it is now a parking lot.

[350] It was located in Nashville on 8th Avenue South.

[351] Williams, 31 March 1995.

[352] Moore, 31 August 1994.

[353] Interview with Sara Jane Meeks, 7 June 1994.

[354] Spiller, 10 May 1994; Moore, 31 August 1994.

[355] *Chicago Daily News*, 14 April 1940.

[356] *Nashville Banner*, 15 May 1940. At the time of this review, *Adventures in Good Eating* was in its seventh edition and *Lodging for a Night* was in its third.

[357] Spiller, 16 August 1993 and 10 May 1994.

[358] Frank J. Taylor, "America's Gastronomic Guide," *Scribner's Commentator* 10/6 (June 1941): 15. In 1940 the only notable lodging in Bowling Green was the Helm Hotel.

[359] Meeks, 7 June 1994.

[360] Spiller, 16 August 1993 and 10 May 1994.

[361] One of the newest members of Hines's household was a large Doberman named Bruno. The dog viciously snarled at every stranger he met at the door until Hines told him to stop. No one liked Bruno, except Hines. The dog's behavior terrified the members of Hines's immediate family. Bruno was, by all accounts, afraid of nothing; the dog possessed a natural assurance that the world should *and would* obey his every command. The world was his to do with as he pleased. One day Bruno gave this assumption the ultimate test. According to family members, the dog wandered onto the nearby railroad track, stepped before an approaching locomotive, ordered the gargantuan, onrushing machinery to stop—and was shocked when it did not. As a result of this miscalculation, Bruno was evenly spread across the train track for the next quarter-mile. Interview with Duncan Welch, 7 March 1995.

[362] Later Davis became both a Kentucky state legislator and an undergraduate dean of two colleges.

[363] Interview with Paul Ford Davis, 9 April 1993.

[364] By the time the guidebooks ceased publication in 1962, the total number of restaurants and lodgings had increased to approximately 9,000 listings.

[365] Davis, 9 April 1993.

[366] A country ham generally weighs between 15-20 lbs. and Hines made $15-$20 each time he sold one.

[367] Spiller, 16 August 1993.

[368] Davis, 9 April 1993; Spiller, 10 May 1994.

[369] Interview with Robert Wright, 25 May 1994.

[370] Davis, 9 April 1993.

[371] Duncan Hines to A.C. Roberts, 23 December 1946.

[372] Davis, 9 April 1993.

[373] Wright, 25 May 1994.

[374] The dinners were usually held at Chicago's Sheraton Hotel at 505 North Michigan Avenue; the event was usually held on a Tuesday in either March or May, but at the first dinner in 1941 it was held in October.

[375] Duncan Hines speech at Duncan Hines Family Dinner, Chicago IL, 7 October 1941, 1-8.

[376] Duncan Hines, speech for Regional Meetings of Listed Places, June 1942.

[377] Meeks, 7 June 1994.

378 In 1948 Hines published *Duncan Hines' Vacation Guide*; pine green was the color he assigned to both book and rental signs.

379 Ibid.; Duncan Hines speech before Regional Meetings of Listed Places, June 1942.

380 Meeks, 7 June 1994.

381 *Courier-Journal* (Louisville KY), 16 April 1941.

382 Frank J. Taylor, "America's Gastronomic Guide," *Scribner's Commentator*, vol. 10, no 6 (June 1941), p. 13.

383 Taylor, "America's Gastronomic Guide," 16.

384 Ibid., 17.

385 Ibid., 17-18.

386 *Courier-Journal* (Louisville KY), 16 April 1941.

387 MacKaye, "Where Shall We Stop for Dinner?," 80.

388 Interview with Cora Jane Spiller, 16 August 1993.

389 MacKaye, "Where Shall We Stop for Dinner?," 80. That comment was made in 1938. Some people have argued that, despite the passage of over six decades, nothing has changed.

390 David M. Schwartz, "Duncan Hines: He Made Gastronomes Out of Motorists," *Smithsonian* 15 (November 1984): 92.

391 Paddleford, "60,000 Miles of Eating," 12.

392 Hines, *Adventures in Good Eating*, 296.

393 Paddleford, "60,000 Miles of Eating," 12.

394 Interview with Cora Jane Spiller, 16 August 1993 and 10 May 1994.

395 Undated Philadelphia newspaper clipping.

396 MacKaye, "Where Shall We Stop for Dinner?," 84.

397 *Park City Daily News*, 7 December 1945.

398 MacKaye, "Where Shall We Stop for Dinner?," 84.

399 Ibid., 84.

400 Ibid., 82.

401 Duncan Hines speech at Regional Meeting of Listed Places, June 1942.

402 Interview with Cora Jane Spiller, 10 May 1994.

403 Anna Rothe, ed., *Current Biography 1946* (New York: H. W. Wilson Company, 1946) 259.

404 Duncan Hines speech for Regional Meetings of Listed Places, June 1942.

405 Duncan Hines testimony given before the Ohio State Health Commissioner' Conference, Columbus OH, 24 September 1942.

406 Duncan Hines Rotary Club speech, Cave City KY, 18 August 1943.

407 *Park City Daily News*, 29 September 1943.

408 Duncan Hines to members of Duncan Hines Family, 15 February 1943.

409 Interview with Sara Jane Meeks, 7 June 1994.

[410] Press release, "History of the School of Hotel Administration," Cornell University, 3.

[411] In a letter to Robert V. Menifee, dated 16 November 1949, Hines insisted that he never profited from his company beyond expenses. He wrote that he gave "the entire capital stock of [Adventures in Good Eating, Inc.]...to the Duncan Hines Foundation, which is an irrevocable trust.... The foundation receives all the dividends. I personally do not participate."

[412] "As Duncan Hines Sees It," Table Topics 7/4 (July 1944): 1-2.

[413] Duncan Hines speech at Duncan Hines Family Dinner, Chicago, Illinois, October 1945.

[414] Marion Edwards, "They Live to Eat," Better Homes and Gardens 23/3 (March 1945): 31. It was at this time that Hines also began including in his guidebooks eating and lodging accommodations in the American territories of Alaska and Hawaii, as well as Mexico and Canada.

[415] Park City Daily News, 11 December 1945.

[416] Edwards, "They Live to Eat," 30.

[417] Ibid., 30-31.

[418] Ibid., 31.

[419] Ibid., 70.

[420] Hines, 30 August 1993.

[421] Spiller, 16 August 1993.

[422] Park City Daily News, 6 December 1945.

[423] Interview with Edward Beebe, 7 March 1995.

[424] Death certificate of Emelie Tolman Hines, 9 November 1986. She died at the Manor Care retirement home in Boynton Beach, Florida. She was buried in Lakeworth, Florida.

[425] Interview with Cora Jane Spiller, 16 August 1993.

[426] Ibid., 10 May 1994.

[427] Ibid., 16 August 1993.

[428] Spiller, 16 August 1993.

[429] Park City Daily News, 5 October 1944.

[430] Interview with Robert Wright, 23 May 1995. While published accounts claim her mother died in 1905, Wright believes the mother of his half-sister, Clara, died in 1907.

[431] Spiller, 10 May 1994; Wright, 25 May 1994.

[432] Her father was Cumberland College's first academic dean.

[433] Telephone interview with Charles Shackelford, Cumberland College, Williamsburg, Kentucky, 23 May 1995.

[434] Courier-Journal (Louisville KY), 9 August 1983.

[435] *The Talisman*, Western Kentucky Normal School, 1930, 21; 1931, 23; 1932, 17.

[436] *Courier-Journal*, 9 August 1983.

[437] *Park City Daily News*, 5 October 1944. Clarence Nahm was buried in a family plot in Louisville's Adath Israel cemetery.

[438] *Warren County, Kentucky Marriages (1918-1965), Groom's List, A-J 1* (Bowling Green KY): 1992.

[439] Spiller, 10 May 1994.

[440] Ibid., 16 August 1993.

[441] *Park City Daily News*, 16 March 1959.

[442] Spiller, 16 August 1993.

[443] Clementine Paddleford, "60,000, Miles of Eating," *This Week Magazine* (12 January 1947): 12.

[444] Phyllis Larsh, "Duncan Hines," *Life* 21/2 (8 July 1946): 17.

[445] *Courier-Journal*, 9 August 1983.

[446] Wright, 25 May 1994.

[447] Duncan Hines, *Adventures in Good Eating*, (Bowling Green KY: Adventures in Good Eating, Inc., 1946) xvi-xix. In this latest edition he also listed 173 dinner detectives.

[448] Duncan Hines to J. A. Frohock, 11 December 1942.

[449] Duncan Hines speech, 29 March 1946, 3.

[450] Larsh, "Duncan Hines," *Life*, 16-17.

[451] Ibid. Mrs. McKay told *Life* she knew better than to offer Hines a free meal or to serve him large portions; nor did he want special treatment. He preferred to be served like any other.

[452] Ibid., 16.

[453] Ibid., 17.

[454] Spiller, 16 August 1993.

[455] *Park City Daily News*, 29 September 1946.

[456] Clementine Paddleford, "60,000 Miles of Eating," 10-11.

[457] This was an exaggeration, but if stretching the truth led to cleaner restaurants, so much the better.

[458] Paddleford, "60,000 Miles of Eating," 12.

[459] Duncan Hines, "How to Find a Decent Meal," *Saturday Evening Post* (26 April 1947): 99.

[460] Paddleford, "60,000 Miles of Eating," 10-11.

[461] *Herald-Tribune* (New York), 12 May 1947.

[462] Hines, "How to Find a Decent Meal," 18.

[463] Ibid., 18-19.

[464] Ibid., 19.

[465] Ibid., 97.

[466] Duncan Hines speech, December 1947, 6.

[467] Ibid., 100.

[468] Frank J. Taylor, "America's Gastronomic Guide," *Scribner's Commentator* 10/6 (June 1941): 16.

[469] To better appreciate the changes that swept through the emerging motel industry between 1940 and 1960, consult Warren James Belasco, *Americans on the Road: From Autocamp to Motel, 1910-1945* (Cambridge and London: MIT Press, 1979).

[470] Duncan Hines, *Lodging for a Night* 23rd ed. (Bowling Green KY: Adventures in Good Eating, Inc., 1947) ix.

[471] Belasco, *Americans on the Road: From Autocamp to Motel, 1910-1945*, 170.

[472] Interview with Cora Jane Spiller, 10 May 1994.

[473] Duncan Hines, "How to Find a Decent Meal," *Saturday Evening Post* (26 April 1947): 100.

[474] Ibid., 102.

[475] Ibid.; Spiller, 10 May 1994.

[476] Hines, *Adventures in Good Eating* 17th ed., 111.

[477] Ibid., 295.

[478] Ibid., 107.

[479] Ibid., 224.

[480] Ibid., 254.

[481] Ibid., 70.

[482] *Park City Daily News*, 4 September 1947.

[483] Carol Lynn Gilmer, "Duncan Hines: Adventurer in Good Eating," *Coronet* 23/1 (November 1947): 100-101.

[484] Horace Sutton, "The Wayfarer's Guardian Angel," *Saturday Review of Literature* 31/27 (November 1948): 38.

[485] Gilmer, "Adventurer in Good Eating," 104.

[486] Ibid., 102-104.

[487] Ibid., 104.

[488] Ibid., 104-105. *Coronet* magazine also reported Hines had been involved in two lawsuits during his career. One from 1940 involved a man named Carl A. Barrett, who had published a restaurant guide, portions of which had obviously been lifted from *Adventures in Good Eating*. Hines proved plagiarism in court by pointing out planted typographical errors which had been copied verbatim. On the other occasion Hines brought suit against a racketeer who was representing himself as one of his representatives and was selling "Recommended" by Duncan Hines" signs to listed restaurants. Ibid., 105-106.

[489] Hines all along anticipated the coming economic boom. On 18 August 1943, he told members of the Cave City, Kentucky Rotary Club that "as soon as the war is over, there will be the largest [market for] tourist travel this country has ever known."

[490] The book was copyrighted 1948 but did not reach the public until early 1949.

[491] Spiller, 10 May 1994.

[492] Duncan Hines, *Duncan Hines Vacation Guide* (Bowling Green KY: Adventures in Good Eating, Inc., 1948) i.

[493] Interview with Sara Jane Meeks, 7 June 1994.

[494] Horace Sutton, "The Wayfarer's Guardian Angel," 38.

[495] Hines, *Duncan Hines' Food Odyssey* (New York: Thomas Y. Crowell, 1955) 173.

[496] Sutton, "The Wayfarer's Guardian Angel," 38-39.

[497] *Greensboro Daily News* (North Carolina), 31 July 1960.

[498] Anne Murray, "History of Roy Park," 1992.

[499] *Greensboro Daily News*, 31 July 1960.

[500] Roy Park speech, Cornell University Graduate School of Business and Public Administration, 2 November 1976, Kroch Library, Cornell University, Ithaca, New York, file # 3981.

[501] Roy H. Park, "When Dangerous Opportunity Knocks," *Ithaca College Quarterly* (December 1987): 21.

[502] "An Adventure in Food Marketing: A Case Study of a New Entrant in America's Biggest, Fastest Growing Industry," *Tide: The Newsmagazine for Advertising Executives* (3 August 1951): 2.

[503] *Greensboro Daily News*, 31 July 1960.

[504] "An Adventure in Food Marketing," 2.

[505] *Greensboro Daily News*, 31 July 1960.

[506] Roy Park press release, n. d.

[507] *Greensboro Daily News*, 31 July 1960.

[508] Roy Park press release, n. d. Cooperative chores were not the only thing occupying Park's mind. On 3 October 1936, Park married Dorothy Goodwin Dent, a native of Raleigh; the two were married for fifty-six years.

[509] Roy Park, "Notes from Lempret, Former Editor of the *Omaha* Magazine," typescript, n. d., Park Communications, Ithaca, New York.

[510] "An Adventure in Food Marketing," 2.

[511] *North Carolina State College News*, August 1955.

[512] Roy Park press release, n. d.

[513] The cooperative is now known as Agway.

[514] Park, "When Dangerous Opportunity Knocks," 22.

[515] Park, "Notes from Lempret," n. d.

[516] "An Adventure in Food Marketing," 3; *Greensboro Daily News*, 31 July 1960; *North Carolina State College News*, August 1955.

[517] According to another undated Roy Park press release, some of his clients, in addition to the Dairyman's League, included "the American Cranberry Growers, Southern States Cooperative, the Pennsylvania Farm Cooperative, the North Carolina Farmers Cooperative Exchange, the Philco Corporation, and the agricultural interests of Victor Emmanuel."

[518] "An Adventure in Food Marketing," 3.

[519] Park, "Notes from Lempret," n. d.

[520] "An Adventure in Food Marketing," 3.

[521] Roy Park speech, 2 November 1976.

[522] "An Adventure in Food Marketing," 3.

[523] Park, "Notes from Lempret," n. d.

[524] "An Adventure in Food Marketing," 3.

[525] Roy Park speech, 2 November 1976.

[526] David M. Schwartz, "Duncan Hines: He Made Gastronomes Out of Motorists," *Smithsonian* 15/8 (November 1984): 87-88.

[527] Murray, "History of Roy Park," 1992.

[528] Park, "Notes from Lempret," n.d.

[529] "An Adventure in Food Marketing," 3.

[530] Roy Park speech, 2 November 1976.

[531] *North Carolina State College News*, August 1955.

[532] *Daily News* (Bowling Green, Kentucky), 5 May 1988.

[533] Roy Park speech, 2 November 1976.

[534] "An Adventure in Food Marketing," 3.

[535] *Greensboro Daily News*, 31 July 1960.

[536] *North Carolina State College News*, August 1955.

[537] *Greensboro Daily News*, 31 July 1960.

[538] "An Adventure in Food Marketing," 3.

[539] *Greensboro Daily News*, 31 July 1960.

[540] Roy Park speech, 2 November 1976.

[541] *Greensboro Daily News*, 31 July 1960.

[542] *Ithaca* [N.Y.] *Journal*, 15 May 1963; "An Adventure in Food Marketing," 4. The name Park abandoned, Agricultural Advertising & Research, became Hines-Park's marketing research arm, popularly known thereafter as Ag Research.

[543] *Greensboro Daily News*, 31 July 1960.

[544] "An Adventure in Food Marketing," 3.

[545] *North Carolina State College News*, August 1955.

[546] "An Adventure in Food Marketing," 3-4.

[547] *North Carolina State College News*, August 1955.

[548] "An Adventure in Food Marketing," 3-4.

[549] *Park City Daily News*, 4 June 1950.

[550] Park, "Notes from Lempret," n. d.

[551] "An Adventure in Food Marketing," 3-4.

[552] Schwartz, "Duncan Hines," 96.

[553] Press release, Duncan Hines Institute, Ithaca NY, 1 October 1957, 3.

[554] *Park City Daily News*, 4 June 1950.

[555] "An Adventure in Food Marketing," 4.

[556] Earlier in the year Hines had approved a coffee, a butter, and even an oleomargarine bearing his name; the latter must have possessed an unforgettable flavor given his low opinion of margarine.

[557] *Park City Daily News*, 4 June 1950.

[558] "Duncan Hines Is A Big Success As Label," *Food Mart News* (November 1952): 78.

[559] Advertisement, *Look* (17 July 1951).

[560] J. Allen, *Northwestern Miller*, "Duncan Hines Cake Mix Line to Enter Market," (3 July 1951).

[561] *Courier-Journal* (Louisville, Kentucky), 25 September 1949.

[562] Duncan Hines to Mrs. Leslie R. Groves, 11 March 1950.

[563] *Park City Daily News*, 23 April 1950.

[564] Duncan Hines, *Duncan Hines' Food Odyssey* (New York: Thomas Y. Crowell, 1955) 155.

[565] Duncan Hines scrapbooks, private collection.

[566] Duncan Hines speech, 10th Annual Duncan Hines Family Dinner, Chicago IL, 8 May 1951, 6.

[567] Ibid., 3-4.

[568] Hines, *Food Odyssey*, 133.

[569] Duncan Hines speech, 8 May 1951, 3-4.

[570] Hines, *Food Odyssey*, 134.

[571] Interview with Duncan Welch, 7 March 1995 and 28 March 1995; diary of Clarence Welch, January 1946 to 2 November 1946.

[572] Interview with Robert Wright, 25 May 1994; Vincent P. Barabba, Director, *Historical Statisticals of the United States: Colonial Times to 1970, Part 1*, (Washington D C: Bureau of the Census, United States Department of Commerce, 1975) 296, 303.

[573] Wright, 25 May 1994.

[574] Interview with Sara Jane Meeks, 7 June 1994.

NOTES 291

[575] Wright, 25 May 1994. Robert Wright also said the average order not from individuals was usually for about 10 books. Bookstores and establishments that Hines recommended received a 40% discount. The Williams company handled all large orders; a typical order to Marshall Field in Chicago, for example, was for 200-300 books.

[576] Ibid.; interview with Paul W. Moore, 31 August 1994.

[577] Wright, 25 May 1994.

[578] Interview with Mary Herndon Cohron, 16 February 1995.

[579] Meeks, 7 June 1994.

[580] Cohron, 29 August 1994.

[581] Ibid., 16 February 1995.

[582] Ibid., 29 August 1994.

[583] Meeks, 7 June 1994.

[584] Cohron, 29 August 1994.

[585] Meeks, 7 June 1994.

[586] Interview with J. T. Orendorf, 2 September 1994.

[587] Interview with Margaret Jackson, 2 March 1995.

[588] Meeks, 7 June 1994.

[589] Obituary, Edith M. Wilson, [Bowling Green, Kentucky] *Daily News*, 3 October 1993.

[590] Jackson, 2 March 1995. Edith Wilson is buried in a family plot in Scottsville, Kentucky.

[591] Interview with Wanda Eaton, 7 June 1994.

[592] Meeks and Eaton, 7 June 1994.

[593] Cohron, 29 August 1994.

[594] Meeks and Eaton, 7 June 1994; interview with Cora Jane Spiller, 10 May 1995.

[595] Orendorf, 2 September 1994.

[596] Donald H. Molesworth v. Adventures in Good Eating, Inc., United States District Court, docket 422, 81.

[597] Eaton, 7 June 1994.

[598] Spiller, 26 February 1995.

[599] Meeks, 7 June 1994.

[600] Orendorf, 2 September 1994.

[601] *Park City Daily News*, 16 November 1952.

[602] Donald H. Molesworth v. Adventures in Good Eating, Inc., 81.

[603] Meeks, 7 June 1994.

[604] Cohron, 29 August 1994.

[605] Meeks, 7 June 1994.

[606] Cohron, 29 August 1994.

[607] *North Carolina State College News* (Raleigh NC), August 1955.

[608] "Meet Duncan Hines," *Moonbeams* (November 1958): 7-8.

[609] Press release, "Duncan Hines Mixes," Nebraska Consolidated Mills, Inc., Omaha, Nebraska, ca. 1953; *New York Journal of Commerce*, 24 June 1953.

[610] David M. Schwartz, "Duncan Hines: He Made Gastronomes Out of Motorists," *Smithsonian* 15/8 (November 1984): 96.

[611] Ibid., 88.

[612] *Greensboro Daily News* (Greensboro NC), 31 July 1960.

[613] *Park City Daily News*, 23 March 1952.

[614] "An Adventure in Food Marketing: A Case Study of a New Entrant in America's Biggest, Fastest Growing Industry," *Tide: The Newsmagazine for Advertising Executives* (3 August 1951): 5; *Grocer's Spotlight*, 12 June 1952.

[615] *Ice Cream Trade Journal*, July 1952.

[616] "An Adventure in Food Marketing,", 5.

[617] "Duncan Hines Is A Big Success As Label," *Food Mart News*, 78.

[618] *Park City Daily News*, 23 March 1952.

[619] "An Adventure in Food Marketing," 4.

[620] Ibid., 5.

[621] *North Carolina State College News*, August 1955.

[622] David Schwartz, "Duncan Hines," *Smithsonian* (November 1984): 96.

[623] *North Carolina State College News*, August 1955.

[624] *Park City Daily News*, 19 October 1952. The author has not been able to obtain any recorded copies of the five-minute program but has been informed that transcripts of the program are in Ithaca, New York.

[625] "Duncan Hines, Adventurer," *Tide: The Newsmagazine for Advertising Executives* (3 August 1951): 3.

[626] Press release, Duncan Hines Institute, Ithaca, New York, 1 October 1957, 3.

[627] *Park City Daily News*, 16 March 1959. The 1954 edition of *Adventures in Good Eating* was the final version that Hines fully supervised and edited; it contained 2,365 recommended restaurants.

[628] "Meet Duncan Hines," *Moonbeams* (November 1958): 6. Park located the Duncan Hines Institute in one of Ithaca's largest old mansions, a 100-year-old two-story Georgian structure at 408 East State Street.

[629] Duncan Hines, *Duncan Hines' Food Odyssey* (New York: Thomas Y. Crowell, 1955) 26.

[630] Duncan Hines Institute, Inc., *Adventures in Good Eating* (Ithaca NY: Duncan Hines Institute, 1959), iv-v.

[631] *Greensboro Daily News* (Greensboro NC), 31 July 1960.

[632] Duncan Hines Institute, *Adventures in Good Eating*, vi.

[633] Ibid., x.

[634] Several years later the *Mobil Travel Guides* solved this difficulty by publishing books broken down into geographical regions. Park experimented with this concept as well, but there is no data available to indicate its success.

[635] *Chicago Daily Tribune*, 5 January 1954.

[636] Duncan Hines, "Duncan Hines Picks Ten Best Motels in U. S. A.," *Look* 18 (12 January 1954): 31-34.

[637] Hines, *Food Odyssey*, 258.

[638] *Courier-Journal*, 4 April 1954.

[639] *Chicago Daily Tribune*, 5 January 1954.

[640] Interview with Cora Jane Spiller, 10 May 1994.

[641] *Courier-Journal*, 4 April 1954.

[642] Roy Park's interview with Duncan Hines, ca. 1954.

[643] Nelle Palmer was widowed by this time; her husband, Arthur, had died in 1951.

[644] Duncan Hines, *Duncan Hines' Food Odyssey* (New York: Thomas Y. Crowell, 1955) 226.

[645] *Chicago Daily Tribune*, 5 January 1954.

[646] "Best," *The New Yorker* 30 (17 April 1954): 26-27.

[647] *Park City Daily News*, 27 June 1954.

[648] Hines, *Food Odyssey*, 229.

[649] *Park City Daily News*, 27 June 1954.

[650] Horace Sutton, "What Do You Want, Oomph in Your Butter?," *Saturday Review* 37 (17 July 1954): 31.

[651] In *Duncan Hines' Food Odyssey* (229), Hines said he later discovered that the ham was "also a popular Italian delicacy, called *prosciutto*, although it's usually reserved for special occasions because the ham is so expensive."

[652] *Park City Daily News*, 27 June 1954.

[653] Hines, *Food Odyssey*, 229-31.

[654] *Park City Daily News*, 27 June 1954.

[655] *Park City Daily News*, 27 June 1954; Hines, *Food Odyssey*, 231-32.

[656] Hines, *Food Odyssey*, 232.

[657] *Park City Daily News*, 27 June 1954.

[658] Sutton, "What Do You Want?" 31.

[659] *Park City Daily News*, 27 June 1954.

[660] Hines, *Food Odyssey*, 232.

[661] *Park City Daily News*, 27 June 1954.

[662] Hines, *Food Odyssey*, 232.

[663] *Park City Daily News*, 27 June 1954.; Hines, *Food Odyssey*, 233-34.

[664] Hines, *Food Odyssey*, 233.

[665] *Park City Daily News,* 27 June 1954.

[666] Hines, *Food Odyssey,* 233-34.

[667] *Park City Daily News,* 27 June 1954.

[668] "Hines Abroad," *The New Yorker* 30 (24 July 1954): 15-16.

[669] *Park City Daily News,* 27 June 1954.

[670] Hines, *Food Odyssey,* 234.

[671] Ibid., 236.

[672] *Park City Daily News,* 27 June 1954.

[673] "Hines Abroad," 15-16.

[674] Hines, *Food Odyssey,* 236.

[675] Sutton, "What Do You Want?" 31.

[676] Hines, *Food Odyssey,* 237.

[677] *Park City Daily News,* 27 June 1954.

[678] Hines, *Food Odyssey,* 112.

[679] *Park City Daily News,* 27 June 1954.

[680] Hines, *Food Odyssey,* 237.

[681] Ibid. Some publications erroneously reported at the time that Hines returned to America on the *Queen Elizabeth.*

[682] Ibid., 238.

[683] *Park City Daily News,* 27 June 1954.

[684] "Hines Abroad," pp. 15-16.

[685] Sutton, "What Do You Want?" 31.

[686] Hines Abroad," 15-16.

[687] Sutton, "What Do You Want?" 32.

[688] *Park City Daily News,* 27 June 1954.

[689] Hines, *Food Odyssey,* 238.

[690] *Park City Daily News,* 16 March 1959.

[691] "Setup & Style of Duncan Hines Dessert Book."

[692] *Park City Daily News,* 15 September 1955.

[693] "Notes For Duncan Hines Book, *There's No Accounting For Tastes,*" from interview conducted by Roy Park with Duncan Hines, ca. 1954, 1.

[694] "Eating for a Living," *Newsweek* 45/21(23 May 1955): 75.

[695] "Trends Affecting the Food Service Industry," *American Entertainment Magazine* (June 1955).

[696] Duncan Hines speech, 14th Annual Duncan Hines Family Dinner, Chicago, Illinois, 9 May 1955.

[697] Interview with Robert Wright, 25 May 1994.

[698] *North Carolina State College News* (Raleigh NC), August 1955, 6-7.

[699] *Park City Daily News,* 15 September 1955.

[700] *North Carolina State College News,* August 1955.

[701] Duncan Hines, *Duncan Hines' Food Odyssey* (New York: Thomas Y. Crowell, 1955) 262.

[702] *Ithaca Journal* (Ithaca NY), 17 August 1956.

[703] Duncan Hines speech, Duncan Hines Family Dinner, Chicago, Illinois, 7 May 1956.

[704] *Wall Street Journal*, 18 August 1956.

[705] *Northwestern Miller* (Minneapolis MN), 21 August 1956.

[706] *Journal of Commerce* (New York NY), 20 August 1956.

[707] *Washington* [D.C.] *Post-Times-Herald*, 18 August 1956.

[708] *Journal of Commerce*, 20 August 1956.

[709] Press release, 17 August 1956.

[710] "Duncan Hines Joins the Family," *Moonbeams* (September 1956): 4.

[711] *Park City Daily News*, 16 March 1959. When Procter and Gamble acquired the rights to the Duncan Hines name, Roy Park chose the least costly way of disposing with food suppliers whose products still displayed the Duncan Hines name. According to Ed Rider, archivist at Procter and Gamble, rather than waste money on protracted litigation, Park wrote the president of each licensed company and asked them to stop using the Duncan Hines name. While many companies complied with his request, others refused, citing the terms of their contract. Rather than fight them in court, Park decided to let them use the name until their contracts expired. The last contract lapsed around 1969. After that time, Procter and Gamble owned exclusive rights to the name.

[712] Duncan Hines Institute to Duncan Hines Family members, 30 November 1956.

[713] Interview with Sara Jane Meeks, 7 June 1994.

[714] *Monterey* [California] *Herald*, 2 March 1956.

[715] Meeks, 7 June 1994.

[716] Interview with Caroline Tyson Hines, 27 July 1994.

[717] *Monterey Herald*, 2 March 1956. Whether Hines really ate this concoction is highly improbable, but he gave a good reason for the practice, stating there was no need to put milk and sugar on corn flakes when ice cream could produce the same result.

[718] The company was founded in October 1837.

[719] New product presentation material, Procter and Gamble, Inc., November 1957.

[720] *Courier-Journal* (Louisville KY), 7 July 1957. The royalty agreement with Procter and Gamble was the same as the one Hines had made with Roy Park in 1949; under that contract he also received one-half cent per 24 units of every product sold.

[721] Duncan Hines Family Newsletter, 28 March 1958, 1.

[722] *North Carolina State College News* (Raleigh NC), August 1955.

[723] Meeks, 7 June 1994.

[724] *Chicago Sun-Times* (Illinois), 3 December 1957.

[725] *Dallas News* (Texas), 22 December 1957.

[726] Duncan Hines Family Newsletter, 28 March 1958, 7.

[727] "Duncan Hines Deluxe," *Moonbeams* (October-November 1959): 12.

[728] Interview with Cora Jane Spiller, 12 July 1995.

[729] Meeks, 7 June 1994.

[730] Interview with Mary Herndon Corhon, 29 August 1994.

[731] Spiller, 16 August 1993; interview with Robert Wright, 25 May 1994.

[732] *Park City Daily News*, 16 March 1959; death certificate, Kentucky Registrar of Vital Statistics, 15 March 1959.

[733] Rev. H. Howard Surface conducted Hines's funeral ceremony in an Episcopal church at 12th and State Streets in Bowling Green, not far from his late sister's home. Beside the church today stands the Duncan Hines Chapel, so named because Clara Hines donated monies to have it built in her husband's memory.

[734] *Park City Daily News*, 16 March 1959; interview with Cora Jane Spiller, 10 May 1994. The only sibling not buried in the family plot was Annie Hines. She was laid to rest next to her husband, Scott Hines, in December 1951, in another section of the same cemetery.

[735] *Park City Daily News*, 19 April 1959.

[736] Ibid., 16 March 1959.

[737] [Louisville, Kentucky] *Courier-Journal*, 17 March 1959.

[738] *Ithaca* [N.Y.] *Journal*, 16 March 1959.

[739] *Park City Daily News*, 19 March 1959.

[740] Interview with Robert Wright, 25 May 1994. Her house was located at 728 Richland Drive.

[741] *Park City Daily News*, 1 June 1960.

[742] In the Hardy living quarters is a bathroom Hines had built, which remains virtually untouched; it resembles a 1930s-style hotel bathroom, complete with white-tiled floors and walls and glass doorknobs. It also has an unusual septic tank, which is a freight train car Hines had buried in the back yard.

[743] Roy H. Park to Duncan Hines Family, 23 November 1962.

[744] *New York Herald-Tribune*, 24 November 1962.

[745] *Ithaca Journal*, 15 May 1963.

[746] *Times-Union* (Rochester NY), 16 August 1973.

[747] *Courier-Journal* (Louisville KY), 25 November 1962.

[748] *Daily News* (Bowling Green KY), 5 May 1988.

[749] *Park City Daily News*, 8 August 1983.

[750] *New York Times*, 27 October 1993, D23.

[751] David M. Schwartz, "Duncan Hines: He Made Gastronomes Out of Motorists," *Smithsonian* 15 (November 1984): 97.

[752] Duncan Hines, *Duncan Hines' Food Odyssey* (New York: Thomas Y. Crowell) 243.

[753] Milton MacKaye, "Where Shall We Stop for Dinner?" *Saturday Evening Post* 211 (3 December 1938): 80.

BIBLIOGRAPHY

Books

Andriot, John L., ed. *Population Abstract of the United States, Volume 1*, McLean VA: Andriot Associates, 1983.

Apple, Charles, ed. *1884 Cheyenne, Wyoming City Directory*. Cheyenne WY: Leader Steam Printing Co., 1884.

————. *1895 Cheyenne, Wyoming City Directory*. Cheyenne WY: Leader Steam Printing Co., 1895.

Belasco, Warren James. *Americans on the Road: From Autocamp to Motel, 1910-1945*. Cambridge and London: Massachusetts Institute of Technology Press, 1979.

Descendants of Henry Hines, Sr. 1732-1810 Louisville KY: John Morton & Company, 1925.

Dunning, Joseph. *Tune in Yesterday: The Ultimate Encyclopedia of Old-Time Radio, 1925-1976*. Englewood Cliffs NJ: Prentice Hall, 1976.

Duncan Hines Institute, Inc. *Lodging for a Night*, 1960 ed. Ithaca NY: Duncan Hines Books, 1959.

Duncan Hines Institute, Inc. *Lodging for a Night*, 1961 edition. Ithaca NY: Duncan Hines Books, 1960.

Edgerton, John. *Southern Food: At Home, on the Road, in History*. New York: Knopf, 1987.

Hines, Duncan. *Adventures in Good Cooking*, first ed. Bowling Green KY: Adventures in Good Eating, Inc., 1939.

————. *Adventures in Good Eating*, first ed. Chicago: Adventures in Good Eating, Inc., 1936.

————. *Adventures in Good Eating*, 2nd ed. Chicago: Adventures in Good Eating, Inc., 1937.

————. *Adventures in Good Eating*, 17th ed. Bowling Green KY: Adventures in Good Eating, Inc., 1941.

————. *Adventures in Good Eating*, 30th ed. Bowling Green KY: Adventures in Good Eating, Inc., 1946.

————. *Duncan Hines' Food Odyssey*. New York: Thomas Y. Crowell, 1955.

————. *Lodging for a Night*, 2nd ed. Bowling Green KY: Adventures in Good Eating, Inc., 1939.

————. *Lodging for a Night*, 23rd ed. Bowling Green KY: Duncan Hines Books, 1947.

————. *Lodging for a Night*, 1954 ed. Bowling Green KY: Duncan Hines Books, 1953.

————. *Duncan Hines Vacation Guide*, first ed. Bowling Green KY: Duncan Hines Books, 1948.

Lawren, William. *The General and the Bomb: A Biography of General Leslie R. Groves, Director of the Manhattan Project*. New York: Dodd, Mead & Company, 1988.

Poling-Kempes, Lesley. *The Harvey Girls: Women Who Opened the West*. New York: Paragon House, 1989.

Roberts, Phil, David L. Roberts and Steven L. Roberts. *Wyoming Almanac*. Laramie WY: Skyline West Press, 1994.

Rothe, Anna ed,. *Current Biography* New York: H. W. Wilson, 1946.

Schremp, Gerry. *Kitchen Culture: Fifty Years of Food Fads*. New York: Pharos Books, 1991.

Magazines

Advertisement, *Look* (17 July 1951), Duncan Hines Collection, Kroch Library, Cornell University, Ithaca NY, file #3981.

Advertisement, *Successful Grocer* (April 1951), Duncan Hines Collection, Kroch Library, Cornell University, Ithaca NY, file #3981.

Allen, J. *Northwestern Miller* (3 July 1951).

"An Adventure in Food Marketing: A Case Study of a New Entrant in America's Biggest, Fastest Growing Industry." *Tide: The Newsmagazine for Advertising Executives* (3 August 1951).

"As Duncan Hines Sees It." *Table Topics* 4/7 (July 1944).

"Best." *The New Yorker* 30 (17 April 1954).

Cartoon, *Moonbeams* (December 1958).

Cox, James A. "How good food and Harvey 'skirts' won the West." *Smithsonian* 18/6 (September 1987).

"Duncan Hines, Adventurer." *Tide: The Newsmagazine for Advertising Executives* (3 August 1951).

"Duncan Hines: The Adventures of a Good Eater." *Friends* (March 1942).

"Duncan Hines Deluxe" *Moonbeams* (October-November 1959), Procter and Gamble Duncan Hines manuscript collection, FP H-mm.

"Duncan Hines Is A Big Success As Label." *Food Mart News* (November 1952).

"Duncan Hines Joins the Family." *Moonbeams* (September 1956), Procter and Gamble Duncan Hines manuscript collection, FP H-mm.

"Duncan Hines Week." *Bowling Green-Warren County Tourist Convention Commission* 21 (November-December 1986).

"Eater." *American Magazine* 131 (April 1941).

"Eating for a Living," *Newsweek* 45/21 (23 May 1955): 75.

Edwards, Marion. "They Live to Eat." *Better Homes and Gardens* 23/3 (March 1945).

"From Hobby to Publishing." *Publisher's Weekly* 134 (6 August 1938).

Gilmer, Carol Lynn. "Duncan Hines: Adventurer in Good Eating." *Coronet* 23/1 (November 1947).

Grocer's Spotlight, 12 June 1952.

Gustaitis, Joseph. "Prototypical Talk Show Host." *American History* 28/6 (Jan/Feb. 1994).

Hines, Duncan. "Adventures in Good Eating." *Coronet* 23/2 (December 1947).

————. *Flower Grower* 45/5 (May 1958).

————. "How to Find a Decent Meal." *Saturday Evening Post* (26 April 1947): 18-19, 97, 99-100, 102.

————. "Duncan Hines Picks Ten Best Motels in the U.S.A." *Look* 18 (12 January 1954): 31-34.

"Hines Abroad." *The New Yorker* 30 (24 July 1954): 15-16.

"The Hines-Park Varsity." *Tide: The Newsmagazine for Advertising Executives* (3 August 1951).

Ice Cream Trade Journal, July 1952, Duncan Hines Collection, Kroch Library, Cornell University, Ithaca, New York, file #3981.

Johnston, Patricia Condon. "Nelle Palmer of Stillwater: Entertainer and Innkeeper." *Minnesota History* 45/5 (Spring 1983).

Knox, Bob. "State Man Uses Magical Name To Build $50 Million Idea." *North Carolina State College News* (August 1955).

Larsh, Phyllis. "Duncan Hines." *Life* 21/2 (8 July 1946).

MacKaye, Milton. "Where Shall We Stop for Dinner?." *The Saturday Evening Post* 211 (3 December 1938).

"Meet Duncan Hines." *Moonbeams* (November 1958).

New York Journal of Commerce (May 1951), Duncan Hines Collection, Kroch Library, Cornell University, Ithaca NY, file #3981.

Northwestern Miller (21 August 1956).

Paddleford, Clementine. "60,000 Miles of Eating." *This Week Magazine* (12 January 1947).

Park, Roy H. "When Dangerous Opportunity Knocks." *Ithaca College Quarterly* (December 1987).

Pebbrook, Paul. "Full Time Hobby." *Airlanes* (September 1946).

Prey, Hal. "What Life Was Like During the Troubling Forties." *Reminisce* (Spring 1991).

Printer's Ink (August 1951), Duncan Hines Collection, Kroch Library, Cornell University, Ithaca NY, file #3981.

"Procter Buys Duncan Hines Line of Mixes," *New York Journal of Commerce* (20 August 1956), Procter and Gamble Duncan Hines manuscript collection, FP H-m.

Schwartz, David M. "Duncan Hines: He Made Gastronomes Out of Motorists." *Smithsonian* 15/8 (November 1984).

Sutton, Horace. "Wayfarer's Guardian Angel." *Saturday Review of Literature* 31 (27 November 1948).

———. "What Do You Want, Oomph in Your Butter?." *Saturday Review* 37 (17 July 1954): 31-32.

———. *Saturday Review* 31 (27 November 1948).

The Talisman, Bowling Green KY (1930): 21.

The Talisman, Bowling Green KY (1931): 23.

The Talisman, Bowling Green KY (1932): 17.

Taylor, Frank J. "America's Gastronomic Guide." *Scribner's Commentator* 10/6 (June 1941).

"Trends Affecting the Food Service Industry." *American Entertainment Magazine* (June 1955), Duncan Hines Collection, Kroch Library, Cornell University, Ithaca, New York, file #3981.

Interviews

Beebe, Edward. Interview by author, telephone interview, 7 March 1995.
Brainerd, Jean. Interview by author, telephone interview, Wyoming State Museum, Cheyenne WY, 2 September 1994.
Cohron, Mary Herndon. Interview by author, North Salem ID, 29 August 1994.
Dedman, Thomas C.. Interview by author, Harrodsburg KY, 19 May 1994.
Eaton, Wanda. Interview by author, Louisville KY, 7 June 1994.
Groves, Major Gen. Richard. Interview by author, telephone interview, 10 August 1994.
Groves, Major Gen. Richard. Interview by author, telephone interview, 8 September 1994.
Hartley, Mrs. Radio interview with Mrs. Hartley Transcript. WSB, Atlanta GA, 1947, Procter and Gamble Duncan Hines manuscript collection, FP xH-f.
Hines, Caroline Tyson. Interview by author, Tape recording, Bowling Green KY, 27 July 1994.
Hines, Elizabeth Duncan. Interview by author, Bowling Green KY, 30 August 1993.
Jackson, Margaret. Interview by author, Bowling Green KY, 2 March 1995.
Meeks, Sara Jane. Interview by author, Louisville KY, 7 June 1994.
Moore, Paul W. Interview by author, Hendersonville TN, 31 August 1994.
"Notes for Duncan Hines Book. *There's No Accounting For Tastes.*" From interview conducted by Roy Park with Duncan Hines, ca. 1954, Procter and Gamble Duncan Hines manuscript collection, FP xH-g.
Orendorf, Jo T. Interview by author, telephone interview, 2 September 1994.
Shackelford, Charles. Interview by author, telephone interview, 23 May 1995.
Spiller, Cora Jane. Interview by author, Bowling Green KY, 16 August 1993.
———. Interview by author, Bowling Green KY, 25 March 1994.
———. Interview by author, Bowling Green KY, 10 May 1994.
———. Interview by author, telephone interview, Bowling Green KY, 29 June 1994.

————. Interview by author, telephone interview, Bowling Green KY, 12 July 1995.

Tyson, Caroline Hines. Interview by author, Bowling Green KY, 27 July 1994.

Welch, Duncan. Interview by author, telephone interview, 7 March 1995.

Williams, Larry. Interview by author, telephone interview, Franklin TN, 31 March 1995.

Wright, Robert. Interview by author, Frankfort KY, 25 May 1994.

Newspapers

Book Reviews, "Duncan Hines' Guides to Good Eating, Lodging," *Nashville* (TN) *Banner*, 15 May 1940.

Bush, Peggy. "Early President of Wells Fargo has his roots in Bowling Green," *Park City Daily News*(Bowling Green KY), 9 November 1986.

Cleveland (OH) *Plain Dealer*, 11 October 1955, Duncan Hines Collection, Kroch Library, Cornell University, file #3981.

Columbus (OH) *Dispatch*, 24 October 1955, Duncan Hines Collection, Kroch Library, Cornell University, file #3981.

Creason, Joe. "Please Mr. Hines, Won't You Try Some of This Nice Whale Blubber?," *Courier-Journal* (Louisville KY), 7 July 1957.

————. "The Time? Ask Duncan Hines," *Courier-Journal* (Louisville KY), 4 April 1954.

Cushman, Howard. possibly *Philadelphia Inquirer*, ca. 1941, Procter and Gamble Duncan Hines manuscript collection, FP H-m.

"Death Claims John J. Valentine," *Times-Journal* (Bowling Green KY), 21 December 1901.

"Divorce Granted," *Park City Daily News* (Bowling Green KY), 6 December 1945.

"Duncan Hines Firms Plan To Leave City," *Ithaca* (NY) *Journal*, 15 May 1963, 3, Procter and Gamble Duncan Hines manuscript collection, FP H-m.

"Duncan Hines, Food Expert, Dies at 79," *Ithaca* (NY) *Journal*, 16 March 1959.

"Duncan Hines Is Synonymous with Good Food in U.S." *Park City Daily News* (Bowling Green KY), 29 September 1943.

"Duncan Hines' Kin." *Waterways Journal* (St. Louis MI), 4 April 1959.

"Duncan Hines," *Chicago Sun-Times*, 3 December 1957, Procter and
    Gamble Duncan Hines manuscript collection, FP 2H-a.
"Duncan Hines, Travel, Food Authority, Dies," *Park City Daily News*
    (Bowling Green KY), 16 March 1959, 49a
Editorial, "A Lifelong Adventure In Good Eating," *Courier-Journal*
    (Louisville KY), 17 March 1959.
"Fame of Local Resident as Food Authority Not Confined to US," *Park
    City Daily News* (Bowling Green KY), 16 July 1939.
"Fed Up: Duncan Hines Halts Food Guides." *Courier-Journal* (Louisville
    KY), 25 November 1962.
"Food Is An Adventure to No. 1 Gourmet; He Travels Just to Eat,"
    Oklahoma City Times, 4 December 1939, Procter and Gamble
    Duncan Hines manuscript collection, FP H-m.
"Former Employee of Adventures in Good Eating Wins Judgment," *Park
    City Daily News* (Bowling Green KY), 16 November 1952, 10.
Gaines, Ray. "Duncan Hines Gets New Watch," *Park City Daily News*
    (Bowling Green KY), 13 May 1957.
———. "Eulogies Are Put In Record," *Park City Daily News* (Bowling
    Green KY), 19 March 1959.
———. "Park Row Paragraphs," *Park City Daily News* (Bowling Green
    KY), 23 March 1952.
———. "Park Row Paragraphs," *Park City Daily News* (Bowling Green
    KY), 19 October 1952.
———. "Park Row Paragraphs," *Park City Daily News* (Bowling Green
    KY), 25 February 1954.
———. "Park Row Paragraphs," *Park City Daily News* (Bowling Green
    KY), 15 September 1955.
———. "Park Row Paragraphs," *Park City Daily News* (Bowling Green
    KY), 10 October 1961.Miller, Lucy Key. "Front Views & Profiles:
    Farmer Hines," *Chicago Daily Tribune*, 5 January 1954, Procter and
    Gamble Duncan Hines manuscript collection, FP H-m.
"Hines Property Sold To F.B. Hardy For $32,500," *Park City Daily News*
    (Bowling Green KY), 1 June 1960.
"Home Wedding." *Times-Journal* (Bowling Green KY), 7 October 1905.
Horstman, Judith. "Ithacan Buying Newspapers," *Times-Union*
    (Rochester NY), 16 August 1973, Procter and Gamble Duncan Hines
    manuscript collection, FP H-m.

"J. Porter Hines Retires After 28 Years Service." *College Heights Herald*
    (Bowling Green KY), 13 January 1956, 8.
"J. Porter Hines Rites Conducted Here Today." *Park City Daily News*
    (Bowling Green KY), 19 June 1961.
Knox, Joseph. "Farm Boy Becomes Multimillionaire," *Greensboro* (NC)
    Daily News, 31 July 1960, section D.
Listens, Linda. "What D'Ya Know," *Park City Daily News* (Bowling Green
    KY), 29 September 1946.
————. "The Duncan Hines' Travel Again," *Park City Daily News*
    (Bowling Green KY), 4 September 1947.
————. "What D'Ya Know," *Park City Daily News* (Bowling Green KY),
    26 March 1952.
Niles, R. "He showed His Digestion What He Thought of It," *Courier-*
    Journal (Louisville KY), 16 April 1941.
Manthie, Josephine. "Duncan Hines Orders Ham and Eggs for First Meal
    in US after Gastronomic Tour of Europe," *Park City Daily News*
    (Bowling Green KY), 27 June 1954.
Mason, Jim. "Park Row Paragraphs," *Park City Daily News* (Bowling
    Green KY), 10 January 1961.
Mills, Marjorie. *Boston* (MA) *Herald*, 23 June 1939, Duncan Hines
    Collection, Kroch Library, Cornell University, file #3981.
Minneapolis Morning Tribune, 23 July 1955, Duncan Hines Collection,
    Kroch Library, Cornell University, file #3981.
Morningstar, Jane. "Park Row Paragraphs," *Park City Daily News*
    (Bowling Green KY), 5 January 1965.
————. "Roy H. Parks [sic] Visits With Mrs. Duncan Hines," *Park City*
    Daily News (Bowling Green KY), 4 February 1962, 10.
"Mrs. Duncan Hines Succumbs." *Park City Daily News* (Bowling Green
    KY), 7 September 1938, n.p.
"Name of Duncan Hines to Be Used on Quality-Controlled Food
    Products," *Park City Daily News* (Bowling Green KY), 4 June 1950.
Obituary. "Mrs. Clara Hines dies." *Park City Daily News* (Bowling Green
    KY), 8 August 1983.
Obituary for Duncan Hines, *Courier-Journal* (Louisville KY), 26 March
    1959.
Obituary. "Clarence Nahm Taken By Death." *Park City Daily News*,
    (Bowling Green KY), 5 October 1944.

Obituary. "Clara Wright Hines, 79, dies; was widow of noted food critic."
Courier-Journal (Louisville KY), 9 August 1983, A-3.

Obituary. "Captain Hines Passed Away Sunday 1 P.M.." *Park City Daily
News* (Bowling Green KY), ca. February 1920, 1, c. 1.

Obituary. "Life's Close To Captain E. L. Hines." *Times-Journal* (Bowling
Green KY), 16 February 1920, 1, c. 4.

Obituary. "Relieved: Mrs. Edward L. Hines' Spirit Takes its Flight."
Bowling Green Gazette (Bowling Green KY), 31 December 1884, 3, c.
1.

Obituary. "Hines Rites Are To Be Held Here At His Sisters; Dr. Whitaker
To Conduct Services at Home of Mrs. A. Scott Hines." *Park City
Daily News* (Bowling Green KY), 6 December 1935, 1, c. 8.

Obituary. "Duncan Hines, Electric Board Member Dies." *Park City Daily
News* (Bowling Green KY), 18 January 1971, 1.

Obituary. "Heart Attack is Fatal to Warner Hines." *Park City Daily News*
(Bowling Green KY), 18 August 1948.

Obituary. "A. Scott Hines Funeral Will Be Tomorrow." *Park City Daily
News* (Bowling Green KY), 20 May 1942.

Obituary. "Widow of Former May Dies at City Hospital." *Park City Daily
News* (Bowling Green KY), 4 December 1951.

Obituary. "Illness Fatal to Mrs. Hines: Succumbs at Home on Park Street;
Funeral Tomorrow." *Park City Daily News* (Bowling Green KY), 30
July 1941.

Obituary. "Mrs. J. Hines Dies Today at City Hospital." *Park City Daily
News* (Bowling Green KY), 28 March 1950.

Obituary for Edith M. Wilson, *Daily News*, (Bowling Green KY), 3
October 1993.

Obituary. "Harry D. Hines, River Pilot, Dies at Hospital." *Park City Daily
News* (Bowling Green KY), 26 September 1955.

Obituary. Mrs. Florence C. Hines, *Chicago Daily Tribune*, 7 September
1938.

Obituary. New York *Times*, 27 October 1993, 143: D23n.49497.

O'Brien, Howard Vincent. Chicago *Daily News*, 14 April 1940, Procter
and Gamble Duncan Hines manuscript collection, FP H-m.

Paddleford, Clementine. "Home Institute Leafelet Tells What Dishes
Wife Makes for Restaurant Authority," *New York Herald-Tribune*, 12
May 1947.

"Party for Mr. Hines," *Park City Daily News* (Bowling Green KY), 23 April 1950.

"Prepares Story On Duncan Hines," *Park City Daily News* (Bowling Green KY), 11 December 1945.

"Procter & Gamble..." *New York Herald-Tribune*, 18 August 1956, Procter and Gamble Duncan Hines manuscript collection, FP H-m.

"Procter & Gamble Reports It Will Enter Bake Mix Field," *Wall Street Journal*, 18 August 1956, Procter and Gamble Duncan Hines manuscript collection, FP H-m.

Purcell, Denise. "Media mogul got boost from BG's Duncan Hines." Bowling Green *Daily News* (Bowling Green KY), 5 May 1988, 2-A.

Richmond (VA) *Times Dispatch*, 8 October 1955, Duncan Hines Collection, Kroch Library, Cornell University, file #3981.

Richmond (VA) *News Leader*, 7 October 1955, Duncan Hines Collection, Kroch Library, Cornell University, file #3981.

Ross, Don. "A Roadside Change: Duncan Hines Signs Going," *New York Herald-Tribune*, 24 November 1962, Procter and Gamble Duncan Hines manuscript collection, FP H-m.

Saxon, Wolfgang. "R. H. Park, 83, media executive and promoter of Duncan Hines."

Simmons, Jean. "For Twenty-Second Year, It's Time For Duncan Hines," *Dallas News*, 22 December 1957.

"Soap Firm Buying Cake Mix Business," *Post-Times-Herald* (Washington, DC), 18 August 1956, Procter and Gamble Duncan Hines manuscript collection, FP H-m.

St. Paul (MN) *Dispatch*, 20 July 1955, Duncan Hines Collection, Kroch Library, Cornell University, file #3981.

Staten, Vince. "Duncan Hines Approved: Eight of his Kentucky favorites are still in business, still serving delicious meals to road-weary travelers." *Courier-Journal Scene* (Louisville KY), 29 August 1992, 13-16.

Stewart, Doug. "What's a Chicken Dinner Without Sharp Knife, Says Food Specialist." *Park City Daily News* (Bowling Green KY), 25 June 1939.

Talley, Rhea. "New York Is Best Eating Place In U.S., Duncan HInes Says," *Courier-Journal* (Louisville KY), 25 September 1949.

Tolf, Rober. "Chalet Suzanne: Gastronomic Spledor," *Fort Lauderdale News and Sun-Sentinel*, n.d.

Towles, Harry. "Homefolk News and Views," *Park City Daily News* (Bowling Green KY), 20 February 1947.
Prof. Toro, "Peninsula Parade," *Monterey* (CA) *Herald*, 2 March 1956.
"Turkey Basting Info Given By Local Man In Magazine," *Park City Daily News* (Bowling Green KY), 7 December 1945.
"Widow Named Chief Beneficiary In Hines' Will," *Park City Daily News* (Bowling Green KY), 19 April 1959.
Wood, Susan. Book review, "The Harvey Girls." *New York Times Book Review* (10 December 1989).
Whitaker, Dave. "75-Year History of B. G. Business University Presents "Success" Story." *Park City Daily News* (Bowling Green KY), 8 January 1950.

Boston Herald, 23 June 1939.
Bowling Green (KY) *Gazette*, 31 December 1884.
Cheyenne (WY) *Daily Leader*, 28 March 1903.
Cheyenne Daily Leader, 22 December 1903.
Chicago Daily Tribune, 7 September 1938.
Chicago Sun-Times, 3 December 1957.
(Louisville KY) *Courier-Journal*, 4 April 1941.
Courier-Journal, 4 April 1954.
Courier-Journal, 7 July 1957.
Courier-Journal, 17 March 1959.
Courier-Journal, 9 August 1983.
Dallas News, 22 December 1957.
Greensboro (NC) *Daily News*, 31 July 1960.
Ithaca Journal, 16 March 1959.
Ithaca Journal, 15 May 1963.
New York Journal of Commerce, 24 June 1953.
New York Journal of Commerce, 20 August 1956.
Park City Daily News, 16 February 1920.
Park City Daily News, 6 December 1935.
Park City Daily News, 7 September 1938.
Park City Daily News, 6 December 1945.
Park City Daily News, 18 August 1948.
Park City Daily News, 4 June 1950.
Park City Daily News, 4 December 1951.
Park City Daily News, 23 March 1952.

Park City Daily News, 19 October 1952.
Park City Daily News, 15 September 1955.
Park City Daily News, 16 March 1959.
Park City Daily News, 19 March 1959.
Park City Daily News, 19 June 1961.
Wall Street Journal, 18 August 1956
Washington (DC) *Post-Times-Herald,* 18 August 1956.
Untitled Chicago newspaper, 1936.

Letters
Bench, I. A. Letter to Franklin M. Watts. 9 September 1938, Procter and
  Gamble Duncan Hines manuscript collection, FP xH-c.
Black, James H. Letter to Duncan Hines (Chicago IL). 14 October 1956,
  Procter and Gamble Duncan Hines manuscript collection, FP xH-c.
Bruce, Jack of R. R. Donnelley & Sons Company. Letter to Duncan Hines.
  25 April 1939, Procter and Gamble Duncan Hines manuscript
  collection, FP xH-e 6/6.
Duncan Hines Institute. Letter to Duncan Hines Family (Ithaca NY). 30
  November 1956, Procter and Gamble Duncan Hines manuscript
  collection, FP xH-c.
Flanigan, Joseph M. Letter to Duncan Hines. 16 March 1942, Procter and
  Gamble Duncan Hines manuscript collection, FP xH-c.
Glimpse, Fred. Letters between Duncan Hines during preparation of
  Duncan Hines' Food Odyssey, summer 1954-January 1955, Procter
  and Gamble Duncan Hines manuscript collection, FP xH-g.
Hines, Duncan. Letter to Mrs. Leslie R. Groves. 11 March 1950.
———. Letter to I. A. Bench. 9 August 1938, Procter and Gamble
  Duncan Hines manuscript collection, FP x H-c.
———. Letter to Frank M. Watts. 28 December 1939, Procter and
  Gamble Duncan Hines manuscript collection.
———. Letter to Burton G. Feldman of Chicago IL. 8 January 1941,
  Duncan Hines Collection, Kroch Library, Cornell University, Ithaca
  NY file #3981.
———. Letter to Duncan Hines Family. 15 February 1943, Duncan
  Hines Collection, Kroch Library, Cornell University, Ithaca NY, file
  #3981.
———. Letter to I. A. Bench. 27 November 1938, Procter and Gamble
  Duncan Hines manuscript collection, FP xH-c.

————. Letter to I. A. Bench. 11 December 1938, Procter and Gamble Duncan Hines manuscript collection, FP xH-c.

————. Letter to F. H. Marquis. 1 June 1939, Procter and Gamble Duncan Hines manuscript collection, FP xH-c.

————. Letter to Frank M. Watts. 9 June 1939, Procter and Gamble Duncan Hines manuscript collection, FP xH-c.

————. Letter to Frank M. Watts. 28 December 1939, Procter and Gamble Duncan Hines manuscript collection, FP xH-c.

————. Letter to Joseph M. Flanigan. 1 April 1942, Procter and Gamble Duncan Hines manuscript collection, FP xH-c.

————. Letter to J. A. Frohock. 11 December 1942, Procter and Gamble Duncan Hines manuscript collection, FP xH-c.

————. Letter to James H. Black (Bowling Green KY). 10 December 1956, Procter and Gamble Duncan Hines manuscript collection, FP xH-c.

————. Letter to A. C. Roberts. 23 December 1946, Procter and Gamble Duncan Hines manuscript collection, FP xH-c.

————. Letter to Robert V. Menifee (San Diego CA). 16 November 1949, Procter and Gamble Duncan Hines manuscript collection, FP xH-c.

————. Letter to I. A. Bench. 27 November 1938, Procter and Gamble Duncan Hines manuscript collection.

————. Letter to F. H. Marquis. 1 June 1939, Procter and Gamble Duncan Hines manuscript collection.

Park, Roy. Letter to Duncan Hines Family (Ithaca NY). 23 November 1962, Procter and Gamble Duncan Hines manuscript collection, FP xH-c.

————. Letter to Duncan Hines Family. 23 November 1962, Procter and Gamble Duncan Hines manuscript collection.

R. R. Donnelley & Sons Company. Letter to Duncan Hines. 24 April 1939, Procter and Gamble Duncan Hines manuscript collection, FP xH-e 6/5.

————. Letter to Duncan Hines. 15 March 1938.

———— (Crawfordsville IN). Letter to Duncan Hines. 26 April 1939, Procter and Gamble Duncan Hines manuscript collection, FP xH-e 6/7.

————. Letter to Duncan Hines. 1 September 1939, Procter and Gamble Duncan Hines manuscript collection, FP xH-e 6/10.

———. Letter to Duncan Hines. 15 March 1938, Procter and Gamble Duncan Hines manuscript collection.
———. Letter to Duncan Hines. 24 April 1939, Procter and Gamble Duncan Hines manuscript collection.
———. Letter to Duncan Hines. 1 September 1939, Procter and Gamble Duncan Hines manuscript collection.
Schuster, M. Lincoln. Letter to Duncan Hines. 30 November 1938, Procter and Gamble Duncan Hines manuscript collection, FP xH-c.

Speeches

Hines, Duncan. Speech at the Tenth Annual Duncan Hines Family Dinner, Chicago, Illinois, 8 May 1951, Procter and Gamble Duncan Hines manuscript collection, FP H-f.
———. Rotary Club speech, Cave City KY, 18 August 1943, Procter and Gamble Duncan Hines manuscript collection.
———. Speech at Regional Meeting of Listed Places, June 1942, Procter and Gamble Duncan Hines manuscript collection.
———. Speech at Duncan Hines Family Dinner, Chicago IL, 29 March 1946, Procter and Gamble Duncan Hines manuscript collection.
———. ca. 1938-1939, Procter and Gamble Duncan Hines manuscript collection, FP xH-f.
———. Pittsburgh, Pennsylvania, 16 January 1939, Procter and Gamble Duncan Hines manuscript collection, FP xH-f.Transcript, Radio Interview with Miss DIckens, 7 July 1939, Procter and Gamble Duncan Hines manuscript collection, FP xH-f.
———. Seventh World's Poultry Convention, Cleveland, Ohio, 5 August 1939, Procter and Gamble Duncan Hines manuscript collection, FP xH-f.
———. Nashville Rotary Club, Nashville, Tennessee, 21 November 1939, Procter and Gamble Duncan Hines manuscript collection, FP xH-f.
———. Chicago, Illinois, 7 October 1941, Procter and Gamble Duncan Hines manuscript collection, FP H-f.
———. Speech for Regional Meetings of Listed Places, June 1942, Procter and Gamble Duncan Hines manuscript collection, FP H-f.
———. Talk Given Before The Ohio State Health Commissioners' Conference, Columbus, Ohio, 24 September 1942, 1-2, Procter and Gamble Duncan Hines manuscript collection, FP H-f.

————. Talk Given Before Rotary Club, Cave City, Kentucky, 18 August 1943, 2-3, Procter and Gamble Duncan Hines manuscript collection, FP H-f.

————. Speech Given at Duncan Hines Family Dinner, Chicago, Illinois, October 1945, Procter and Gamble Duncan Hines manuscript collection, FP H-f.

————. Address Given at Duncan Hines Family Dinner, Chicago, Illinois, 29 March 1946, Procter and Gamble Duncan Hines manuscript collection, FP H-f.

————. Speech, December 1947, Procter and Gamble Duncan Hines manuscript collection, FP H-f.

————. Speech at the Boone County Ham Breakfast, Columbia, Missouri, 7 September 1948, Procter and Gamble Duncan Hines manuscript collection, FP H-f.

————. Speech at the 14th Annual Duncan Hines Family Dinner, Chicago, Illinois, 9 May 1955, Procter and Gamble Duncan Hines manuscript collection, FP H-f.

————. Speech at the Twenty-First Annual Duncan Hines Family Dinner, Chicago, Illinois, 7 May 1956, Procter and Gamble Duncan Hines manuscript collection, FP H-f.

Park, Roy. Speech at Cornell University Graduate School of Business and Public Administration, 2 November 1976, Kroch Library, Cornell University, Ithaca NY, file # 3981.

Commercial Documents

Bill of receipt. R. R. Donnelley to Duncan Hines, 1 July 1938, Procter and Gamble Duncan Hines manuscript collection.

Company history file. "Valentine: An Oakland Man for President of Wells-Fargo; Succeeds Lloyd Tevis; A Short History of the Great Express Company, Now Forty Years Old" San Francisco CA: 11 August 1892.

Hotel receipt. Walnut Park Plaza, Philadelphia PA: 21 May 1938, no. 20703.

Hotel receipt. Hotel St. Regis, New York NY: 24 May 1938, no. 69128.

Hotel receipt. St. Charles Hotel, New Orleans LA: 18 March 1938, no. 87974.

Hotel receipt. Deshler-Wallick Hotel, Columbus OH: 11 August 1938, J36940 and J36941.

Hotel receipt. Commodore Perry Hotel, Toledo OH: 22 August and 23
    August 1938 nos. E17315 and E17316.
Hotel receipt. Dodge Hotel, Washington, D.C.: 19 October 1938, 2270.
Hotel receipt. Hotel Roanoke, Roanoke VA: 20October 1938, 16290.
Invoice # 5897. Procter and Gamble Duncan Hines manuscript
    collection.
Invoice # 9226. Procter and Gamble Duncan Hines manuscript
    collection.
Invoice # 9558. Procter and Gamble Duncan Hines manuscript
    collection.
Invoice # 9725. Procter and Gamble Duncan Hines manuscript
    collection.
Invoice # 5897. E. Raymond Wright, Inc. 30 June 1936.
Invoice # 9080. E. Raymond Wright, Inc. 28 August 1937.
Invoice # 9226. E. Raymond Wright, Inc. 27 September 1937.
Invoice # 9558. E. Raymond Wright, Inc. 10 November 1937.
Invoice # 9725. E. Raymond Wright, Inc. 22 November 1937.
Morgens, Howard J. Press release, Cincinnati OH: 17 August 1956,
    Procter and Gamble Duncan Hines manuscript collection, FP H-p.
Press release. Duncan Hines Institute, Inc., Ithaca NY: February 1959,
    Procter and Gamble Duncan Hines manuscript collection.
Press release. "History of the School of Hotel Administration," Cornell
    University.
Press release. Duncan Hines Institute, Ithaca NY: 1 October 1957, Procter
    and Gamble Duncan Hines manuscript collection.
Press release. "Duncan Hines Mixes," Nebraska Consolidated Mills, Inc.,
    Omaha NE: ca. 1953, Procter and Gamble Duncan Hines
    manuscript collection.
Press release. Duncan Hines Institute. Ithaca NY: ca. March 1959.
Press release. "Author Forms Corporation," (incorrectly dated 1946;
    probably early 1947.)
Press release. School of Hotel Administration, Cornel University.
Press release. "Duncan Hines Mixes." Nebraska Consolidated Mills, Inc.
    Omaha NE: ca. 1953, Procter and Gamble Duncan Hines
    manuscript collection, FP xH-p.
Press release. Duncan Hines Institute Ithaca NY: 1 October 1957, Procter
    and Gamble Duncan Hines manuscript collection, FP xH-p.

Travel and expense sheet for Duncan Hines, 1937, Duncan Hines Proctor and Gamble manuscript collection, FP xH-a.

Travel and expense sheet for Duncan Hines, 1938, Duncan Hines Proctor and Gamble manuscript collection, FP xH-a.

Woolson Spice Company brochure. Woolson Spice Company, Toledo OH: May 1953.

Government Documents

Adventures In Good Eating, Inc. v. Best Places To Eat, Inc. and Carl A. Barrett, civil action no. 1844 (1940), Duncan Hines collection, Procter and Gamble, Cincinnati, Ohio.

Bureau of Vital Statistics, Marriage certificate. New York State Department of Health, 1391.

Chicago, Illinois city directory, 1906, 1907, 1908, 1909, 1911, 1912, 1913, 1915, 1917, 1928, 1930, 1934.

Contract with R. R. Donnelley & Sons Company. March 1938, Procter and Gamble Duncan Hines manuscript collection, FP xH-c.

Contracts and various documents between R. R. Donnelley and Sons Company and Duncan Hines between 14 February 1938 and 2 May 1938. Procter and Gamble Duncan Hines manuscript collection, FP xH-e.

Death certificate of Emelie Tolman Hines, Boynton Beach FL: 9 November 1986.

Documents concerning Duncan Hines and Adventures in Good Eating, Inc. and R. R. Donnelley & Sons Company, 14 February 1938–2 May 1938, Procter and Gamble Duncan Hines manuscript collection.

Donald H. Molesworth vs Adventures in Good Eating, Inc., United States District Court for Western District of Kentucky. Bowling Green KY, 13 November 1952: Docket 422, 81.

Duncan Hines's testimony given before the Ohio State Health Commissioners' Conference, Columbus OH: 24 September 1942, Procter and Gamble Duncan Hines manuscript collection.

Kentucky Registrar of Vital Statistics, file no. 29188.

Illinois Census, 1920. Cheyenne WY.

Property Transfer. Warren County Deed Book, 11 October 1939, n. 186, 509.

Sign rental contract. Duncan Hines Institute, Ithaca NY: n.d., Procter and Gamble Duncan Hines manuscript collection, FP 2H-a.

Warren County, Kentucky Marriages (1918-1965), Groom's List, A-J (vol. 1), Bowling Green KY: 1992.
Wyoming Census, 1880, Cheyenne, Wyoming.

Additional Sources

Allen, J. *Northwestern Miller* "Duncan Hines Cake Mix Line to Enter Market." 3 July 1951, Duncan Hines Collection, Kroch Library, Cornell University, Ithaca NY, file #3981.

Apple, Charles, ed. *1884 Cheyenne, Wyoming City Directory* Cheyenne WY: Leader Steam Printing Co., ca. 1900.

Apple, Charles, ed. *1895 Cheyenne, Wyoming City Directory.* Cheyenne WY: Leader Steam Printing Co., ca. 1900.

Baird, Nancy. Kentucky Library, Bowling Green, Kentucky, 2 September 1994.

Barabba, Vincent P. Director, Bureau of the Census. *Historical Statisticals of the United States: Colonial TImes to 1970, Part 1.* United States Department of Commerce, Washington DC: 1975, 296, 303.

"Duncan Hines 1880-1959," General files, Kentucky Library, Bowling Green KY: 1959.

Duncan Hines scrapbook. 1953, belonging to Harriet Hines, examined 10 May 1994. Duncan Hines scrapbook, 1950-1951, belonging to Harriet Hines, examined 10 May 1994.

"Duncan Hines 1880-1959," General Files, Kentucky Library, Bowling Green KY: 1959.

The Duncan Hines Family Newsletter. Duncan Hines Institute, 28 March 1958, Procter and Gamble Duncan Hines manuscript collection, FP 2H-a.

Fact sheet. W.(illiam) W.(arner) Hines.

Hartford Dime. Hartford CT: 3 October 1955, Duncan Hines Collection, Kroch Library, Cornell University, Ithaca NY, file #3981.

Hines, Edward Ludlow. Autobiographical paper, n. 1 and n. 2.
———. Autobiographical paper. Bowling Green KY, n.d.

Hines, John Porter. "Reminiscences of Green River," autobiographical paper, 1941.

Matlock Scrapbook, "Nearly Half Million in Valentine Estate," Bowling Green KY, 1902.

Mills, Connie. Kentucky Library, Bowling Green, Kentucky, 14 September 1994.

Morningstar, Jane. Personal reminiscence, Kentucky Library, Bowling Green KY, n.d.

Murray, Anne. "History of Roy Park." 1992.

New product presentation material. Procter and Gamble, Inc., November 1957, Procter and Gamble Duncan Hines manuscript collection, FP IH-a.

"New Duncan Hines Signs Adopted." Duncan Hines Institute, Ithaca NY: September 1958, Procter and Gamble Duncan Hines manuscript collection, FP H-mm.

"Notes For Duncan Hines Book, *There's No Accounting For Tastes*," from interview conducted by Roy Park with Duncan Hines, ca. 1954, Procter and Gamble Duncan Hines manuscript collection.

Original notes for *Duncan Hines' Food Odyssey*, sent to Roy H. Park, 8 September 1954, Procter and Gamble Duncan Hines manuscript collection, FP xH-g.

Park, Roy. "Notes from Lempret, Former Editor of the *Omaha Magazine*," typescript, Park Communications, Ithaca NY: n.d.

Peerless Directory Company, comp. *1902-1903 Cheyenne, Wyoming City Directory*. Greeley CO: Tribune Press, 1902.

"Procter & Gamble Buys Duncan Hines Mix Line From Nebraska Consolidated." *Northwestern Miller* Minneapolis MN: 21 August 1956, 11, Procter and Gamble Duncan Hines manuscript collection, FP H-m.

Pyle, Ernie. "He Makes a Living by Eating And Writing About Eating: Traveling Gourmet Covers 60,000 Miles and 2,000 Meals Every Year." Scripps-Howard news service, 10 September 1938, Procter and Gamble Duncan Hines manuscript collection, FP H-m.

———. Scripps-Howard news service, 10 September 1938, Procter and Gamble Duncan Hines manuscript collection.

Rupp, Carla Marie. "How Roy Park Got Into Publishing." *Editor and Publisher*, 19 November 1977.

"Setup & Style of *Duncan Hines' Dessert Book*." Duncan Hines Institute, Ithaca NY: 10 July 1954, Procter and Gamble Duncan Hines manuscript collection, FP xH-g.

Supermarket News. 8 September 1952, Duncan Hines Collection, Kroch Library, Cornell University, Ithaca NY, file #3981.

INDEX

Silver Mine Tavern 171
Simon and Schuster 81
Simon, Richard 82
Smith, Grace 66
Smith, Kate 61
Southern Illinois University xi
Southern Tea Room 157
Spiller, Cora Jane ix
Spinning Wheel Tea Room 69
Spur Oil Distributing Company
    10, 119
S. S. Pierce Company 188, 192
St. Charles Hotel 75
St. Columba 14, 15
St. Mary's Company 194
Staley Sign Company 129
Stone, Anna 93
Stone's Restaurant 93
Stout, Wesley 81
Street, Julian 62
Stute's Chicken Inn 52
Sunkist 187

Table Topics 144
Tatum, Terry xii
Taylor, Frank J. 131, 132, 159
Technician, The 180
This Week 158
Thornapple Lodge 170
Tibbett, Lawrence 61
Time 183
Toll House 91, 92, 170, 201
Toll House Cookie 92
Tolman, Emelie 50, 58, 105, 106,
    107, 114, 115, 116, 117,
    122, 127, 150, 211

Union Oyster House 170

Urbana-Lincoln Hotel 169

Valentine, John J. 18, 19
Valley Green Lodge 136
Vanderbilt University 153
Virginia McDonald's Tea Room
    67

Wakefield, Kenneth 91, 201
Wakefield, Ruth 78, 91, 92, 171,
    201
Waldorf-Astoria 76, 171, 177,
    198
Walker, Edgar and Irene 117
Walnut Park Plaza 76
Ward Seminary 9
Warren College 6
Watts, Frank M. 82, 198
Welch, Clarence Herbert 206,
    207, 208, 211
Welch, Duncan xi
Wells, Carveth 62
Wells-Fargo Express Company
    18, 19, 21, 27, 29, 29, 30
Western Kentucky State
    Teachers College 11
Western Kentucky University ix,
    xi, 11
Wheaton, Shirley xii
White Fence Farm 68, 69, 71, 73
Wilkinson, E. F. 117
Willard Library xi
Williams Printing Firm xi, 119,
    145, 174
Williams, Larry xi, 119, 120
Williams, Tom 120, 121
Wilson, Edith 174, 211, 215,
    216, 220